Florent Manelli

Florent is a committed illustrator and author from Perpignan. It was at the age of fourteen, discovering the work of Andy Warhol, that he decided to take an interest in the visual arts. From a fine line with black felt-tip to a colourful painting, his drawings are the reflection of a vivid imagination. As well as being an illustrator, he is an activist fighting for LGBTQI+ rights and the environment. Manelli has been a columnist for Radio Nova. He published his first book, *40 LGBT+ qui ont changé le monde* (Volume 1) in 2019, followed by a second volume in 2020. His third book, *Fire or Nothing: Portrait of a Committed Generation,* was published in March 2022.

Clare Summerskill

Clare Summerskill is a freelance academic, an oral historian, a playwright and a lesbian comedienne and singer-songwriter. Her publications include *Gateway to Heaven: Fifty Years of Lesbian and Gay Oral History* (Tollington Press, 2012), *Creating Verbatim Theatre from Oral Histories* (Routledge, 2019), and she co-edited *New Directions in Queer Oral History. Archives of Disruption* (Routledge, 2022). Her plays include *Rights of Passage,* based on interviews with lesbian and gay asylum seekers in the UK, and *Hearing Voices,* based on the experiences of patients on a secure psychiatric ward. She regularly tours her one-woman comedy shows to theatres around the UK and the US, bringing lesbian humour to the forefront of alternative comedy. She co-founded the Oral History Society's LGBTQ Special Interest Group and is a patron of several LGBTQ organizations including Kenric, London Gay Symphony Orchestra, East London Out Project (ELOP), Mind Out, Diversity Choir, and Educate & Celebrate.

First published in the UK in 2023 by Supernova Books, an imprint of Aurora Metro Publications Ltd. 80 Hill Rise, TW10 6UB, UK; www.aurorametro.com
t: @aurorametro F: facebook.com/AuroraMetroBooks
50 LGBTQI+ who changed the world © 2023 Florent Manelli
Introduction © 2023 Clare Summerskill
Cover image © 2023 Florent Manelli
Cover design: © 2023 Supernova Books/Aurora Metro Publications Ltd.
Editors: Laura Burgess, Yasmeen Doogue-Khan, Cheryl Robson
With thanks to: Chelsea Louise Berlin, Tony Malone, Graham Lewis and Stop Hate, Claire Summerskill and ELOP.
This book has an accompanying exhibition which can be booked for display in libraries, arts centres and educational institutions, supported by Arts Council, England. To book the exhibition please contact: info@aurorametro.com
All rights in this book are strictly reserved.
For rights enquiries please contact the publisher: info@aurorametro.com
Permission to reproduce the original French editions granted for volume 1
© 2019 Florent Manelli and les éditions lapin and for volume 2 © 2020 Florent Manelli and les éditions lapin
All the illustrations and photographs in this volume are reprinted with permission or presumed to be in the public domain. Every effort has been made to ascertain and acknowledge copyright status, but should there have been any oversight on our part, we will endeavour to rectify the error in subsequent printings.
Contact: info@aurorametro.com
No part of this publication may be reproduced, stored in or introduced into a retrieval system, or transmitted in any form, or by any means (electronic, mechanical, photocopying, recording or otherwise) without the prior permission of the publisher. Any person who does any unauthorised act in relation to this publication may be liable to criminal prosecution and civil claims for damages.
This paperback is sold subject to the condition that it shall not, by way of trade or otherwise, be lent, resold, hired out, or otherwise circulated without the publisher's prior consent in any form of binding or cover other than that in which it is published and without a similar condition being imposed on the subsequent purchaser.
Printed by Short Run Press, Exeter, UK on sustainably resourced paper.
ISBN: 978-1-913641-28-3 (print) ISBN: 978-1-913641-29-0 (ebook)

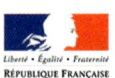 Ministère de la Culture

We gratefully acknowledge financial support from the French Ministry of Culture through the French Institute Literary Assistance Programme.

Florent Manelli

50 LGBTQI+ who changed the world

Introduced by Clare Summerskill

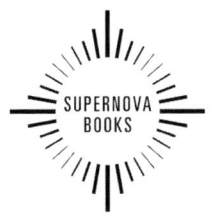

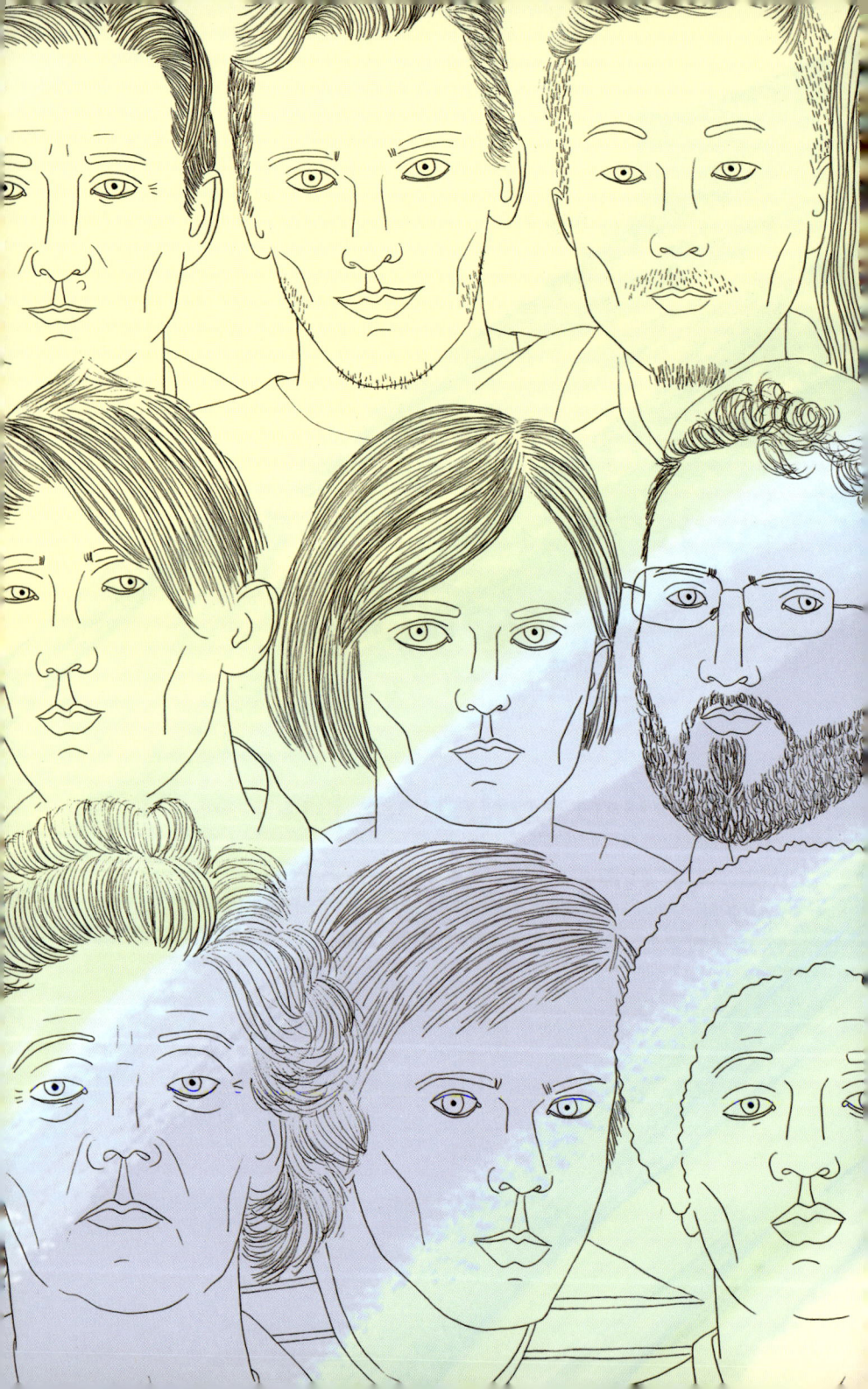

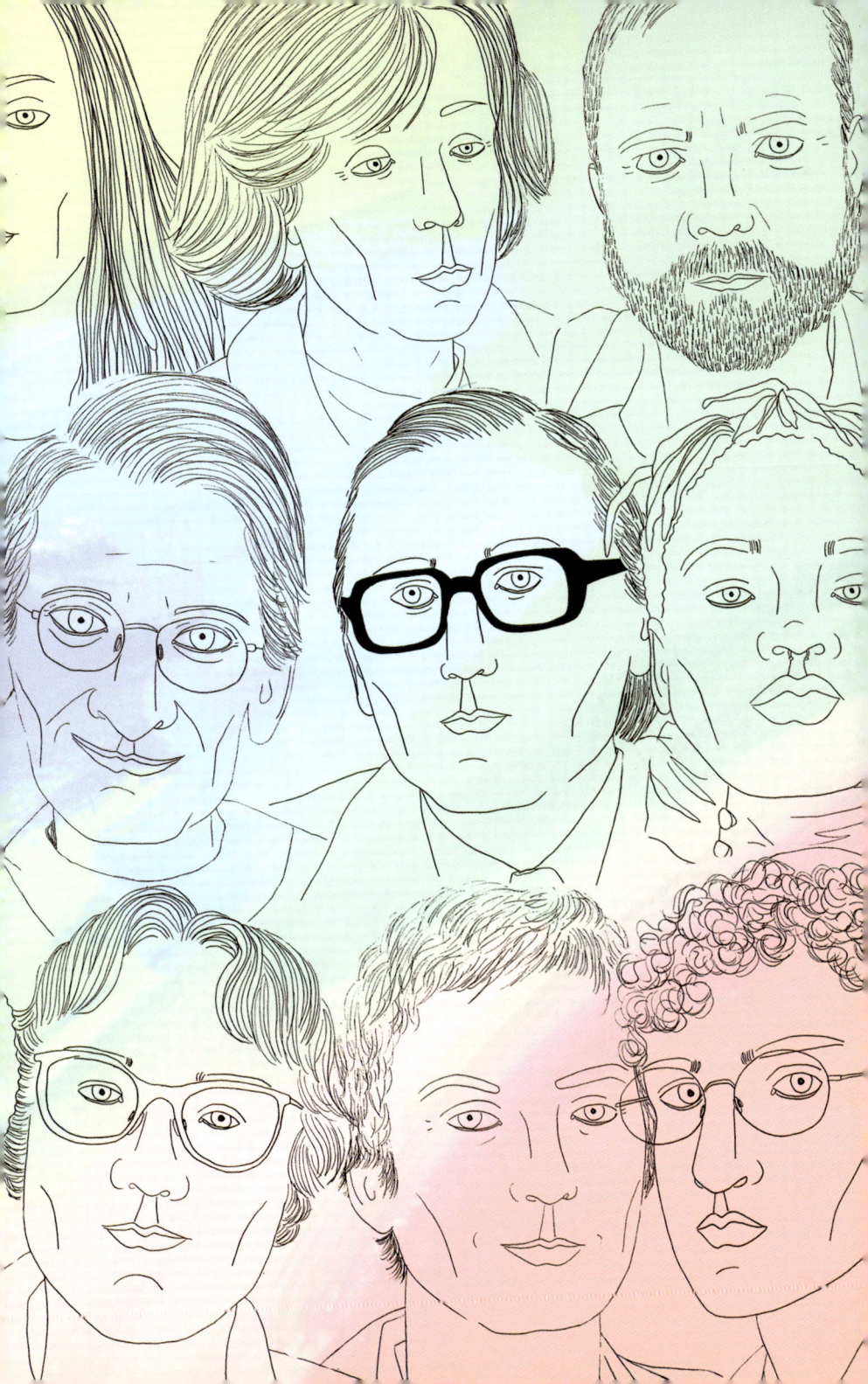

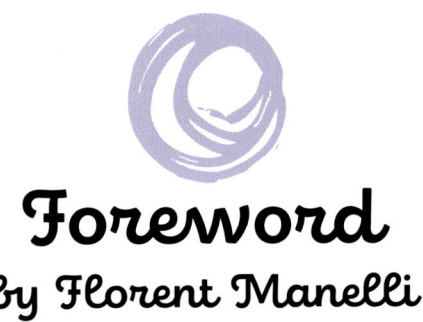

Foreword
by Florent Manelli

I wish that I'd had a book like this one during my teenage years, as I often had questions about my sexuality that went unanswered. Today, the topics of gender and sexuality continue to generate violence, demonstrations, and hate speech, and I hope this book will contribute to the fight for freedom and human rights for the LGBTQI+ community.

By highlighting the on-going struggle for LGBTQI+ rights both at home and abroad, in countries where these rights are often wilfully ignored, or painfully denied, I wanted to both honour and pay tribute to those who have fought for change, and those who are still fighting for our human rights today, all over the world. The fight for the recognition and the protection of LGBTQI+ people around the globe is crucial. It demonstrates our humanity to one another, in the face of political, cultural and religious opposition.

Learning about our shared LGBTQI+ history is essential because it helps us understand that LGBTQI+ people have long existed and that we have been fighting for our rights, for equality and freedom, for generations. Historical records play an important part in the way identities and personal histories are perceived, and I believe that we need to engage with the way we define ourselves in relation to the world, and to others, to be in charge of our own history, and of what will be recorded today for future generations.

50 LGBTQI+ who changed the world

From American civil rights leader Bayard Rustin to Belgian intersex model Hanne Gaby Odiele, from British political activist Phyllis Akua Opoku-Gyimah to the first openly gay Indian prince Manvendra Singh Gohil, this book highlights the unparalleled lives of those who said "No!" – individuals who have challenged the norms of their cultures and societies.

With these 50 LGBTQI+ portraits, I want to celebrate courage, the beauty of being, and the rage to live openly as your true self.

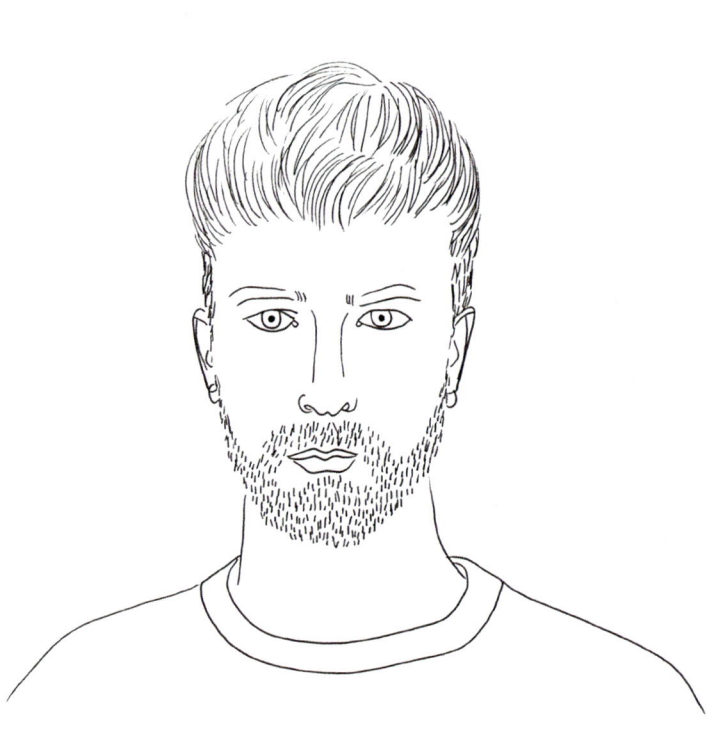

Florent Manelli

Contents

Foreword	7
Introduction	11

Profiles

Bayard Rustin	24
Alan Turing	30
Tom of Finland	38
Edith Windsor	46
Harvey Milk	50
Barbara Gittings	58
Audre Lorde	62
Renée Richards	68
Nancy Cárdenas	72
Larry Kramer	76
Miss Major Griffin-Gracy	82
Craig Rodwell	86
Armistead Maupin	92
Marsha P. Johnson	98
Brenda Howard	106
Jean Le Bitoux	112
Pedro Almodóvar	118
Michael Cashman	126
Sylvia Rivera	130
Peter Tatchell	138
Judith Butler	142
Rosanna Flamer-Caldera	146
Martina Navratilova	150
Simon Nkoli	154

Keith Haring	160
Chi Chia-wei	166
Mark Ashton	170
RuPaul	176
Mary Bonauto	184
Manvendra Singh Gohil	188
Hida Viloria	194
Bamby Salcedo	200
Phyllis Akua Opoku-Gyimah	204
Xulhaz Mannan	208
Xiaogang Wei	212
Ludovic-Mohamed Zahed	216
Nikolai Alekseev	220
Yelena Grigorieva	224
Georges Azzi	228
Marielle Franco	232
Kasha Jacqueline Nabagesera	236
David Jay	240
Linda Baumann	244
Megan Rapinoe	248
Elliot Page	252
Hanne Gaby Odiele	256
Olly Alexander	260
Hande Kader	264
Bouhdid Belhadi	268
Aaron Rose Philip	272
Glossary of terms	276
Photo credits	280
Useful Websites	281
Creative Notes and Drawings	284

Introduction
by Clare Summerskill

The LGBTQI+ folk that Florent Manelli has chosen to write about and represent artistically in this publication provide the reader with an exciting collection of people of varying genders and sexualities who have made a significant impact in the world. In his foreword, Florent mentions that, as a teenager, he would have loved to come across a book like this one and I, and many more I'm sure, agree with him wholeheartedly in this respect. Only a few decades ago, it was almost impossible to identify any public figures who could be named as being lesbian, gay, bisexual or transgender – let alone queer, intersex, asexual, or any other definitions to which the '+' after the acronym LGBT now refer.[1]

In the late 1990s I conducted oral history interviews with older lesbians and gay men. When I asked the narrators when they first

---

[1] In my introduction, I have used the LGBTQI+ acronym in different variations. For example, many of the letters encompassed by the plus sign (+) have only been created and/or identified in recent years and are therefore, in my mind, not applicable to certain historical descriptions and discussions. Additionally, some people who identify as lesbian, gay, transgender, for example, may not term themselves LGBTQI+, but instead identify as only one of those descriptions. Also, certain countries specifically criminalize LGBT activities and identities, but not necessarily people who are intersex, asexual, pansexual or other identities that are currently under the LGBTQI+ umbrella term. I have therefore used the letters of the acronym that I deem applicable to the subject addressed, or that the person or organization uses to describe themselves.

thought they might be gay, most replied that they didn't know that they were 'gay' because they'd never come across the word and that any terms they had heard that described the feelings they experienced were used as cruel and demeaning insults. It is a unique situation for any group in society to need to search for a name to describe who they are before they can fully recognize and realize their own identity. When such a step is taken, they can then begin to look for others who might also be partially hidden, in order to become their authentic selves. The issue of visibility, which is the main focus of this publication, is of paramount importance for members of this marginalized population existing in a society where we have historically experienced social prejudice and legal prohibitions against our natural feelings and desires.

This introduction aims to provide a brief overview of those who have not been mentioned in the main body of the book. I will include some notable LGBTQI+ names in history and also explore the role that LGBTQI+ writers, artists and musicians/singers, sports people, politicians and political activists have played in providing representation. It would, of course, be impossible for me to mention all the highly influential members of the LGBTQI+ population around the world, both historically and in the present day. I openly admit that I have made my selection from a highly subjective viewpoint, namely that of a lesbian who has been informed and influenced by LGBTQI+ people and their journeys in my own work as a predominantly LGBTQI+-focused writer, performer and historical researcher. Many of those I mention are people I have come across in the UK, with a sprinkling of names from the States, since artistic and political developments in these two countries have had the greatest influence on my personal and professional life. Under the historical figures, authors, and activists sections of this introduction, I also refer to other key LGBTQI+ figures from different parts of the world.

The courageous actions of all those mentioned in this book have, without doubt, greatly influenced the course of social and political history. But they have also changed other members of the

Introduction

LGBTQI+ population who have learnt about their work and their lives and, as a consequence, may have then felt empowered to come out themselves – a step which can occur because we see others who resemble ourselves, such as those mentioned and celebrated in this book. This, in turn, allows us to feel a sense of strength and pride about belonging to a group which contains these people.

Those cited have either 'come out' or have been identified, historically, as being members of the LGBTQI+ population. 'Coming out' is still, for many, a hugely important personal and sometimes professional choice, even in a society with relatively liberal laws and views. It is also an act that does not just happen once but occurs again and again throughout our lifetimes. Although being lesbian, gay, bisexual or transgender is not criminalized in most Western countries, there are a myriad of reasons why someone – especially in the public eye – may wish to hide their sexual orientation or gender identity. These reasons can range from fearing that close family relationships might be harmed or severed, to losing commercial sponsorship, which could seriously impact a person's ability to continue the work they love and at which they excel. When the tennis player, Martina Navratilova, came out in 1981, she lost around $10 million worth of sponsorship deals. The comedian Ellen DeGeneres came out in 1996, when her sitcom was at the height of its success, but the following year the show was cancelled due to low ratings. The price to be paid was a virtual boycott by the entertainment industry for several years before she managed to revive her career.

Occasionally, an individual might be in a position of publicly declaring that there is something wrong with being LGBTQI+, whilst being LGBTQI+ themselves, in which case, arguably, the personal does indeed become political and some other members of the LGBTQI+ community might wish to 'out' them. For LGBTQI+ folk in the general public who may be looking out for high-profile LGBTQI+ figures as a means of validating their own sexual orientation or gender identity, it therefore makes an enormous difference whether those other famous LGBTQI+ people are in or out of the closet. If they are hiding their true identities, this can reinforce the shame and fear that many of us might already feel about our own inherent natures due to prevalent homophobic and transphobic attitudes. Also, as more and more people come out, heterosexual and cisgender people can see that being LGBTQI+ is far more prevalent than they had perhaps realized.

When I was a teenager, the tennis player, Billie Jean King, was someone I felt sure was a lesbian and I wanted her to declare her sexuality publicly, but in an interview in 1975 she flatly denied that she was a lesbian.[2] I can remember that her statement hit me particularly hard, even though, at the time, I did not fully understand its implications or realize why I needed her to come out as a lesbian. Now I am fully aware that the problem with making any judgements about someone else coming out is that, fundamentally, it is not the LGBTQI+ person who is in any way to blame, but the prejudice or discrimination they encounter from others in society that is making them conflicted about publicly revealing their authentic selves. A person who is, for example, LGB or T might be creating music that is heard by millions, but they may risk losing audience members and record sales if their sexual orientation or gender identity were to be known.

Our LGBTQ History

Unlike many other people from marginalized communities, LGBTQI+ people generally do not grow up in families where stories are told or passed on to younger generations about relatives who might have been LGBTQI+. We therefore have to look outside of our own family networks to search for people who might be similar to us. To counter the homophobia which we might experience within our own families, we will seek out a 'family of choice', consisting of friends and romantic partners who understand and validate our lives and lifestyles.

LGBTQI+ history is rarely a part of any school curriculum, which not only means that we do not have access to our own stories

---

2 Billie Jean King *All In: An Autobiography*, Viking UK, 2021.

Introduction

and information about social and political movements, but neither do heterosexual and cisgender people learn about significant historical developments that have transformed the way we can live our lives. This much-needed body of heritage for LGBTQI+ folk has also been omitted from many social and political records and may appear only in archives documenting medical conditions or criminal convictions.

Prior to 1967, when the Sexual Offences Act was passed, homosexual acts were criminalized in the UK. Meanwhile, the historical silencing of lesbianism has meant that while lesbians' sexual behaviour was not criminalized in the same way as men's, the visibility of women-loving women and, consequently, their political and personal agency, have been severely limited. For the majority of the lifetimes of older lesbians and gay men, homosexuality had been regarded by society as a sickness and, although lesbians were not publicly exposed on the same scale as gay men, their nonconforming lifestyles and identities were often viewed as problematic by society. Some LGBT people were referred to psychiatrists who sought to 'cure' their homosexuality or gender identification, and it was not until 1992 that the World Health Organization (WHO) declassified homosexuality as a mental illness. Furthermore, being lesbian or gay has generally been perceived by Western Christian societies as religiously reprehensible.

Historically, in the UK, there have been some members of the LGBTQ population whose lives have been celebrated in our community and, occasionally, beyond. They include the playwright Oscar Wilde, imprisoned in 1895 for refusing to deny his sexuality, and the writer Radcliffe Hall, whose book *The Well of Loneliness* was published in 1928 but then branded 'obscene' in a subsequent trial. The 'Ladies of Llangollen', Eleanor Butler and Sarah Ponsonby, lived together in Wales and were two upper-class Irish women whose relationship scandalized and fascinated their contemporaries in the late eighteenth and early nineteenth century. The coded diaries of the landowner and non-conforming Anne Lister have recently been adapted into a TV series about her life, Esther Roper was an

Irish English suffragist and social reformer, and Annie Kenney a working-class suffragette and socialist feminist and allegedly a lover of Christabel Pankhurst. Virginia Woolf, arguably one the greatest writers ever, was thought to have had a same-sex relationship with Vita Sackville-West, also a writer; Daphne du Maurier is another renowned British author; and A.E. Houseman, a highly respected poet. There is also the playwright and diarist Joe Orton, the writer, E.M. Forster, and the twentieth century composer Benjamin Britten.

In the States, historically famous LGBTQ writers include James Baldwin; Carson McCullers; Kate Millett; and the poet and novelist Gertrude Stein. In France, there was the author and woman of letters, Colette; Didier Lestrade, an author and AIDS advocate; Monique Wittig, an author, philosopher and feminist theorist; and Guy Hocquenghem, an author and militant who, after 1968, produced the first work on queer theory. Karl Heinrich Ulrichs was a nineteenth century German lawyer, journalist and writer who is regarded today as a pioneer of sexology and the modern gay rights movement. Laurence Michael Dillon was the first man to undergo phalloplasty; and Lili Ilse Elvenes, better known as Lili Elbe, was a transwoman and one of the early recipients of gender-reassignment surgery in 1930.

The Arts

In the world of the arts, there have been so many LGBTQI+ artists, actors, composers, writers, and musicians that many have questioned whether this is a pure coincidence or if there is something more behind this striking phenomenon. It may simply be the case that LGBTQI+ folk are drawn to communities that are made up of people who are more likely to accept them for who they are.

UK writers include Carol Ann Duffy, Maureen Duffy, Jackie Kay, Alan Bennett, Russell T. Davies, Ali Smith, Jeanette Winterson, Sarah Waters, and Alan Ayckbourn. Kae Tempest, a spoken word artist, came out as non-binary in 2020. Celebrated artists from the

Introduction

UK and beyond include the artist and sculptress Maggie Hambling; the collaborative art duo Gilbert and George (Gilbert Proesch, and George Passmore); David Hockney; Frida Kahlo, the Mexican painter; visual artist Andy Warhol; Keith Haring, a New York pop art social activist; and the Irish-born painter Francis Bacon.

In the worlds of film and TV, award-winning LGBTQ activist writers and producers include Derek Jarman, a British filmmaker and visual artist; Nik Sheehan, the Canadian filmmaker who produced the first major documentary on AIDS/HIV; Xiaogang Wei, a Chinese documentary queer film maker; the Kenyan lesbian filmmaker Wanuri Kahui; and Janet Mock, who is a writer and director, and executive producer for the US series *Pose*.

The Theatre World

For over a century in the UK, there has been a general acceptance of gay men working in the theatre world, exemplified by the popularity of the writer, composer and singer, Noel Coward who was out for most of his long career, which ran from 1911 to 1973. Over recent decades, there have been several male actors, such as Ian McKellen, Stephen Fry and Antony Sher who have been vocal about LGBTQ matters. However, lesbian visibility in the acting profession has severely lagged behind. A few years ago, the UK actors' union Equity, asked me to take part in a campaign to increase the visibility of lesbians in theatre, using the slogan, 'I can act, but I can't pretend'. This was launched because research had revealed that many lesbians were concerned that being out in their workplace – or even to their agents – would adversely affect their casting opportunities.

Several well-known lesbians in film and acting have frequently hidden their sexual orientation, or only revealed it publicly in later life when their fame was secured, such as Jodie Foster. The actress and comedian, Lily Tomlin, was not publicly open about her sexual orientation but neither did she think that she kept it a secret. In 2013, she married the writer Jane Wagner, her partner of forty-two years. In recent years, many lesbian and trans actresses have not only been out but also involved in raising LGBTQI+ awareness. They include Miriam Margolyes, Jane Lynch, Laverne Cox, Angelica Ross (also a transgender rights advocate), and Michaela Jaé Rodriguez (the first transgender woman to win a Golden Globe).

In the British world of light entertainment and comedy, Frankie Howerd and Kenneth Williams were known for their camp performances, although Howerd was compelled to hide his potentially career-destroying homosexuality and Williams declared that he was asexual and celibate. Quentin Crisp (1908 – 1999) was an English raconteur, artist's model, actor and writer who cross-dressed and acted intensely effeminate in public, often at great risk to himself. Crisp wrote: 'At the age of ninety, it has finally been explained to me that I am not really homosexual, I'm transgender. I now accept that.'

Openly gay and bisexual comedians have included Julian Clary, Alan Carr and Joe Lycett. It took much longer for lesbians to be accepted on the comedy circuit and on TV but, over the last few years, they have finally been 'allowed' to come into their own. The Australian, Hannah Gadsby is one of the best-known lesbian comedians world-wide due to her Netflix shows, and others include: Rosie O'Donnell, Wanda Sykes, Margaret Cho, Sue Perkins, Sandi Toksvig, Susan Calman, and the pansexual comedian actress Janelle Monae.

There are also a handful of well-known TV presenters who are gay and lesbian who have raised public awareness and visibility such as Clare Balding, Graham Norton, Paul O'Grady and US news anchors Rachael Maddow and Anderson Cooper.

The Music Industry

Since the pop music industry began in the 1950s and 1960s, singers and musicians have had a huge impact on our lives but, again, the prevalence of gay men in that industry has for several decades been far greater than that of lesbians. Elton John is one of the most famous names in music and he has also been recognized internationally for his work on raising funds to support research into AIDS/HIV.

Introduction

Freddie Mercury was another huge presence (naming his band 'Queen'), and other singers such as Jimmy Somerville (from The Communards), and Boy George, were always openly gay. George Michael initially thought that he was bisexual, but later realized that he was completely gay, and the singer and actor Will Young has always been publicly open about his sexual orientation.

But even after the gender-bending pop explosion of the 1970s, there were still very few major female singers who were known to be lesbians. The sexism of the pop industry did not seem to allow women to challenge female stereotypes in the way the men had challenged male ones. The singer Dusty Springfield had several romantic relationships with women, mainly in the US, and in 1982 she married actress Teda Bracci, but it would have been detrimental for her career to have come out when she was at the height of her fame in the late 60s and early 70s. Whilst speculation about people's sexual orientation or gender identity is usually an unhelpful exercise, I do think it worth mentioning that Whitney Houston, one of the best-selling music artists of all time, was widely believed to be bisexual. Her Baptist background and the homophobia of those around her made it difficult for her to publicly express her sexual orientation and live openly with her girlfriend. Whilst the arts in general, and the music industry in particular, undoubtedly contains numerous LGBTQ folk, it is a world where many famous people risk being outed by the press, the most recent example being Rebel Wilson, who came out on Instagram in June 2022.

Other lesbians and bisexual women in the music world worthy of mention are k.d.lang, Lady Gaga, Melissa Etheridge, Janis Ian, and Amy Ray and Emily Saliers, who form the duo The Indigo Girls. In 2016, the singer Anohni (formally in Anthony and the Johnsons) became the first openly transgender performer to be nominated for an Academy Award and another singer, Sam Smith, came out as genderqueer in 2019. Lil Naz (the American rapper and singer) came out as gay and was met with some backlash from the hip hop community. Some members of the Russian band Pussy Riot identify publicly as lesbian and they are from a country where homosexuality is punishable by imprisonment, so even saying that you are a lesbian is not only a political act but a personally dangerous one.

Politicians and Political Activists

If an LGBTQI+ activist is someone who puts their own safety on the line, then those activists who live in countries where there are laws that criminalize LGBT people and behaviour undoubtedly deserve our deepest respect and admiration. Homosexuality is still criminalized in 69 countries; nearly half of these are in Africa. The International Lesbian, Gay, Bisexual, Trans and Intersex Association (ILGA), which monitors the progress of laws relating to homosexuality around the world, states that the death penalty is the legally prescribed punishment for same-sex sexual acts in Brunei, Iran, Mauritania, Saudi Arabia, Yemen and in the northern states in Nigeria.[3]

LGBTQI+ activists operating in countries where they are under the threat of being harmed or imprisoned for their work include Simon Nkoli, a South African anti-apartheid activist who founded Le Saturday Group, the first Black gay organization; Kasha Jacqueline Nabagesera, a Ugandan militant lesbian and a colleague of David Kato; Charlot Jeudy who was involved in the emergence of the LGBT rights movement in Haiti and found murdered in 2019; and Zanele Muholi, a non-binary South African visual activist. The lesbian Jean Chong fought for LGBT rights in Singapore, before the government recently decided to decriminalize sex between men, following similar moves to change the law in Taiwan, India and Thailand.

It is still the case that LGBT people living in Western countries face prejudice in various forms, including in their places of work, social exclusion and family disownment. Discrimination comes in forms other than in enacted laws and can be insidious and harmful. A study by the UK LGBTQ+ charity Stonewall found that half of LGBT people they surveyed had experienced depression,

---

[3] https://ilga.org/ilga-world-releases-state-sponsored-homophobia-December-2020-update Accessed 23rd Nov 2022.

Introduction

three in five had experienced anxiety, one in eight people aged 18 to 24 had attempted to end their life, and almost half of trans people had thought about taking their life. Additionally, members of the LGBTQI+ community are at a greater risk of experiencing hate crimes compared to heterosexual people.[4] Some older LGBTQ people I have interviewed have expressed deep concerns that laws previously passed, advancing rights that we once thought unassailable, might also be reversed if certain political parties attained power. In a time of rising populism in many European counties, vigilance remains the key word for members of the LGBTQI+ population.

Firsts are always important. As LGBTQI+ people, we look for those who were the first to announce publicly their sexual orientation or gender identity, particularly those in positions of power. Maureen Colquhoun was the first openly lesbian member of the British parliament, but she was deselected by the Labour Party in 1977 due to her sexuality and her feminist views. Chris Smith was the first MP to come out as a gay man in the UK and there are now several openly LGBTQI+ MPs, one of whom, Angela Eagle, threw her hat into the ring of a Labour party leadership bid in 2016. Also worthy of note is Ireland's Leo Varadkar, a Fine Gael politician who was the first openly gay man to serve as Taoiseach (Prime Minister), and in the US, Pete Buttigieg was the first openly gay man to run as a presidential candidate.

In the US, there are many names associated with the LGBTQI+ rights movement, most especially from the 1970s and 1980s. There was the powerful political activist, Angela Davis; Stormé DeLarverie, regarded as the woman who started the fight back against the police during the Stonewall raid of 1969; and Troy Perry, founder of the gay Metropolitan Community Church. More recently in the US, we find Blair Imani, a Muslim, bisexual activist; Mary Bonauto, who was the lead counsel in the legal case which made Massachusetts the first state in which same-sex couples could marry in 2004; and Leonard Matlovich, a gay activist who was the

---

4 https://www.stonewall.org.uk/lgbt-britain-health Accessed 24th Oct 2022.

first to out himself in the military. In France, Adrian de la Vega is a transman who runs a social media YouTube channel and Alexya Salvador is the first trans reverend in Latin America.

Sports People

In contrast to the arts, sport seems to be a relatively safe and welcoming space for lesbians but not for gay men who are, seemingly, remarkably rare. The footballer Megan Rapinoe is one of the highest profile and rewarded stars internationally. In tennis, the French player and coach Amelie Mauresmo is a lesbian and, most courageously, Russian Daria Kasatkina came out in 2022, criticizing her country's homophobic attitudes and laws. The British athlete, Kelly Holmes, came out in 2022, saying that she had known she was a lesbian since 1988 when she was in the army but could not come out then as it was illegal at the time to be gay in the military. Britain's openly lesbian Nicola Adams won her country's first ever female boxing Gold medal.

In the UK, Justin Fashanu was an out gay footballer who played for a variety of clubs between 1978 and 1997 and took his own life in 1998. Gareth Thomas is a retired Welsh rugby player who has talked openly about being HIV positive, and Tom Daly, the Olympic gold medallist diver, recently headed up an awareness campaign about homophobia in Commonwealth countries. In the US, Carl Nassib was the first openly gay man to play in the NFL. Adam Rippon made history as the first openly gay American male figure skater to win a medal at the Winter Olympics. Caitlyn Jenner is a transgender athlete and the transman Kye Allums is a basketball player and LGBTQI+ advocate.

Concluding Thoughts

LGBTQI+ people around the world face inequality, violence and sometimes even death because of who they love, how they look, or who they are. Sexual orientation and gender identity are integral aspects of our selves and should never lead to discrimination or abuse. It would be unthinkable for heterosexual or cisgender people

Introduction

to go about their lives hiding their sexual orientation or gender identity, yet this is what LGBTQI+ people have done and continue to do. The salient theme throughout this book is that, for members of the LGBTQI+ community, visibility is life.

We have the right to be who we are. Discovering other people in our 'tribe' – most especially those who are exceptionally talented or notable in different areas of the arts, politics, sports, and activism – not only creates a wider family and heritage for us but also demonstrates the vast contributions that LGBTQI+ people have made to society, both past and present. Those that have been mentioned, both by myself, and by Florent Manelli in this book, provide badly-needed representation and visibility to members of our LGBTQI+ community and to the wider public. Whether or not they considered themselves activists, famous people who have the courage to come out spearhead the conversation about gender, prejudice, discrimination, and the fight for human rights and, most importantly, their lives and work contribute to a much-needed normalization of the experience of being LGBTQI+.

Bayard Rustin
1912 – 1987

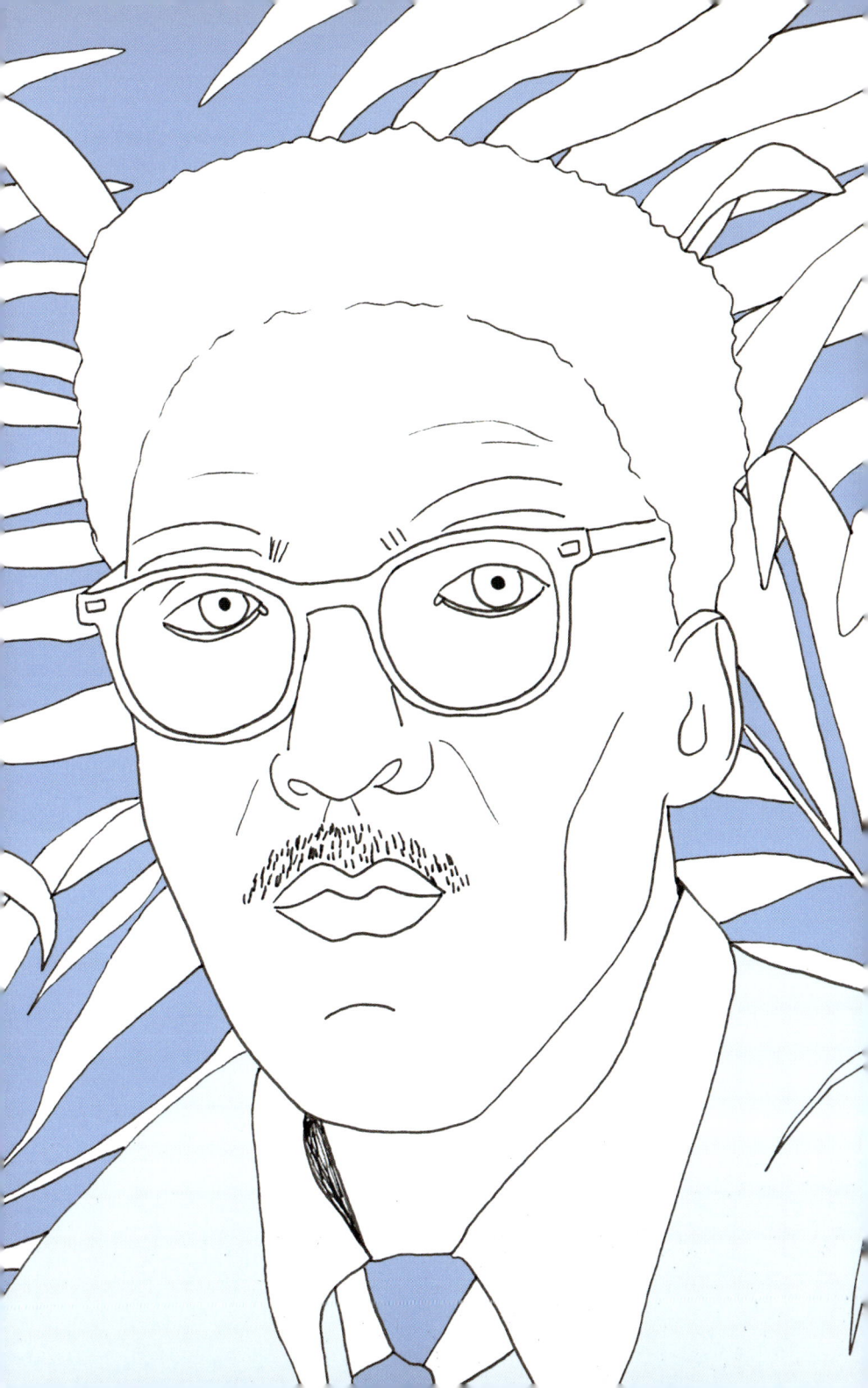

A COMMUNIST AND OPENLY GAY MAN, BAYARD RUSTIN WAS THE DRIVING FORCE BEHIND THE CIVIL RIGHTS MARCH ON WASHINGTON MOVEMENT, ON 28TH AUGUST 1963. ATTRACTING 250,000 PEOPLE AND ENDING WITH MARTIN LUTHER KING JR.'S FAMOUS "I HAVE A DREAM" SPEECH, IT WAS ONE OF THE MOST SIGNIFICANT EVENTS IN THE HISTORY OF THE CIVIL RIGHTS MOVEMENT.

Fifty years later, Barack Obama awarded him the Presidential Medal of Freedom, but Bayard Rustin is still widely unknown.

Throughout his life, Bayard Rustin followed the concept of non-violence, which he learnt in 1948 directly from Gandhi and other leaders in India, but his pacifism sometimes meant paying a high price. For example, he refused to fight in the Second World War in 1944, which resulted in imprisonment. After a few years at the Fellowship of Reconciliation (a non-denominational religious and pacifist organization), he became an advisor to Martin Luther King Jr. and continued to defend his pacifism without losing sight of his fight against racism and racial segregation.

He was arrested in Pasadena in 1953 for having sex with two men in a car, and was incarcerated for sixty days for "vagrancy" and "indecent assault". Consequently, his position as an advisor became more difficult, due to some of Martin Luther King's relatives not approving of a gay man being part of his entourage.

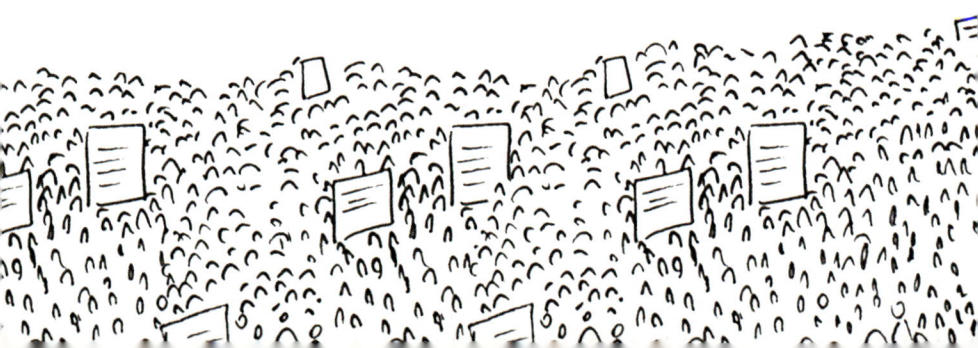

Bayard Rustin

Despite intimidation a month before the Rights March on Washington (Senator Strom Thurmond presented a photo to the Senate showing Martin Luther King. Jr in his bath with Bayard Rustin standing at the side talking to him, giving rise to intense speculation), he worked tirelessly for the eight weeks preceding the march. The purpose of the march was to protest against racial discrimination in employment, going so far as taking over a Harlem church as the temporary headquarters. He planned every detail, from the number of toilets to the 800,000 sandwiches distributed to the crowd on the day of the march (without mayonnaise to prevent participants from getting sick), and was involved in staffing, creating the schedules, and even writing the speech.

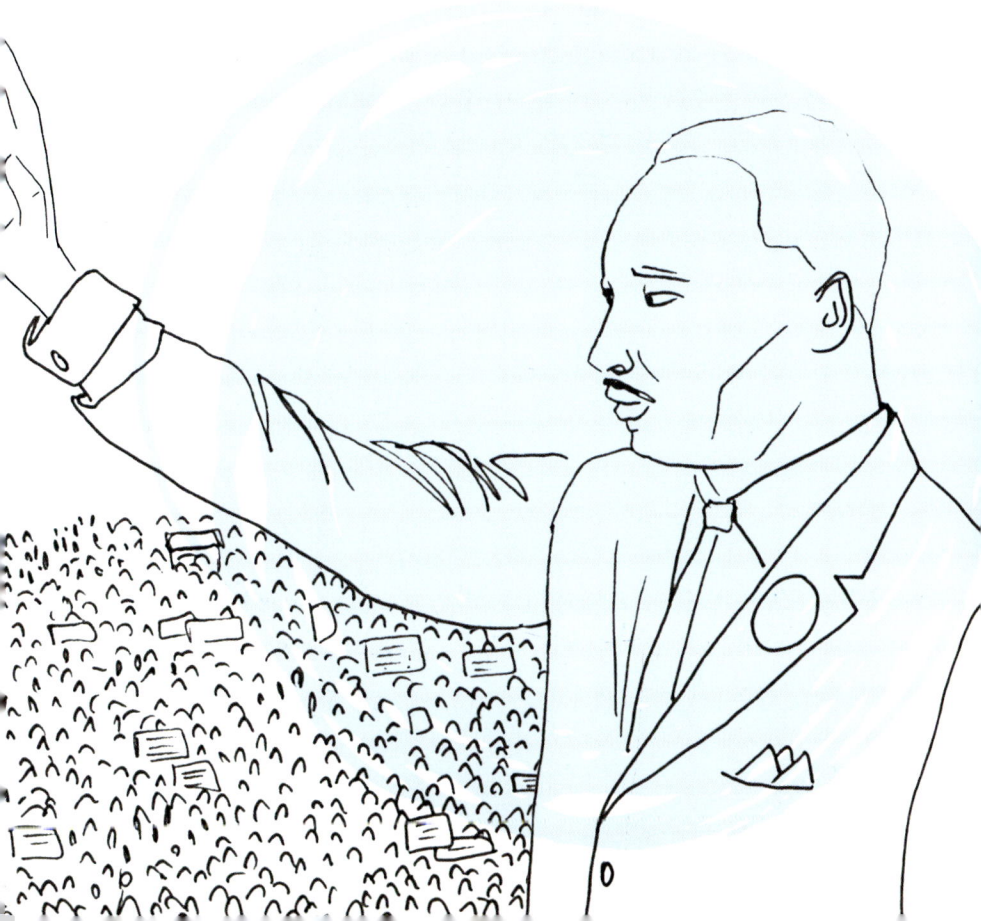

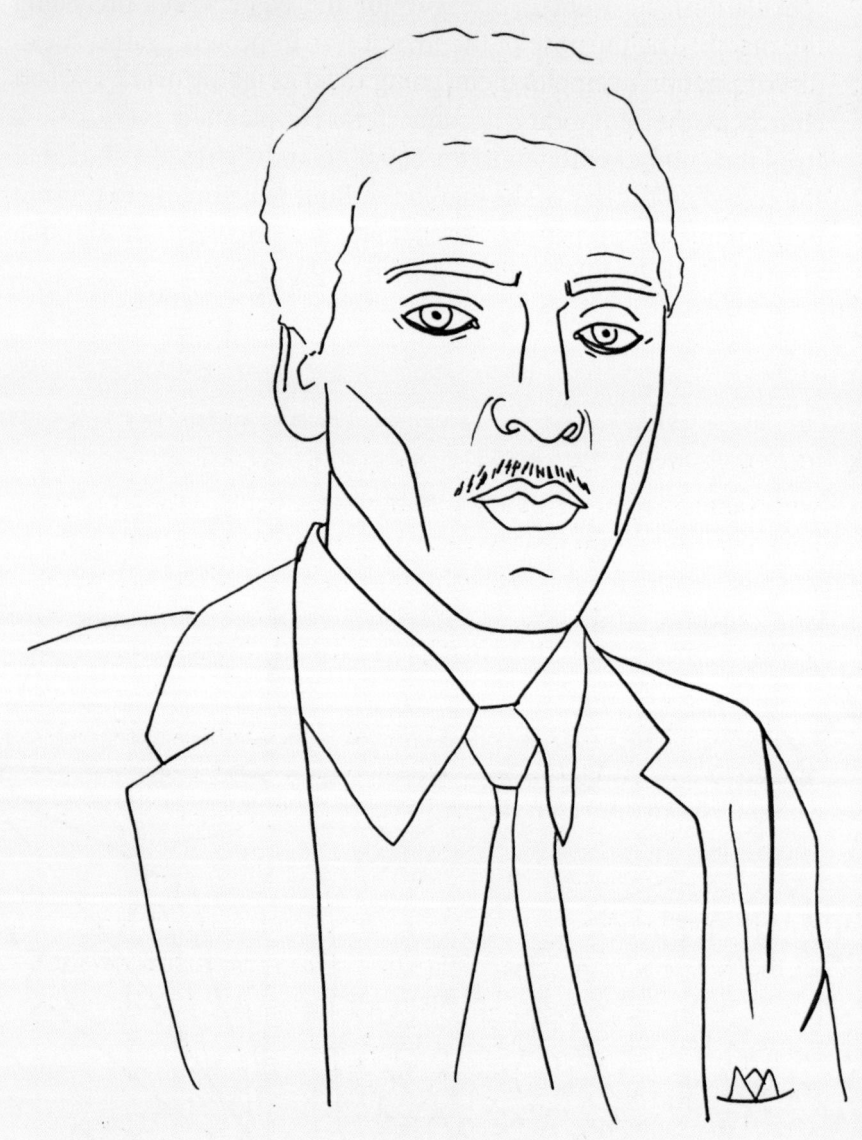

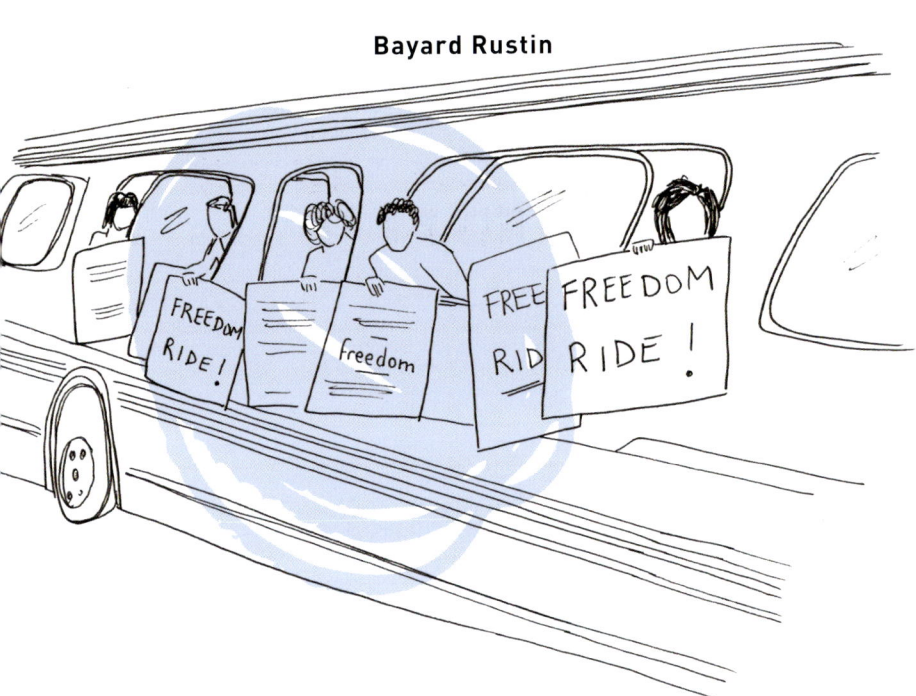

The 1970s onwards were liberating years for Bayard Rustin, who, benefiting from the wave of gay rights demonstrations, was able to speak in public on several occasions, including in 1986 during the debate on New York's anti-discrimination law against homosexuals. At the end of his life, he compared the struggle of gay people to that of Black people a few years earlier:

"Gays are starting to realize what Blacks learned long ago: Unless you are out here, fighting for yourself, then nobody else will help you. I think the gay community has a moral obligation to continue the fight."

Rustin continued to campaign for human rights, and was involved in many projects which helped people who were marginalized or under-represented in society such as refugees, displaced by war. He was on a humanitarian mission in Haiti at the time of his death.

Alan Turing
1912 – 1954

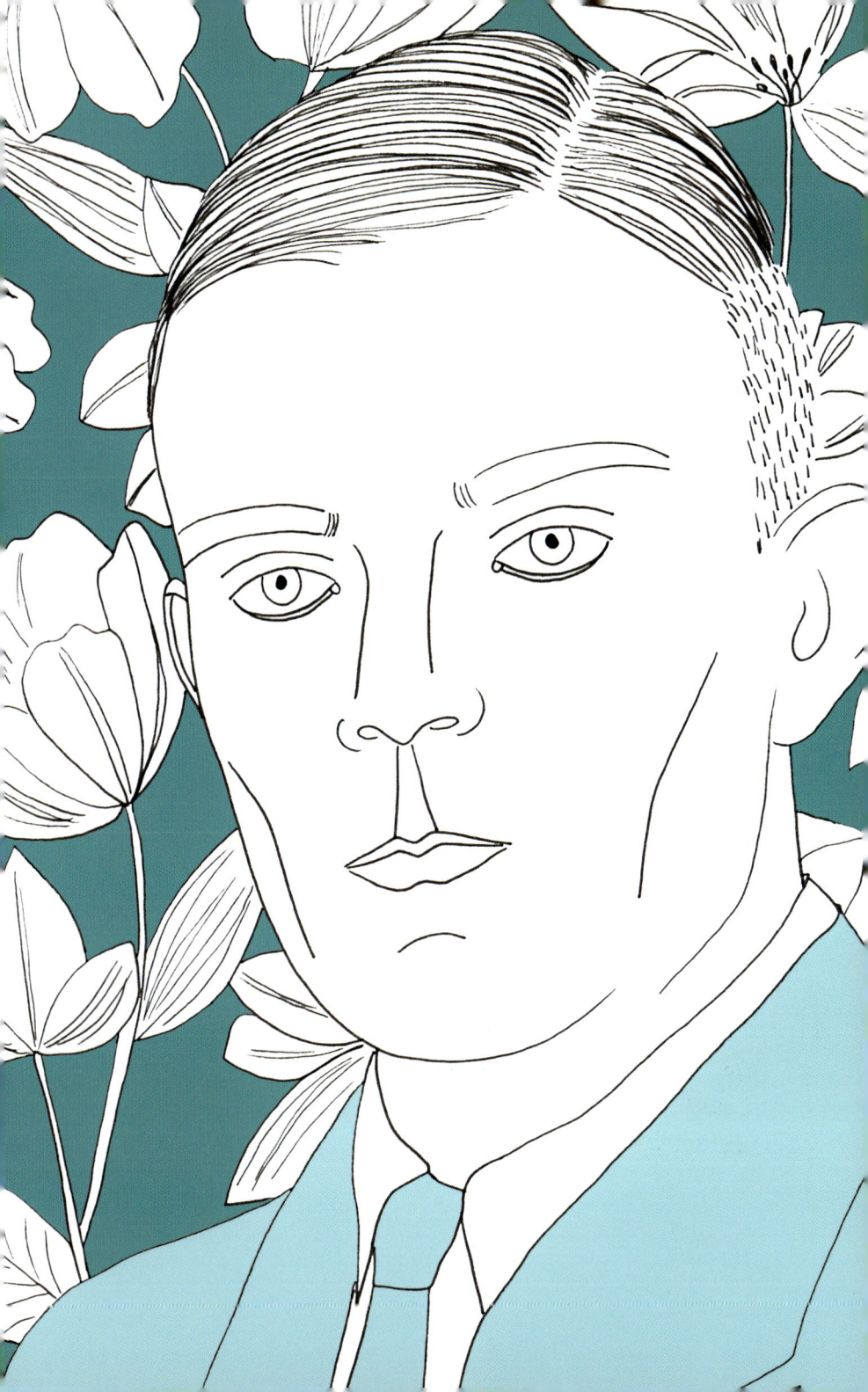

AN ENGLISH MATHEMATICIAN AND COMPUTER SCIENTIST, ALAN TURING STUDIED AND GRADUATED IN MATHEMATICS FROM KING'S COLLEGE, CAMBRIDGE IN 1933.

He won a scholarship and later became a graduate teaching assistant before obtaining his doctorate at Princeton University in the United States. He was passionate about science and mathematics, and some consider him the inventor of the computer and of theoretical modern computing as well as a pioneer of artificial intelligence. However, during his student years, he was regarded as a loner, and was often mocked and rejected by the other students. He immersed himself in his work with great rigour and remained dedicated to it throughout his life. Not only was he extremely strong, mentally, he could run long distances at a speed comparable to that of world-class marathons.

At the beginning of the Second World War, he was recruited by British intelligence and was assigned to work at the secret Bletchley Park centre alongside several hundred

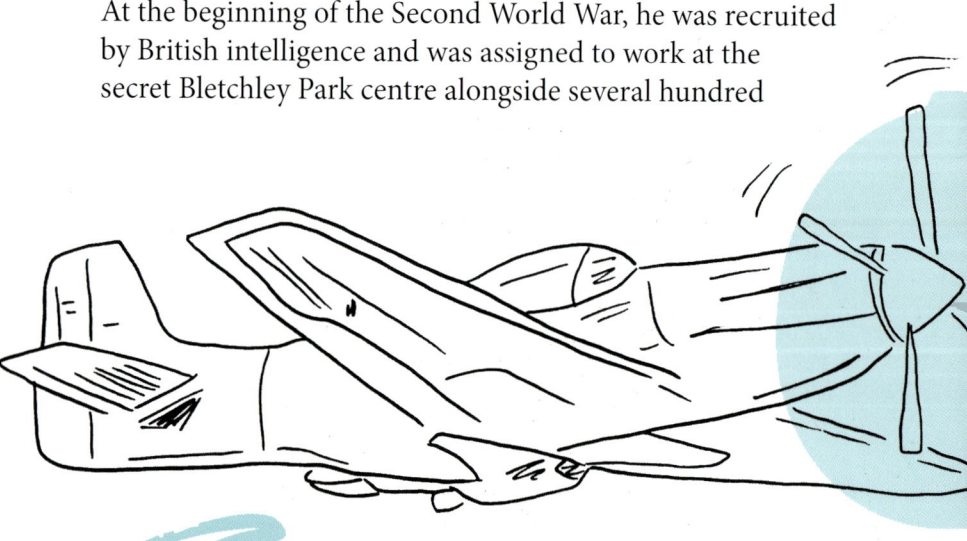

Alan Turing

mathematicians, researchers, and scientists.

Their job wasn't simple: to break the codes used by the German Enigma encryption machine in order to understand the radio messages that the Nazis exchanged with their submarines.

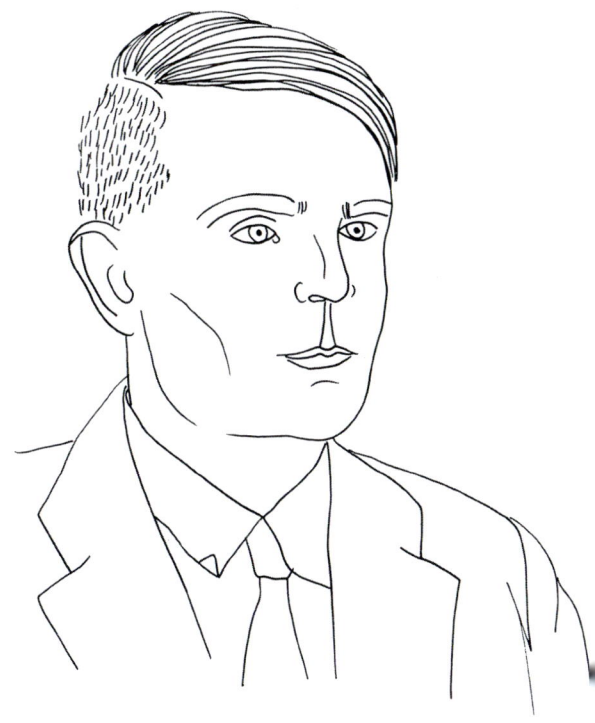

Alan Turing finally managed to decipher the codes used by the Enigma machine in 1942. From that moment, the Germans' attacks could be anticipated, and the Allies were able to plan their retaliation and counter-attacks with this knowledge – aiding their victory, sparing tens of thousands of lives and shortening the war.

> After the war, he continued to work and conduct his research, but those around him began to describe him as "eccentric". His proclivity for hanging out in known cruising spots, at a time when homosexuality was still a crime, aroused suspicion.

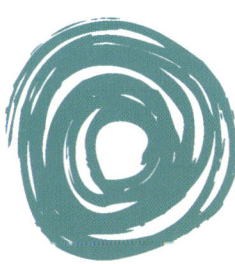

50 LGBTQI+ who changed the world

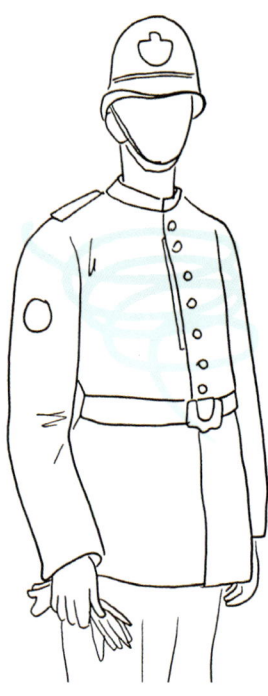

The police arrived at his home one day, after arresting Arnold Murray, a man who had spent the night at Turing's house and then robbed him. In an attempt to escape a conviction, the man denounced Turing for homosexuality, and Turing did not deny spending the night with him.

Tried and convicted in 1952 of "gross indecency", his only choices were either prison or probation – on the condition that he undergo chemical castration. Lawyers advised him to accept the latter.

The process involved regular oestrogen injections which made him impotent and caused him to develop breasts. His mental health and physical condition deteriorated over the months of this supposed "treatment". He died in 1954 after biting into an apple poisoned with cyanide. The coroner's official verdict was suicide.

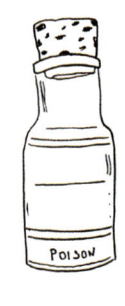
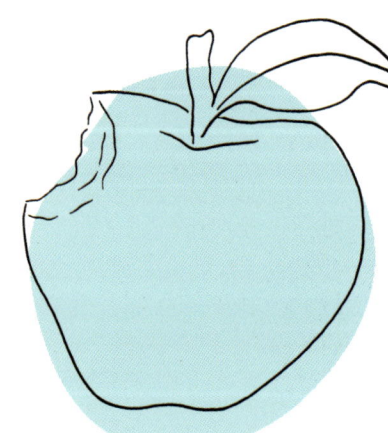

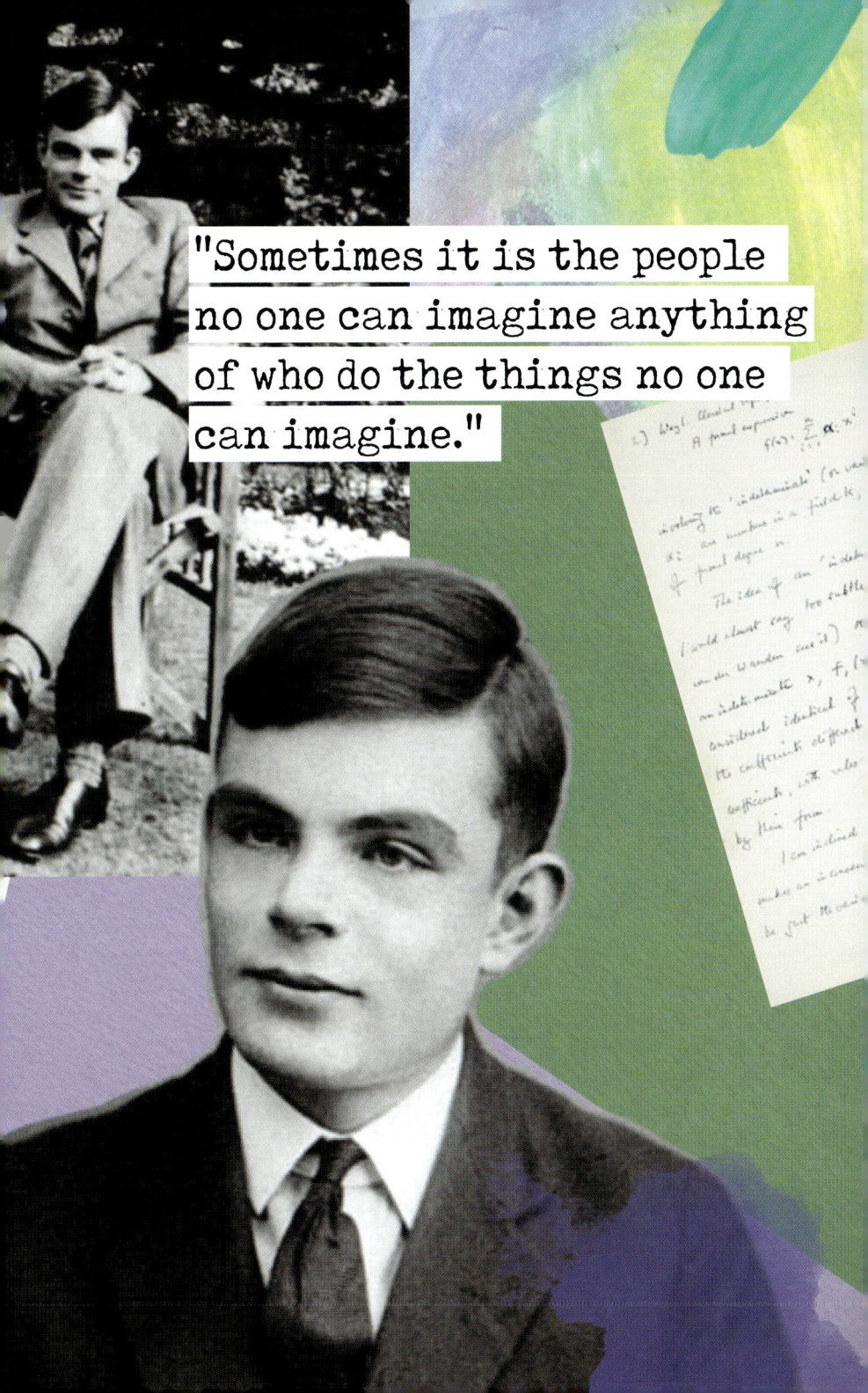

"Sometimes it is the people no one can imagine anything of who do the things no one can imagine."

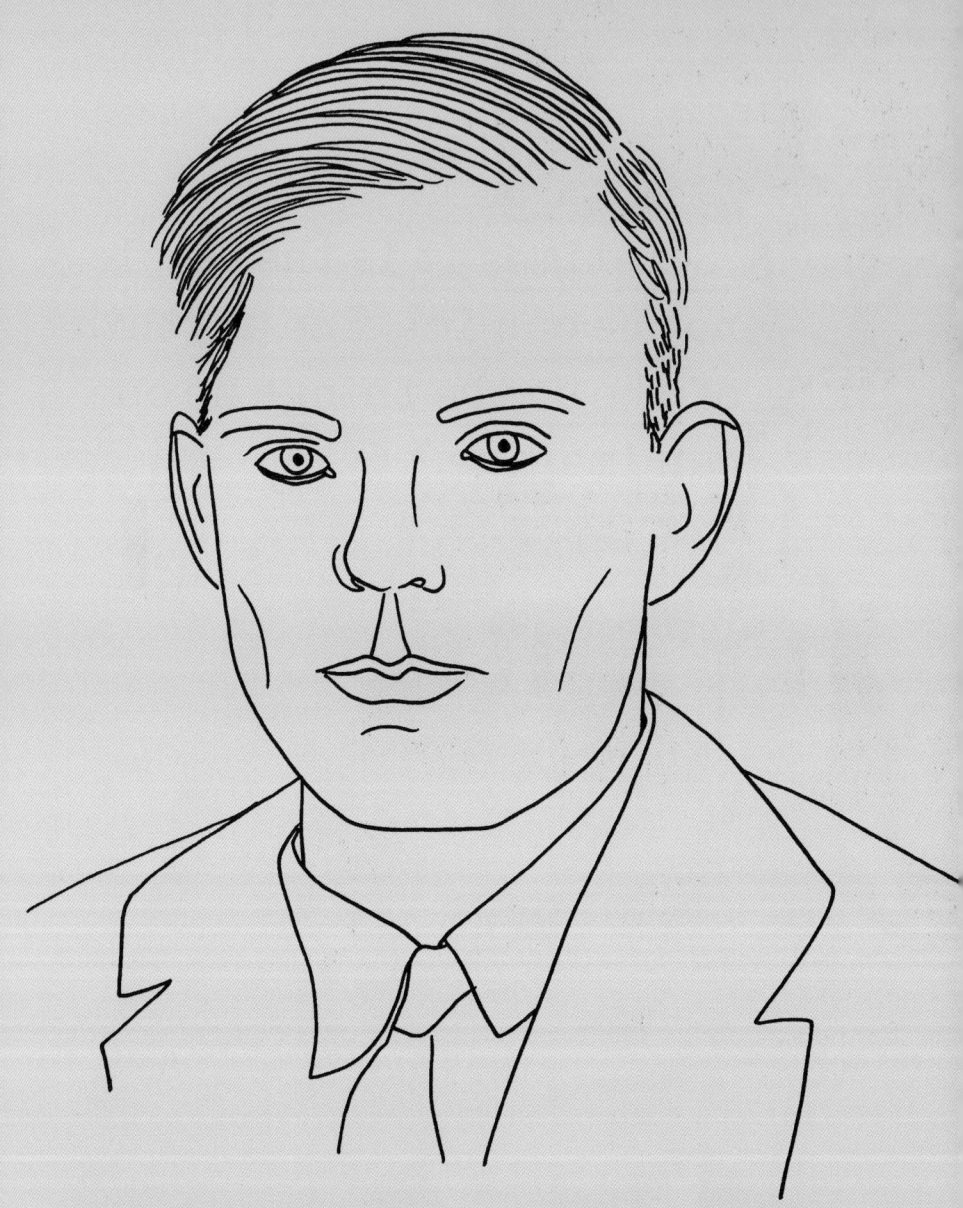

Long forgotten by history, his memory was not rehabilitated until 2013, when he was pardoned by the Queen of England following a petition led by several well-known scholars and scientists. His face began appearing on £50 notes in England in 2021, becoming the first LGBTQI+ person to appear on a bank note in the United Kingdom.

The Alan Turing Institute

A life-size statue of Alan Turing, commissioned by the American philanthropist Sidney Frank and created by sculptor Stephen Kettle, was installed at Bletchley Park in 2007.

The Turing Award, named in his honour, is now known colloquially as the Nobel Prize for Computer Science. It is awarded by the Association of Computing Machinery annually for contributions of lasting and major technical importance to computer science. Since 2014, the award has been accompanied by a prize of US$1 million, with support provided by Google.

The Imitation Game, a movie released in 2014 starring Benedict Cumberbatch, brought Turing's life to the big screen. A national institute for data science and artificial intelligence, headquartered at the British Library in London, was also named in his honour: The Alan Turing Institute.

Tom of Finland
1920 – 1991

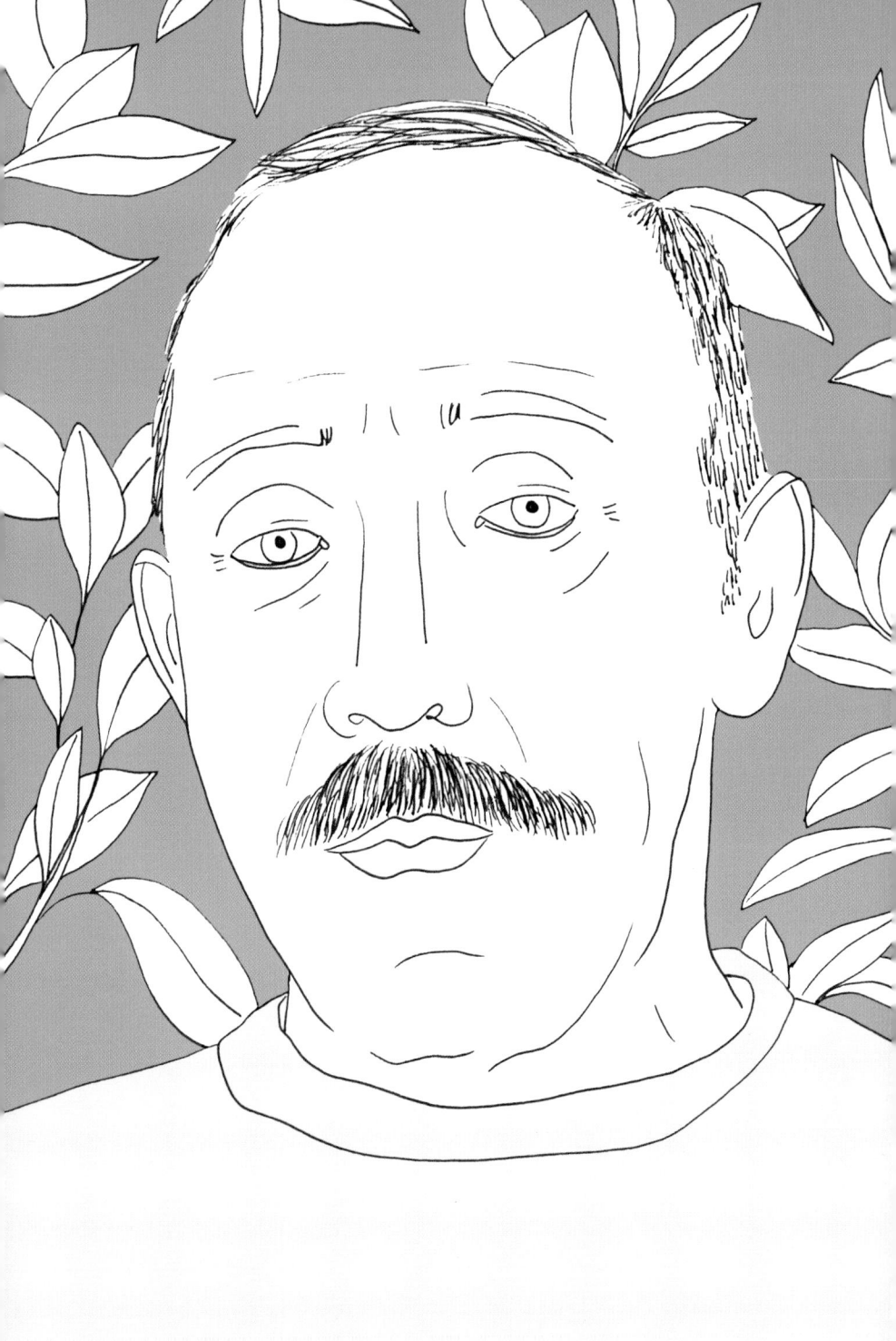

THIS FINNISH ARTIST, WHOSE REAL NAME IS TOUKO LAAKSONEN, LEFT A LASTING MARK ON GAY CULTURE OF THE 1970S AND 80S.

He produced thousands of erotic drawings of men in tight clothing which are still used today to illustrate articles and books. His subjects included policemen, men in leather, soldiers, bikers, and sailors. He had a talent for depicting men with muscular bodies, wearing tight pants and often shirtless.

In 1939, he began studying art, before being conscripted into the Finnish army in 1940 to fight against the Soviet Union. The Nazi armed forces stationed in Finland inspired his taste for uniforms during this period. After the war, he resumed his studies at art school and worked in advertising.

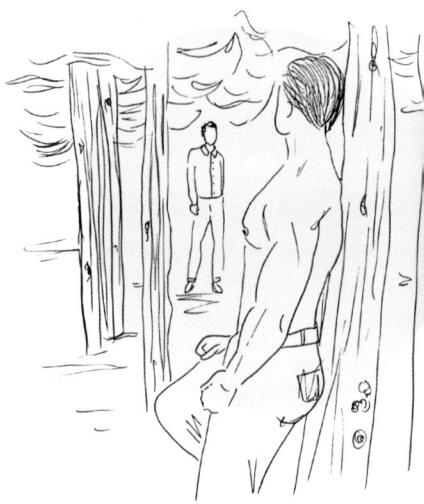

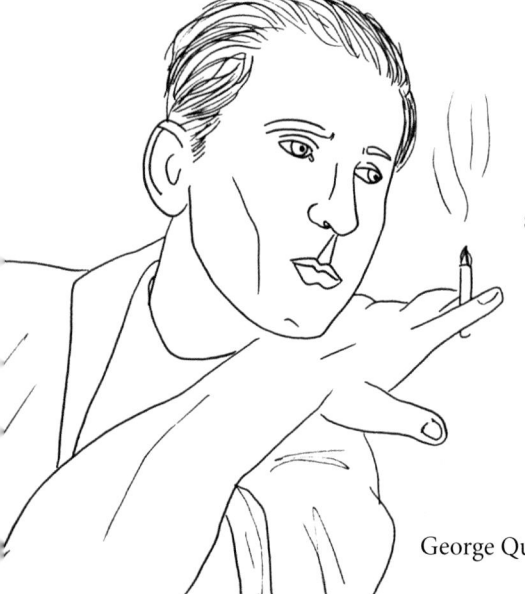

A fan of cruising spots, it was in these clandestine gay social spaces that he found inspiration, as homosexuality was illegal in Finland until 1971. He was also inspired to create his idealized vision of male bodies from the work of other artists such as George Quaintance.

George Quaintance

Tom of Finland

His first drawings were published in the journal *Physique Pictorial* (an American bodybuilding magazine) in 1957. It was at this time that he started using the pseudonym "Tom of Finland", which was less risky under United States censorship laws and easier for readers to remember. His stylized drawings quickly attracted the curiosity of the public and became a success at a time when gay representation in the media was uncommon.

PHYSIQUE   PICTORIAL

The period of censorship in America from the 1950s to the 60s harmed both the development of his career as an artist and his ability to publish his work widely. Although private orders poured in, he continued to work in advertising until 1973.

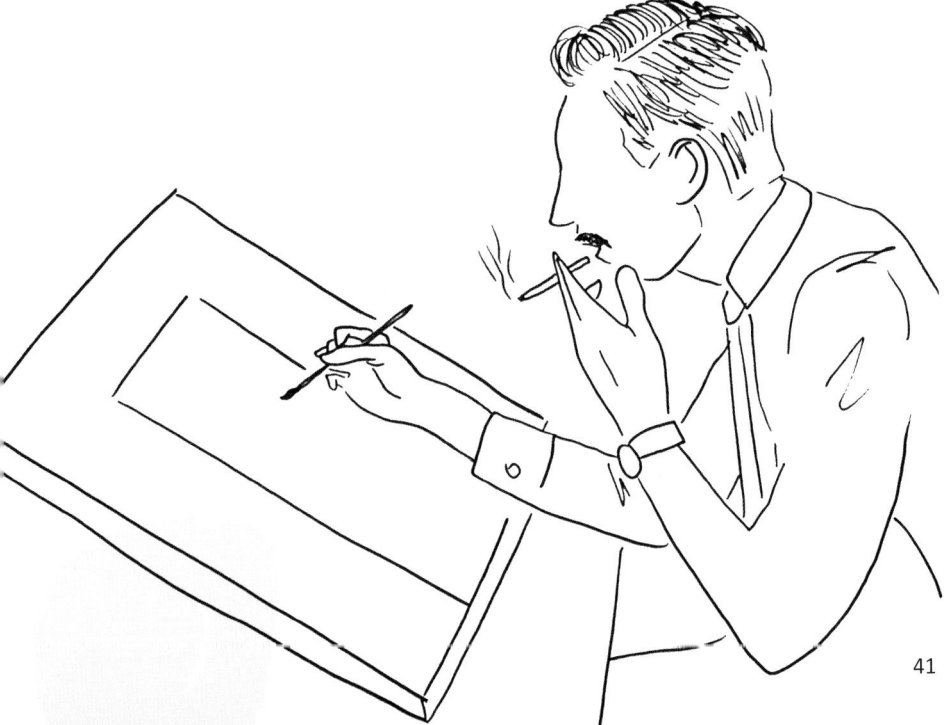

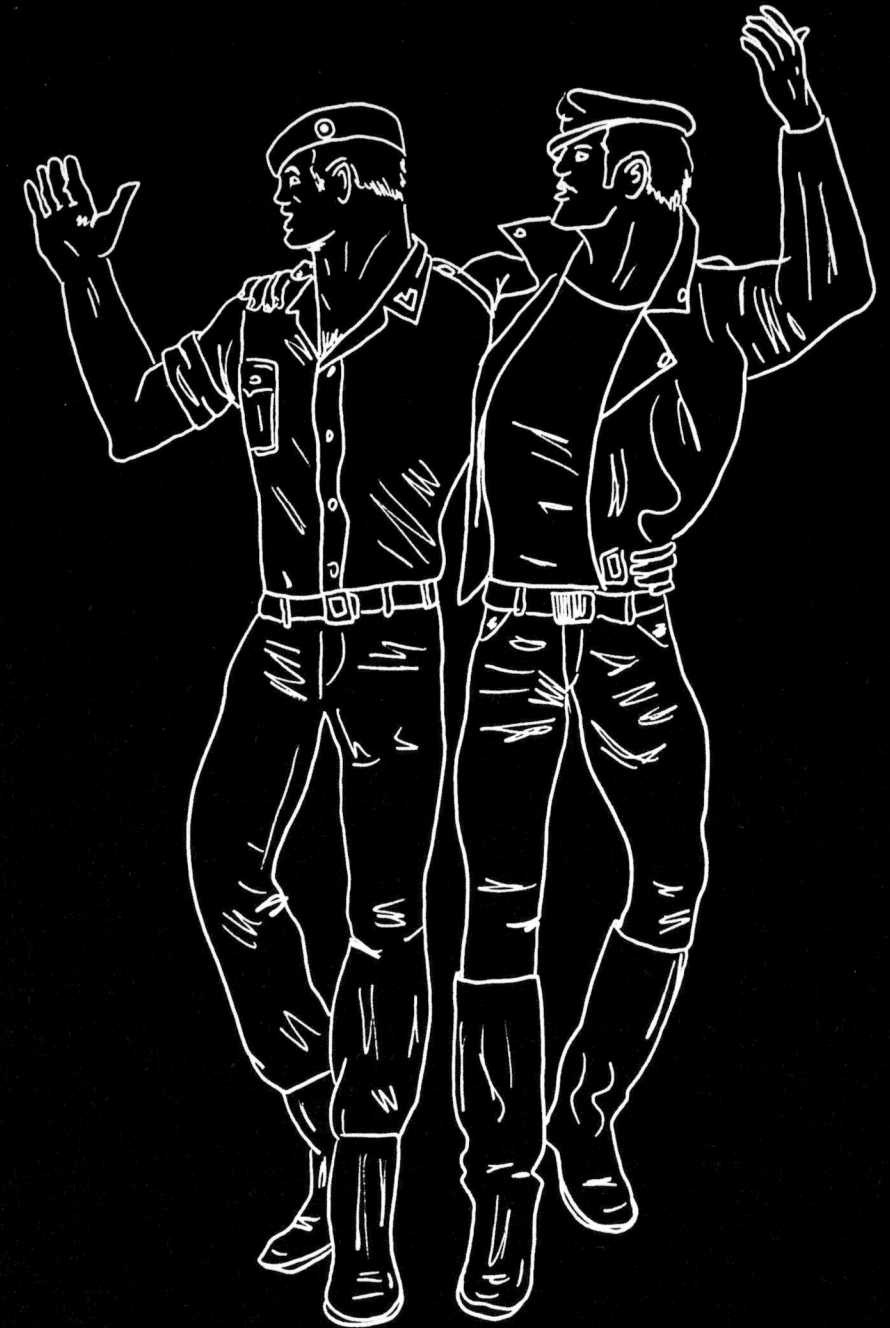

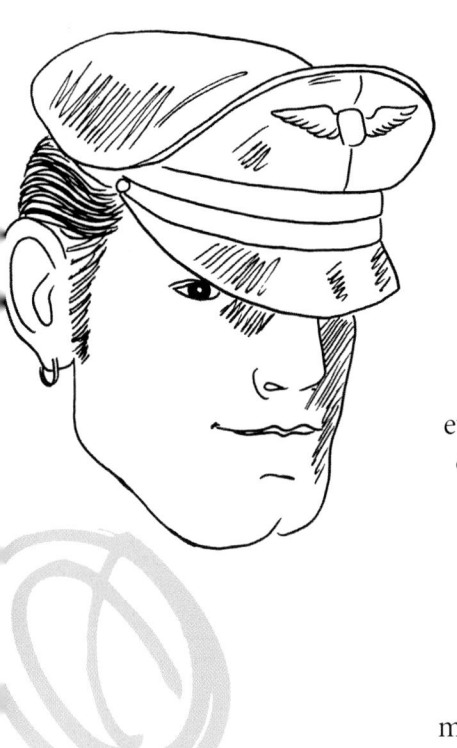

In 1962, the Supreme Court decided that magazines containing images of naked or nearly naked men were no longer considered to be obscene and they lifted the prohibition. This decision paved the way for the free publication of gay magazines in the United States and changed everything for Tom of Finland. His career finally began to flourish; he drew extensively, exhibited, and published his drawings in magazines and books.

Tom of Finland's fetishistic and homoerotic depictions of hyper-masculine bodies have made his art and creations a visual and artistic symbol that is integral to the history of the gay community.

"I ALMOST NEVER DRAW A COMPLETELY NAKED MAN. HE HAS TO HAVE AT LEAST A PAIR OF BOOTS OR SOMETHING ON... DRESS HIM IN BLACK LEATHER OR A UNIFORM – AH, THEN HE IS MORE THAN BEAUTIFUL, THEN HE IS SEXY!"

He co-founded the Tom of Finland Company in 1979, and the Tom of Finland Foundation five years later, to preserve the legacy and archives of his work.

After his death in 1991, his works in turn inspired other artists such as Pierre & Gilles and have become monuments of gay pop culture.

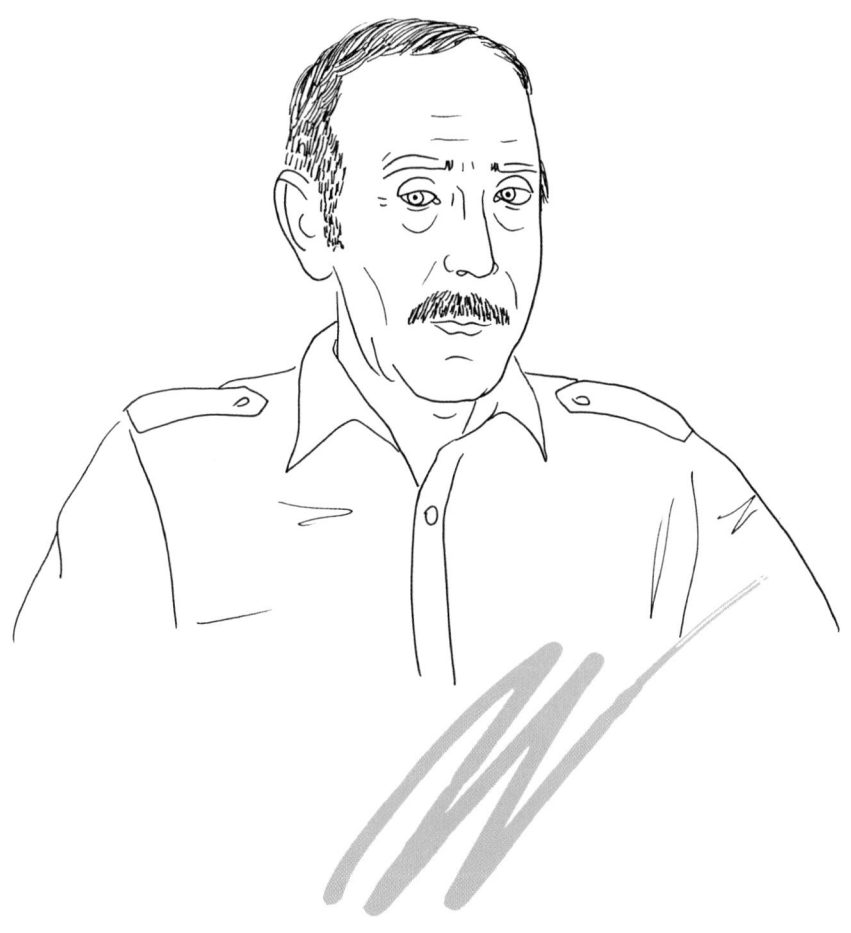

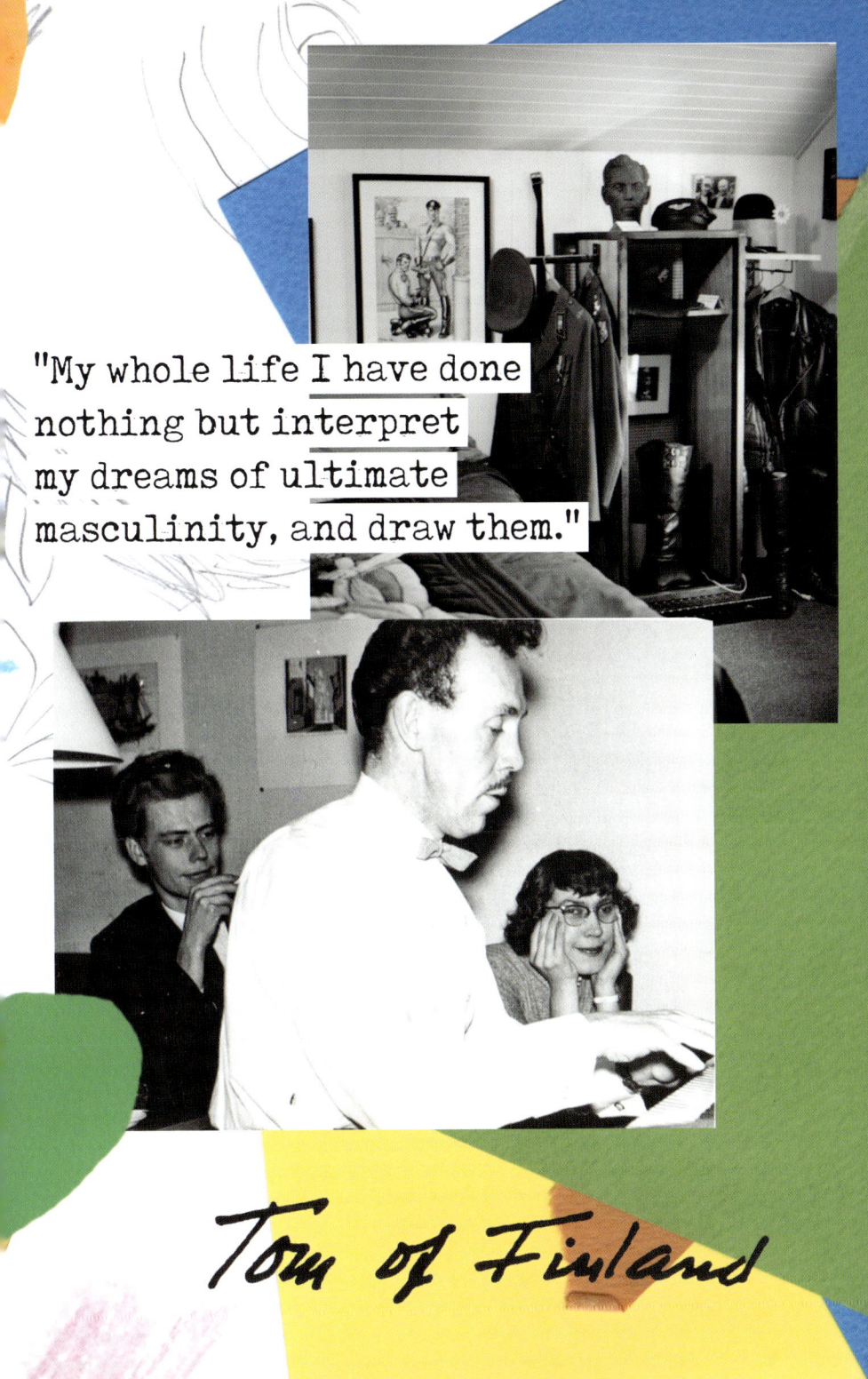

Edith Windsor
1929 – 2017

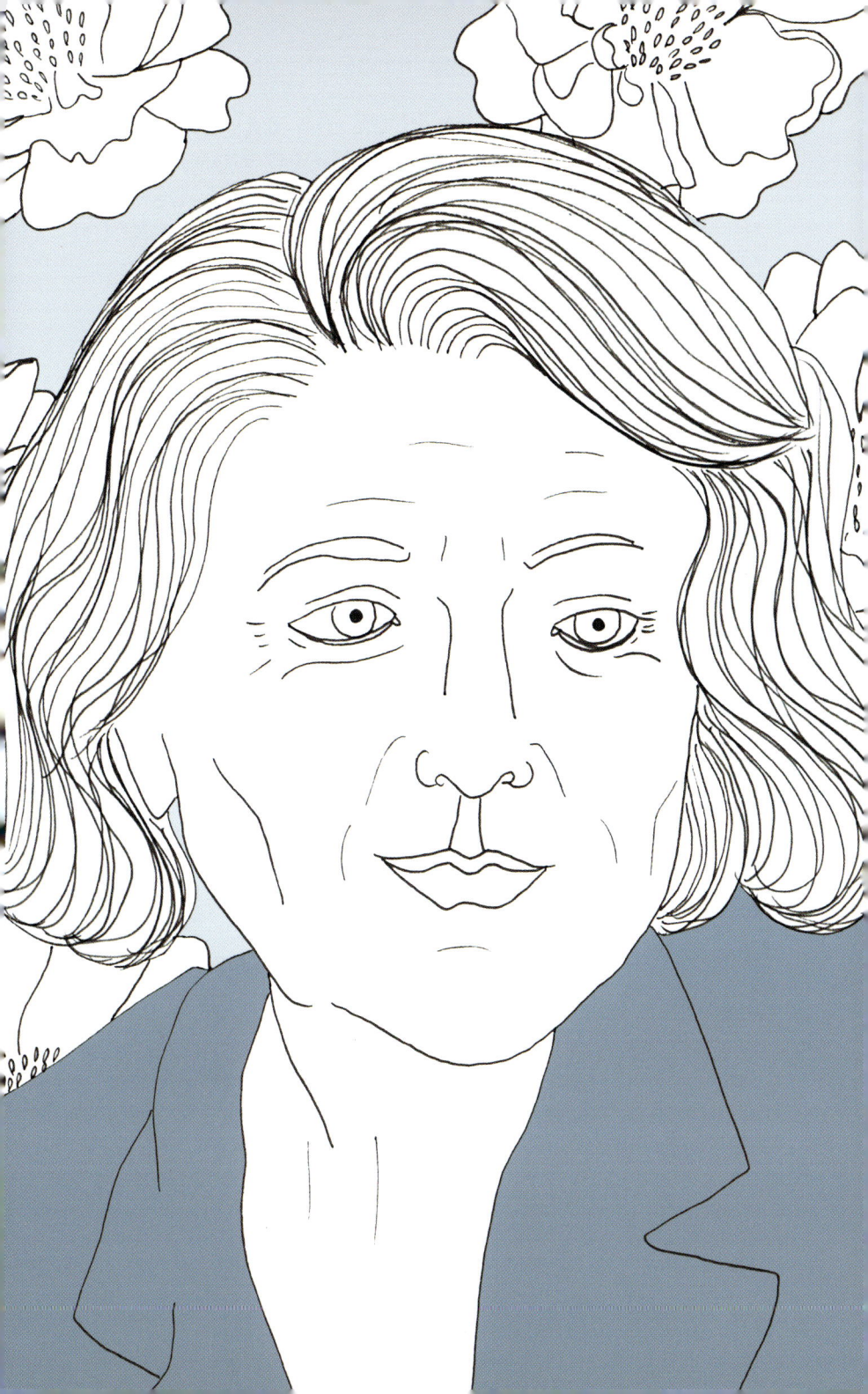

EDITH WINDSOR IS AN ICON OF GAY RIGHTS. IT WAS THANKS TO THIS 84-YEAR-OLD WOMAN THAT, IN 2013, THE FEDERAL LAW OF THE DEFENSE OF MARRIAGE ACT (DOMA) WAS RULED UNCONSTITUTIONAL IN THE UNITED STATES.

DOMA, was a law which came into effect in 1996 under President Bill Clinton, defining marriage at the federal level, as the union of a man and a woman. As a result, many federal rights were not applicable to same-sex couples, particularly in the case of spousal rights after death.

After being married for less than a year to a man, Edith Windsor divorced him in 1952, wishing to live her own life and no longer lie to herself. She knew she was sexually and emotionally attracted to women, but the 1950s was not an easy period to live openly as a lesbian. At around this time, she returned to New York University and studied mathematics there. She became an expert in computer programming and worked for many years for IBM.

In 1963, she met the woman who would become her partner for more than forty years: Thea Spyer. To celebrate their union, Edith Windsor, whom everyone called Edie, offered her an "engagement brooch".
Both were very active in the various gay liberation movements that followed the Stonewall riots.

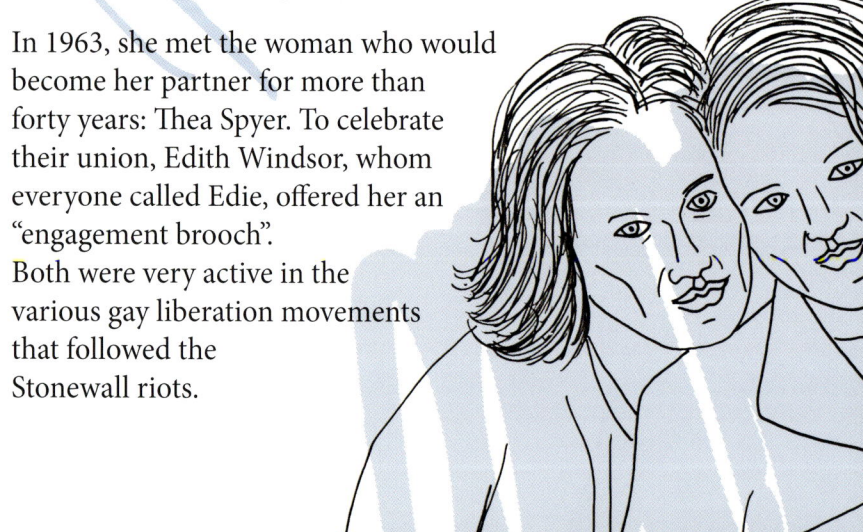

Edith Windsor

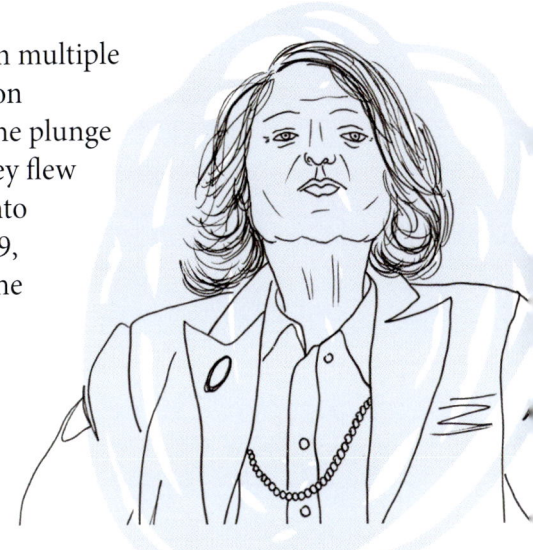

In the early 2000s, suffering from multiple sclerosis and feeling her condition deteriorating, Thea Spyer took the plunge and married Edith Windsor. They flew to Canada and married in Toronto in 2007. When Thea died in 2009, she bequeathed the apartment she owned to Edie. But the United States did not recognize their union, meaning Edith Windsor couldn't benefit from the federal rights applicable to married couples, and tax administration claimed $363,053 in respect of her estate.

She filed a complaint against the state and brought a case before the Supreme Court of the United States. On 26th June 2013, the Court ruled that DOMA was unconstitutional, which laid the foundation for marriage equality in the United States. By making the historic decision to annul DOMA, the Supreme Court had to give same-sex couples access to the same federal benefits as heterosexual couples.

Edith Windsor's victory made her a spokesperson for gay rights. She was even named one of the most influential people of 2013 by *Time* magazine. During the last years of her life, she continued to demonstrate for the legalization of marriage for same-sex couples throughout the United States while providing support and visibility to various LGBTQI+ organizations.

Harvey Milk
1930 – 1978

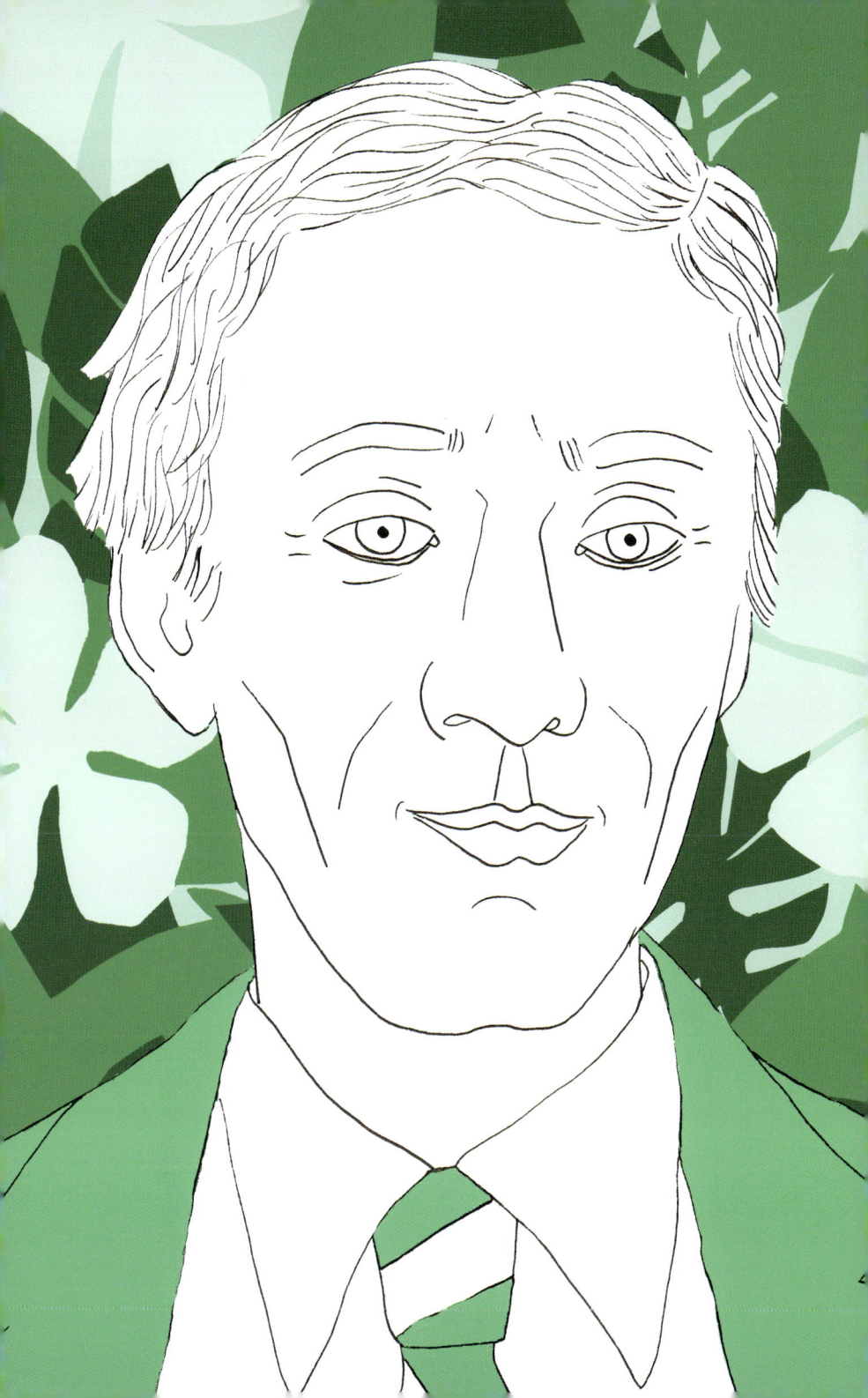

"HOPE WILL NEVER BE SILENT," HARVEY MILK ONCE SAID, AND HOPE ALWAYS GUIDED HIM IN HIS FIGHT FOR GAY PEOPLE'S RIGHTS.

Long before he won the 1977 municipal elections, and made history as the first openly gay person to win an electoral mandate, Harvey Milk left the Navy at the age of twenty-five due to the homophobia he faced.

He worked at a series of jobs in New York and then moved with his partner Scott Smith to San Francisco, like many gay men in the early 1970s. He opened a camera store in the Castro, San Francisco's gay neighbourhood, and quickly became a key figure. He even created the Castro Valley Association of Local Merchants, an association of local traders, leading some people to name him the "Mayor of Castro Street", a far cry from his childhood nickname of "Glimpy".

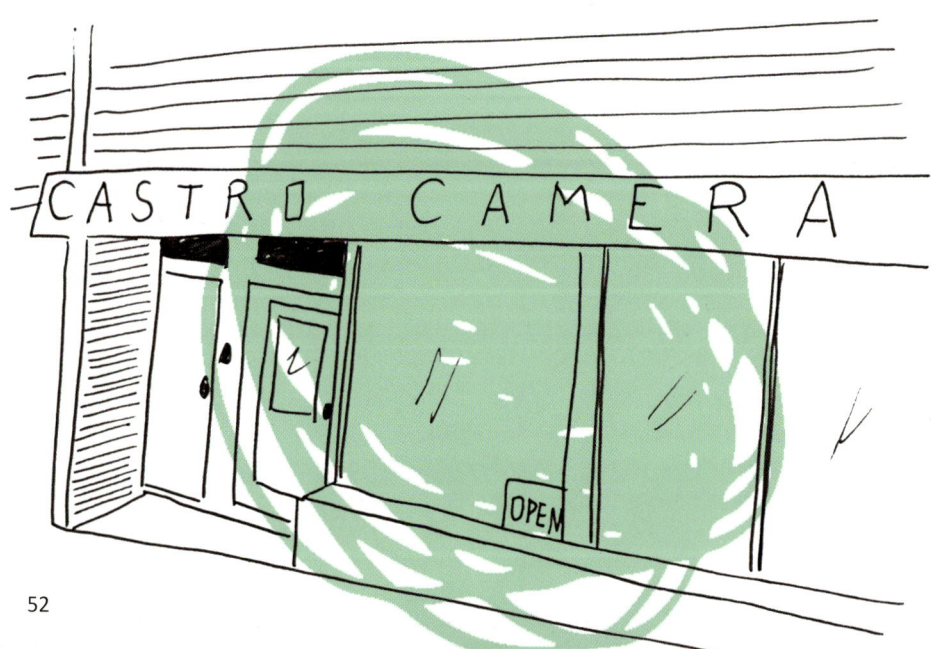

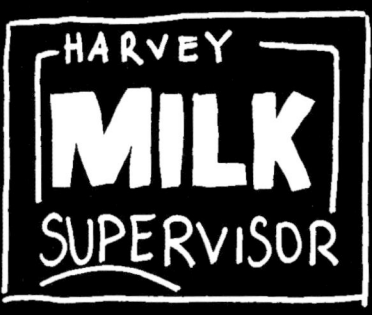

Deeply committed and determined to make the voice of gay people heard, he ran in the San Francisco municipal elections in 1973 and 1975. Whilst these initial attempts failed, he did begin to gain some popularity.

He was eventually elected onto the city's Board of Supervisors in 1977, and helped, during his short term, to defeat a bill led by John Briggs, which would have authorized the dismissal of gay teachers and banned them from the profession. He also waged a fierce battle against the singer Anita Bryant, who was openly homophobic and was involved in campaigns against gay and lesbian people across the country.

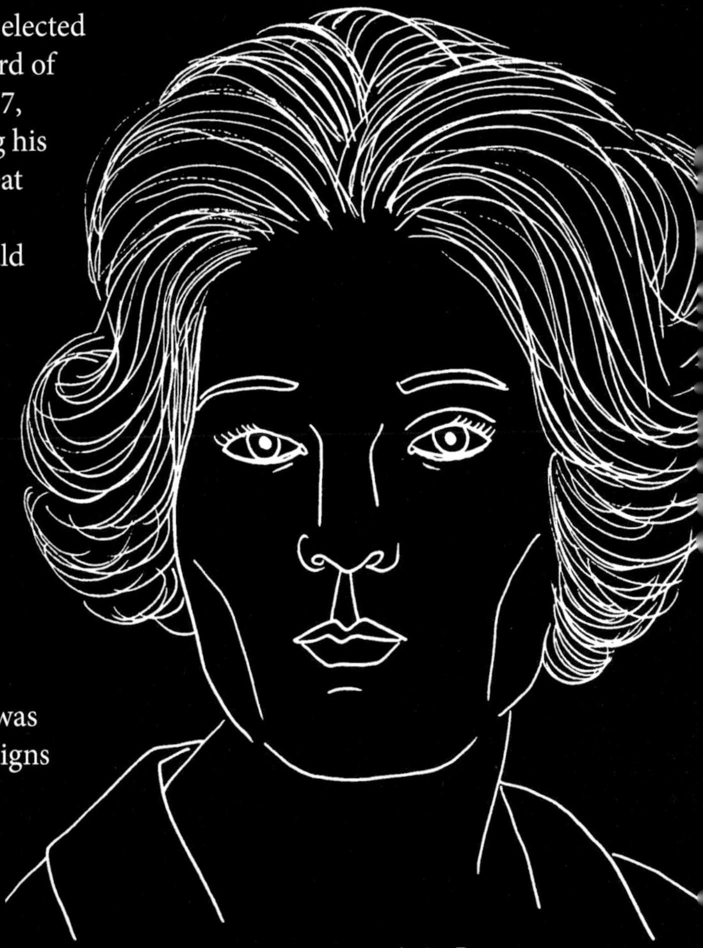

Anita Bryant

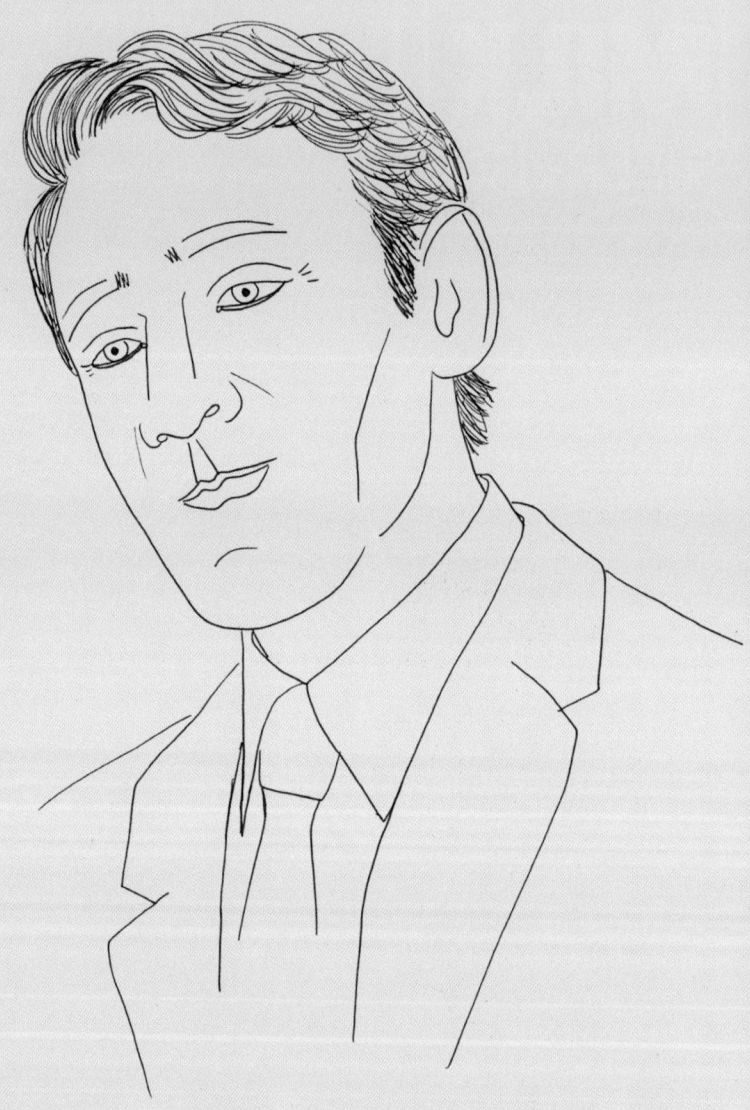

"RIGHTS ARE WON ONLY BY THOSE WHO MAKE THEIR VOICES HEARD."

Harvey Milk

In 1978, Dan White, a Conservative city councillor, assassinated Harvey Milk and San Francisco Mayor George Moscone. It deeply shocked the gay community in America, who have continued to keep Harvey Milk's memory alive and pay tribute to him to this day.

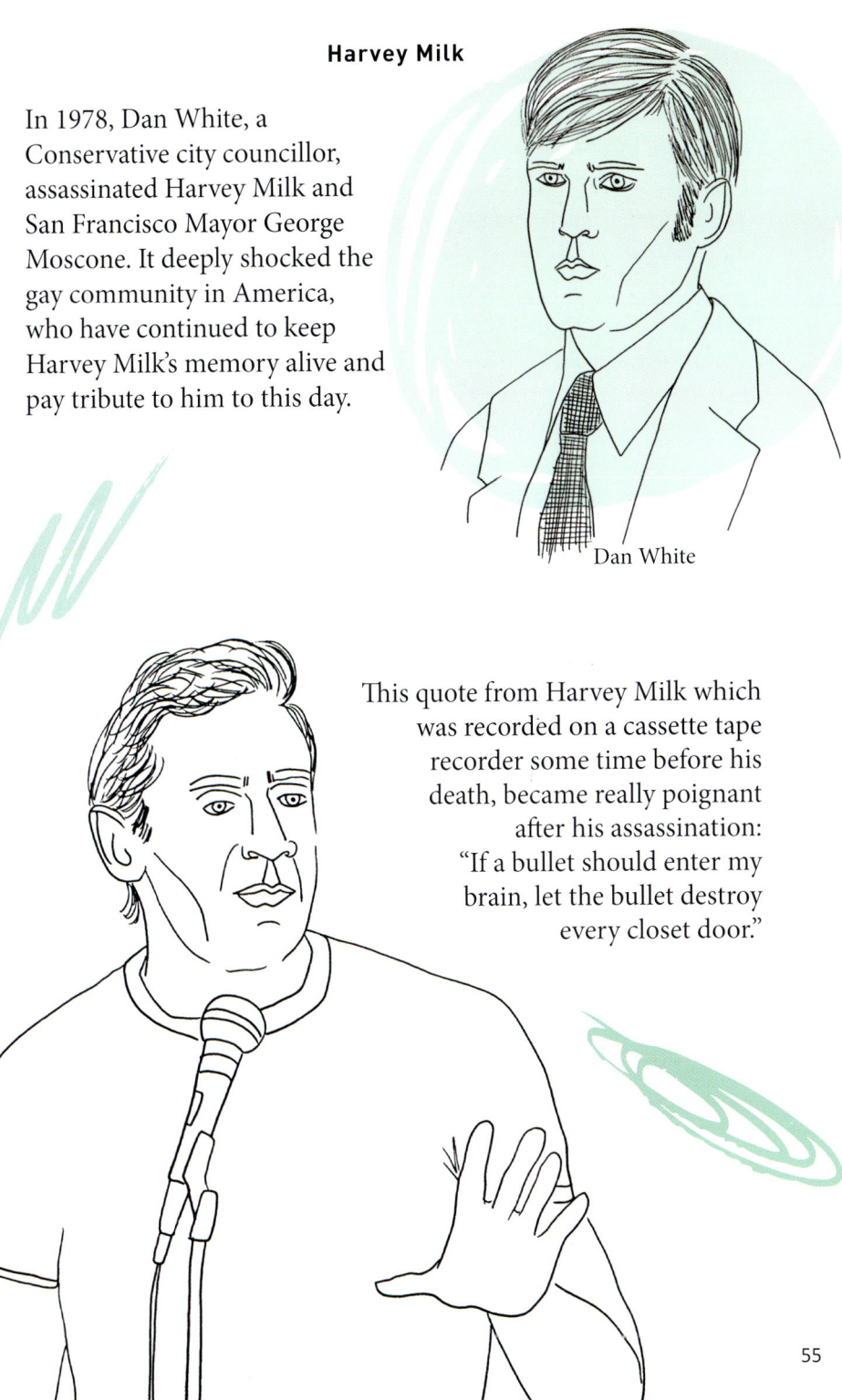

Dan White

This quote from Harvey Milk which was recorded on a cassette tape recorder some time before his death, became really poignant after his assassination: "If a bullet should enter my brain, let the bullet destroy every closet door."

His outspokenness, charisma, and commitment to the gay cause, have become known far beyond the streets of the Castro and have made him an LGBTQI+ icon around the world. A pioneer in the fight for gay rights, various institutions now bear his name.

His story even inspired Hollywood, with Sean Penn starring in the role of Harvey Milk in the biopic *Milk* (2008).

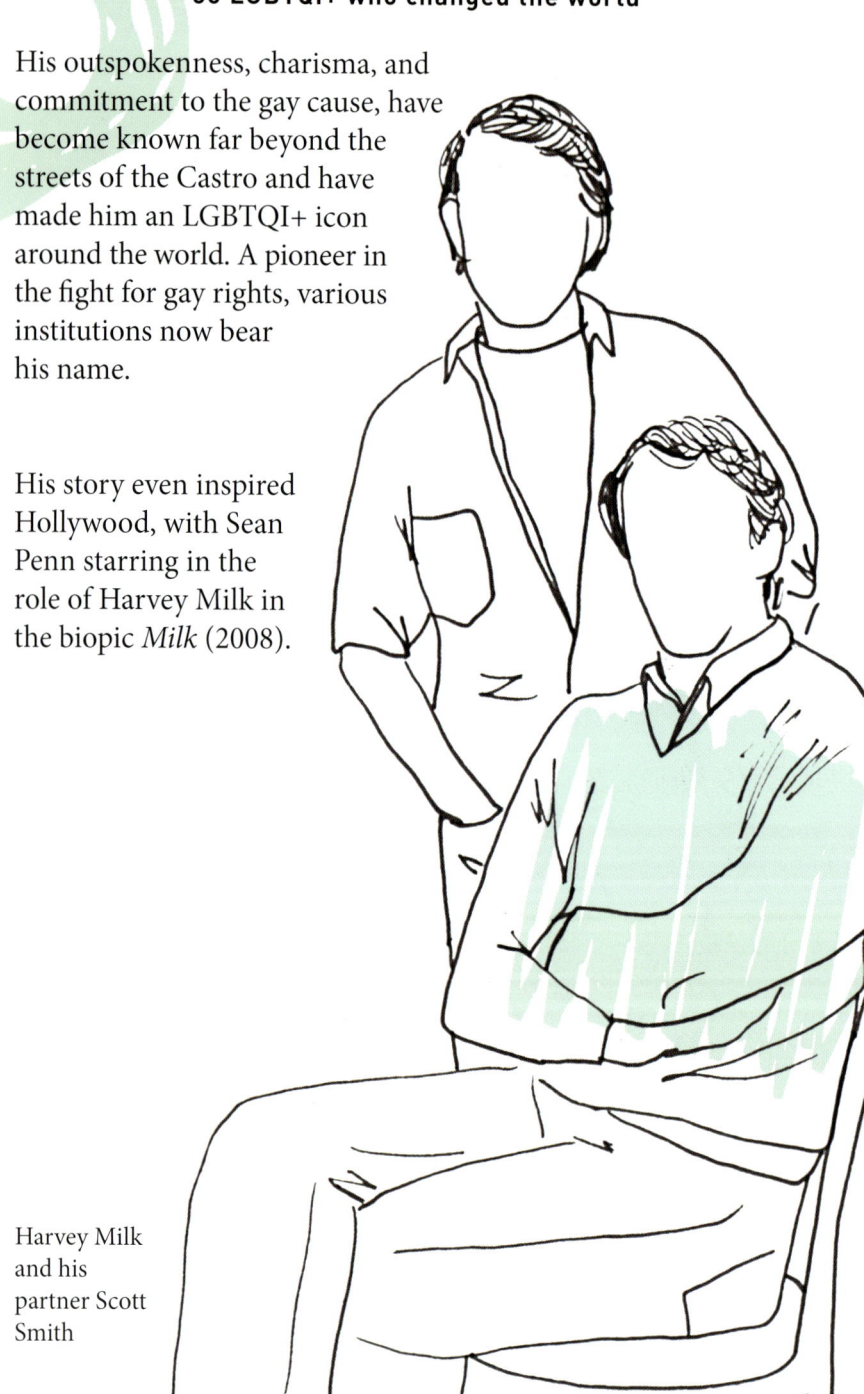

Harvey Milk and his partner Scott Smith

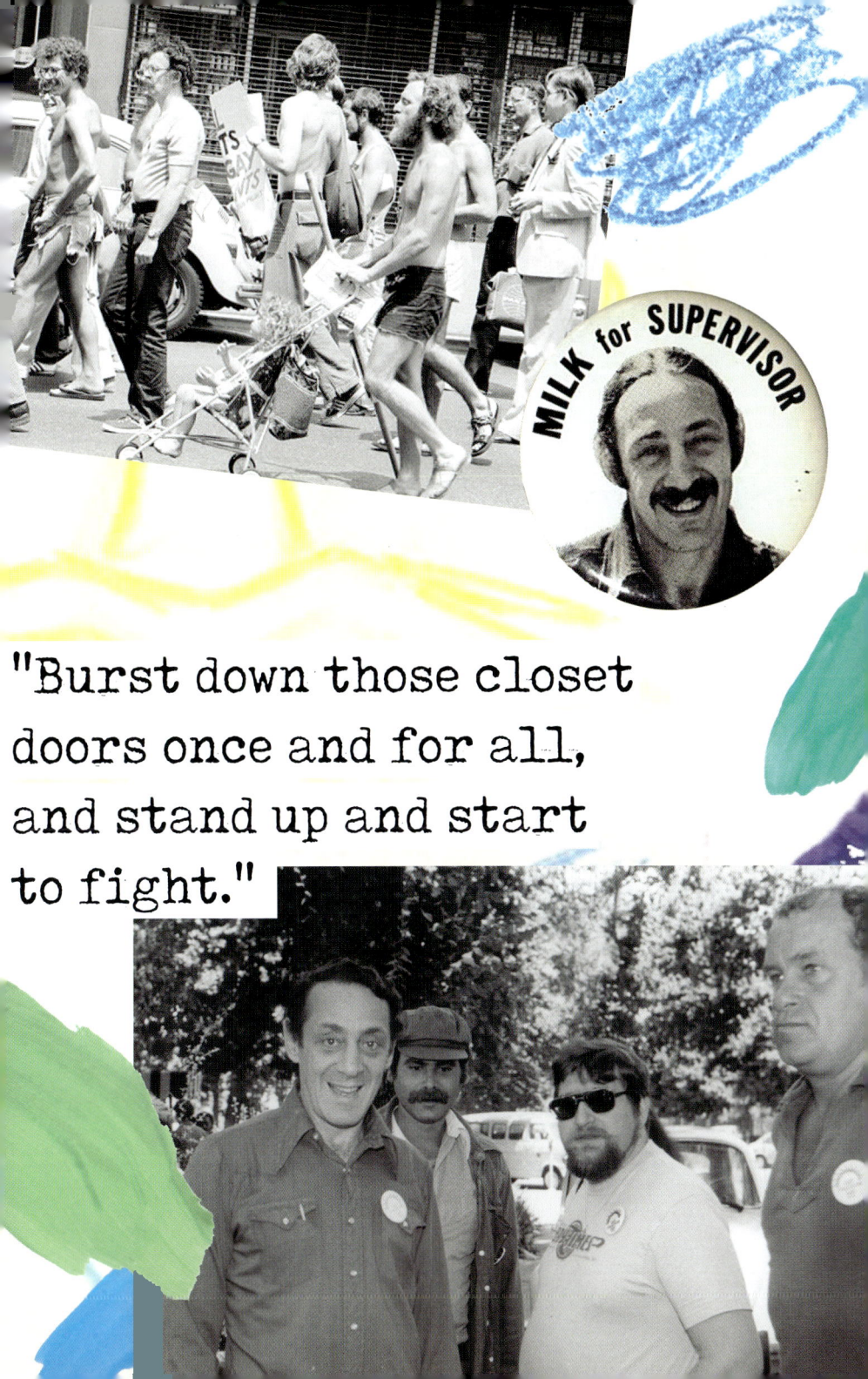

"Burst down those closet doors once and for all, and stand up and start to fight."

Barbara Gittings
1932 – 2007

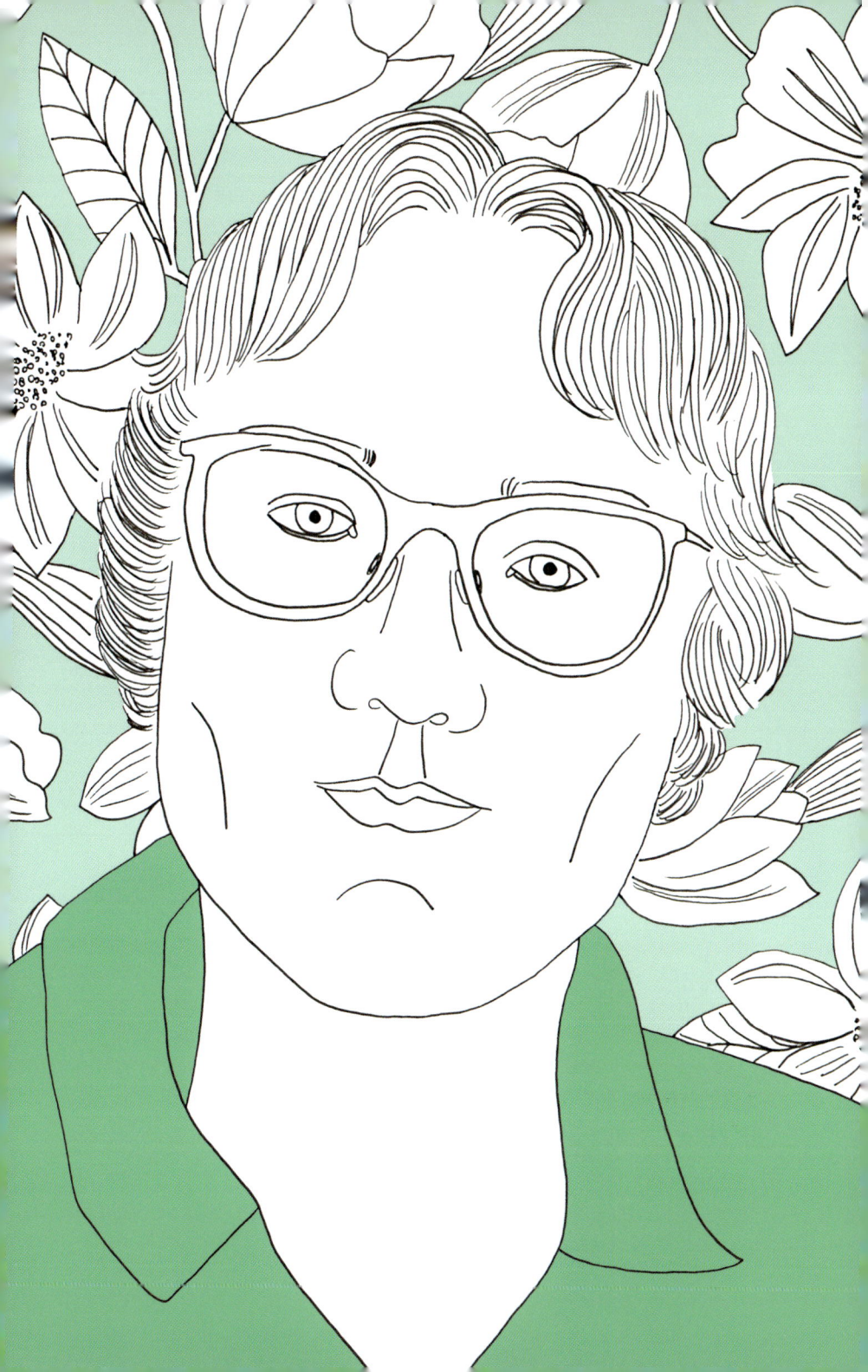

WHILST THE STONEWALL RIOTS ARE A MAJOR EVENT IN THE HISTORY OF LGBTQI+ STRUGGLES, IT IS IMPORTANT TO REMEMBER THAT OTHER GROUPS MOBILIZED LONG BEFORE 1969.

Barbara Gittings began her activism in 1958, at a time when those openly displaying their homosexuality in the United States risked being sent to prison. That year she founded the New York branch of the Daughters of Bilitis (DOB), which was the first lesbian rights organization created in 1955 in San Francisco by Del Martin and Phyllis Lyon.

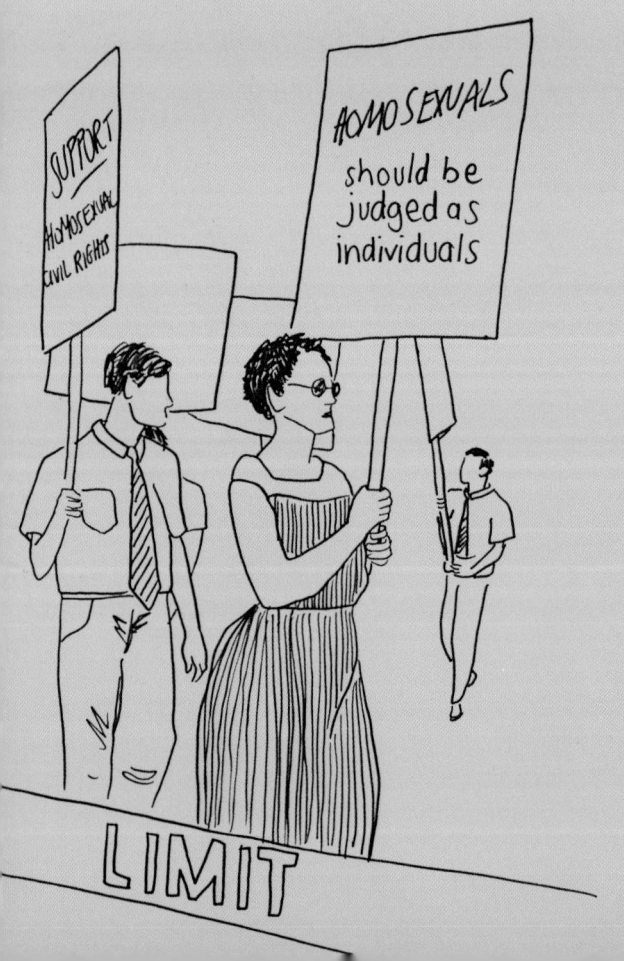

For three years, she was editor-in-chief of the association's magazine, *The Ladder*, the first lesbian magazine distributed monthly throughout the United States. With *The Ladder*, the Daughters of Bilitis enabled many lesbians, who couldn't express their sexuality openly, to see relationships between women represented in the media. Barbara Gittings became more politicized through her writing and editing of the magazine.

Barbara Gittings

In the company of a group of other campaigners, Barbara Gittings led the first public demonstrations in favour of gay and lesbian rights outside Independence Hall in Philadelphia. Whilst the protests were generally conducted by around forty people, these "Annual Reminder" demonstrations that took place every July 4 from 1965 to 1969 paved the way for the Stonewall riots. Subsequently, Barbara Gittings actively participated in the organization of the first Pride March in New York in 1970.

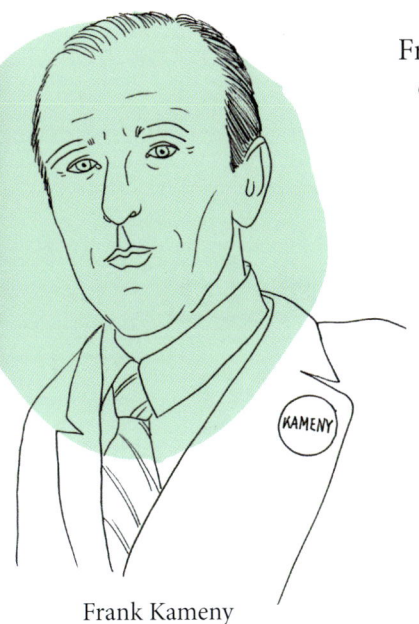

Frank Kameny

From 1970 to 1973, alongside a group of activists including Frank Kameny (another pioneering activist in the gay struggle), she fought to have homosexuality removed from the list of mental illnesses which was published by the American Psychiatric Association. Appearing on the APA list, gave a medical validity to clichés of perversity and madness, that surrounded gay people and lesbians at the time. The activists' victory helped to reduce these stigmas. Barbara Gittings argued that it is society that has a problem with homosexuality, not homosexuals who have a problem with their sexuality.

A great reader, she volunteered to work with the Gay Task Force of the American Library Association and became the group's coordinator for sixteen years. She advocated for more diversity in the book collections of American libraries and for gay and lesbian literature to be more readily available.

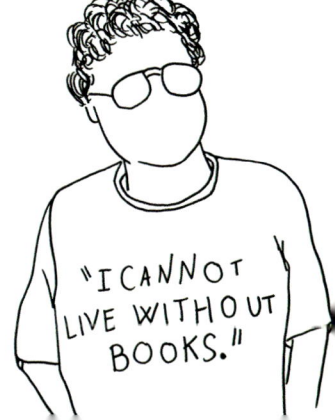

Audre Lorde
1934 – 1992

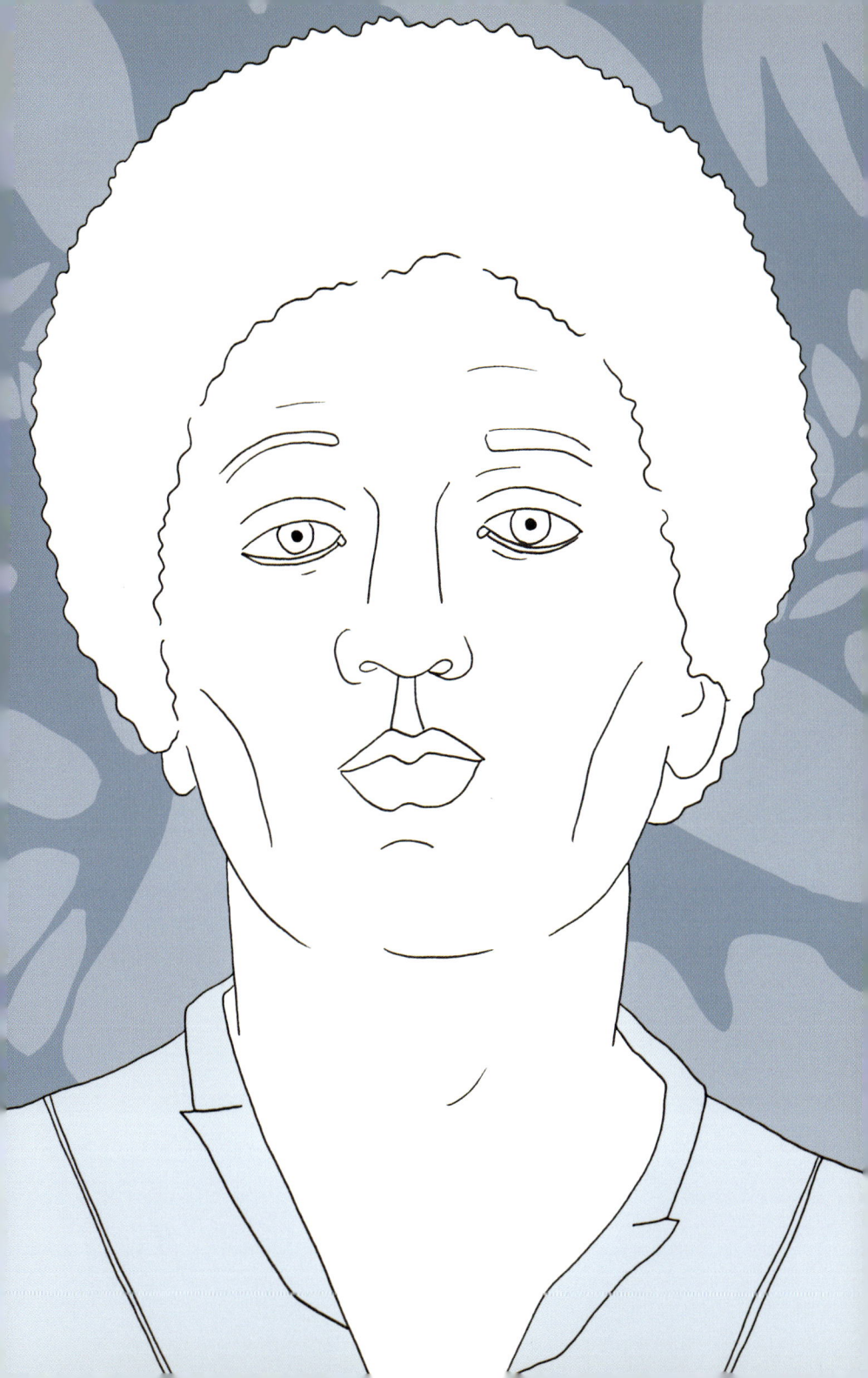

A BLACK POET, AUTHOR, FEMINIST AND A LESBIAN, AUDRE LORDE WAS A MAJOR AMERICAN LITERARY FIGURE IN THE SECOND WAVE FEMINIST MOVEMENT.

She became famous all over the world for her essays, poems, and political texts on racism, feminism, and homophobia. She published her first collection of poems, *The First Cities*, in 1968. A dozen books would follow, focused on motherhood, and her marginalized position as a Black woman and as a lesbian in a society that attemped to erase and silence her.

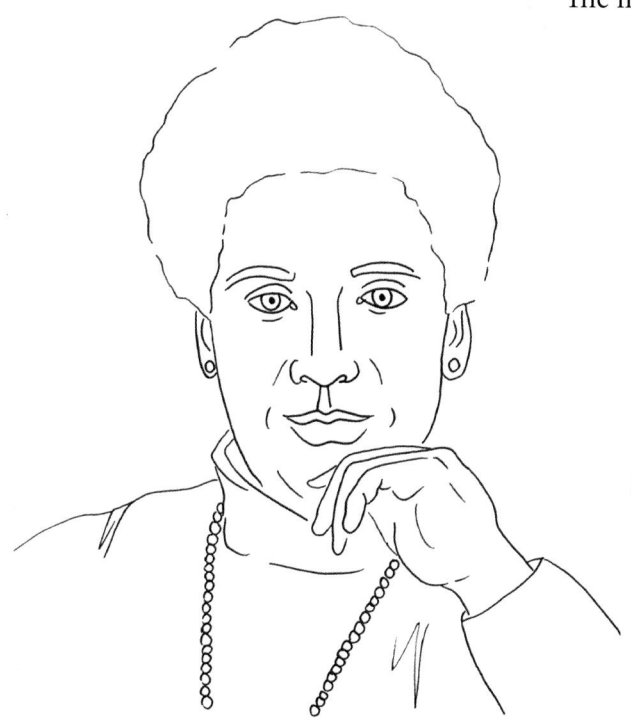

The intersectionality of her struggles was clear to the author, although this word hadn't yet been coined. Black and a lesbian, in a relationship with a white woman, previously married to a man with whom she had two children, Audre Lorde addressed social injustice in her writings with anger, directness, and an incisive pen.

Audre Lorde

"My silences had not protected me. Your silence will not protect you," she wrote. It was the need to speak out about abuse and social injustice that compelled Audre Lorde to write. Although the era was marked by an increase in protests and activism for civil rights, these protests largely ignored LGBTQI+ people and Black women. Although some of her texts were critically received by white feminists, she never changed her convictions that race and difference needed to be acknowledged. In the face of a violent world and a system that crushed marginalized people, writing was her way to fight back.

In *The Cancer Journals* (1980) (which won the American Library Association Gay Caucus Book of the Year Award in 1981), she offered an account of her battle with the disease from biopsy to mastectomy. She described the pain she endured, her relationship with death, as well as the health system, and the way in which female breast cancer survivors are encouraged to use prosthetics to fit in with societal norms of femininity. She wrote: "If I didn't define myself for myself, I would be crunched into other people's fantasies for me and eaten alive."

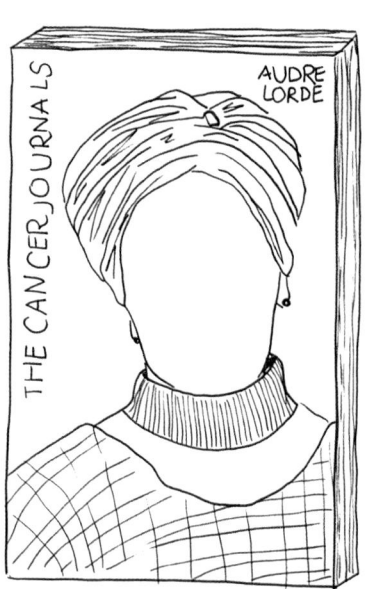

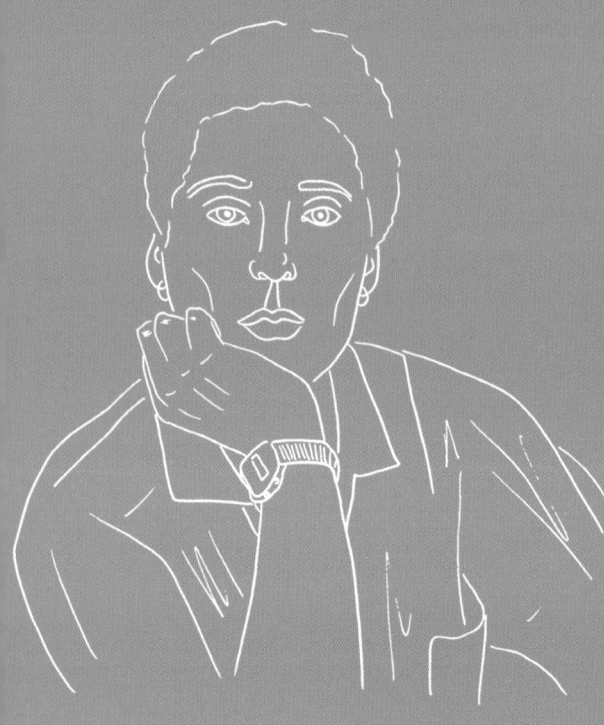
Barbara Smith

In 1981, Audre Lorde and Barbara Smith founded Kitchen Table: Women of Color Press, which specialized in encouraging the writings of other Black feminists.

In 1984, the book *Sister Outsider* was published. It addressed issues of sexism, self-love, police violence, and sisterhood, and questioned the position and attitudes of white feminism in the fight for equality.

She wrote: "If white American feminist theory need not deal with the differences between us, and the resulting difference in our oppressions, then how do you deal with the fact that the women who clean your houses and tend your children while you attend conferences on feminist theory are, for the most part, poor women and women of Color? What is the theory behind racist feminism?"

Audre Lorde

Sister Outsider remains Audre Lorde's most famous work. She was named New York State Poet Laureate in 1991 and took the name Gamba Adisa (which means "Warrior: she who makes her meaning clear") during an African baptism ceremony a few days before her death.

More than twenty-five years after her death, the burning truth of Audre Lorde's writings still resonates with the LGBTQI+ community, by highlighting the intersectional struggles faced by marginalized groups.

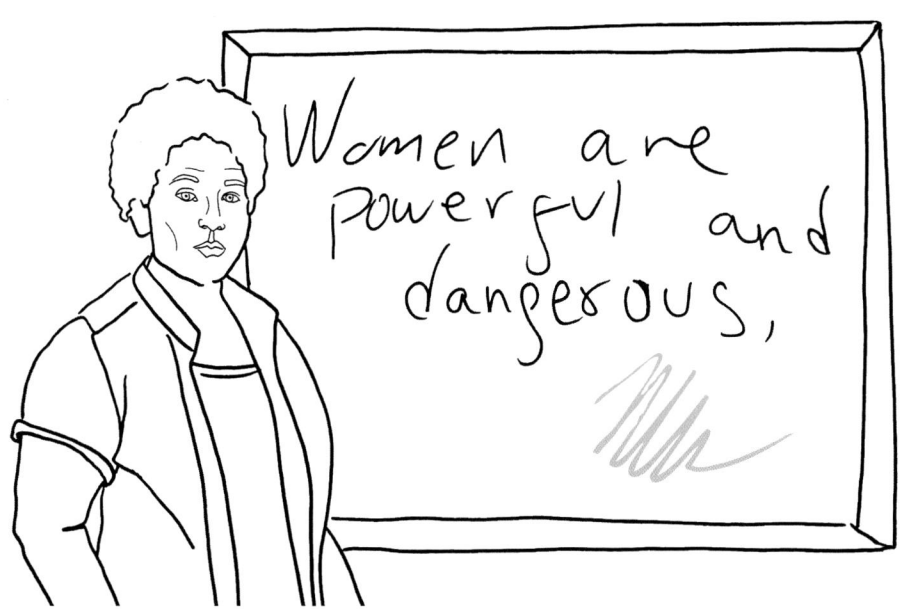

Renée Richards
1934

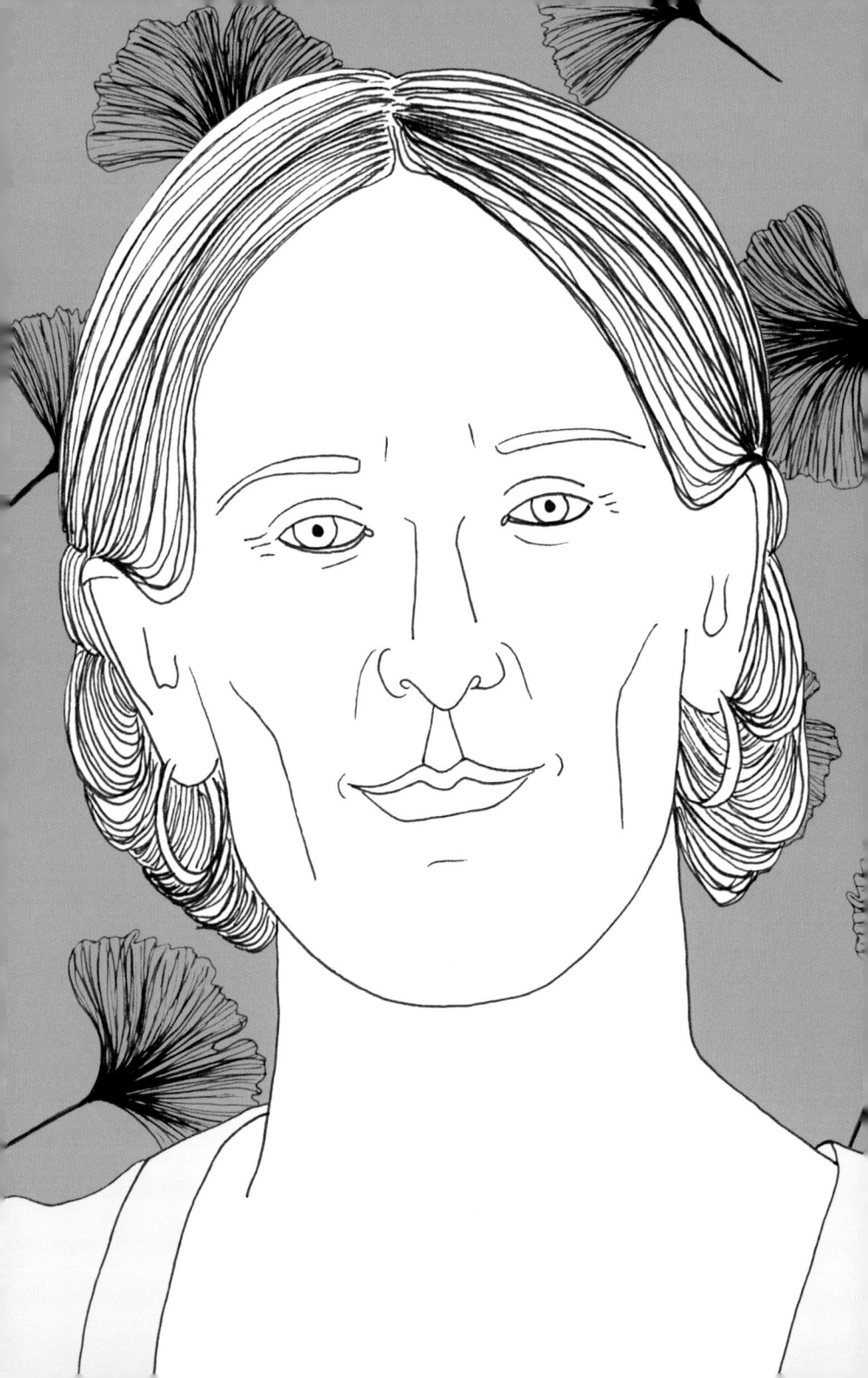

AMERICAN TENNIS PLAYER AND OPHTHALMOLOGIST RENÉE RICHARDS WAS THE FIRST TRANSGENDER WOMAN TO PARTICIPATE IN A PROFESSIONAL TENNIS TOURNAMENT.

Rising to become the captain of the men's tennis team whilst studying at Yale University, then serving in the U.S. Navy, Richards continued to enter and win several tennis tournaments. She then trained as an ophthalmologist, married and had a son, before divorcing a few years later. Tired of living in denial of her trans identity, she began to transition in the 1970s from male to female. In 1975, at the age of 40, she underwent gender reassignment surgery, moved, and returned to the tennis courts on a women's team without mentioning her trans identity to anyone. A year later, a sports journalist outed Renée Richards, leading to an extremely hostile public reaction. The media questioned her presence on a women's tennis team and decried her alleged physical advantages. She suffered boycotts from some opponents and officials in the field, and could not participate in the US Open, at Wimbledon, nor in the Italian Open in 1976.

In 1977, the United States Tennis Federation tried to prevent her from participating in the U.S. Open and wanted to subject her to a chromosomal test, which she refused. She sued them and won her case. She entered the Forest Hills Stadium of the U.S. Open in 1977 and made history (although she lost her match to tennis champion Virginia Wade).

> "I NEVER HAD ANY INTENTION OF PLAYING IN THE U.S. OPEN... BUT, WHEN THEY SAID, 'YOU'RE NOT ALLOWED TO PLAY...' THAT CHANGED EVERYTHING. I SAID, '... I'M A WOMAN AND IF I WANT TO PLAY IN THE U.S. OPEN AS A WOMAN PRO, I'M GOING TO DO IT.'"

Renée Richards pushed the boundaries of gender within the conservative world of tennis, while bringing hope and visibility to transgender people at the time. A few years later, she revealed that she had received death threats, insults, and had experienced opponents walking off court in front of her, just after the judgement rendered in her favour. She continued to coach other players (including Martina Navratilova) after her retirement from sport in 1981, whilst also working as an ophthalmologist. At her peak, she reached 20th place in the world rankings of the Women's Tennis Association.

Nancy Cárdenas
1934 – 1994

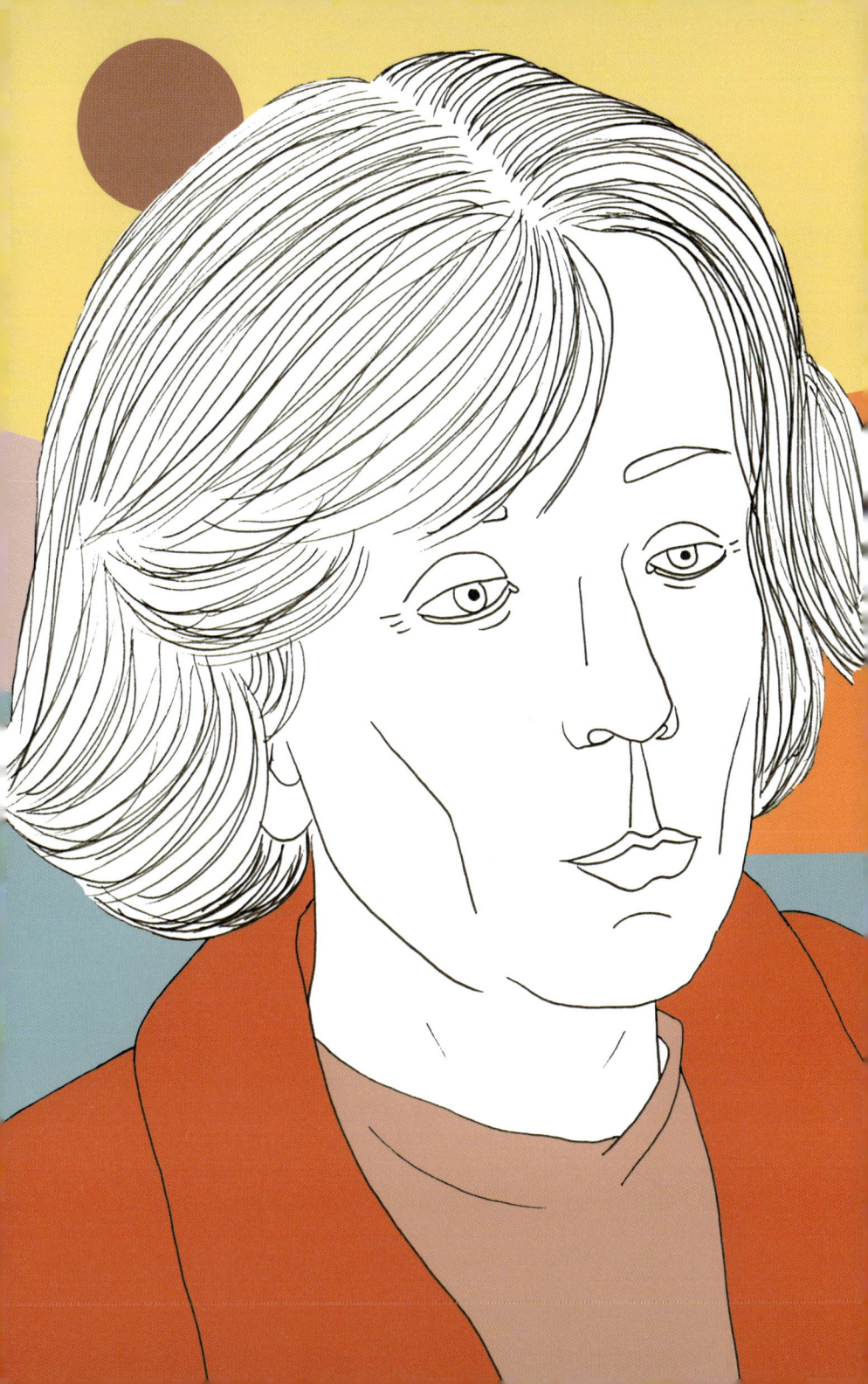

AUTHOR, PLAYWRIGHT, RADIO HOST, AND ACTRESS, NANCY CÁRDENAS WAS ALSO A FEMINIST ACTIVIST, AND PIONEER OF LGBTQI+ MOVEMENTS IN MEXICO.

After studying theatre and film at Yale University in the United States and then spending a few years abroad, Nancy Cárdenas returned to Mexico. She initially became a radio host before taking up acting on the stage. In the 1960s, she switched to writing, published her first play and began a career as a journalist and translator.

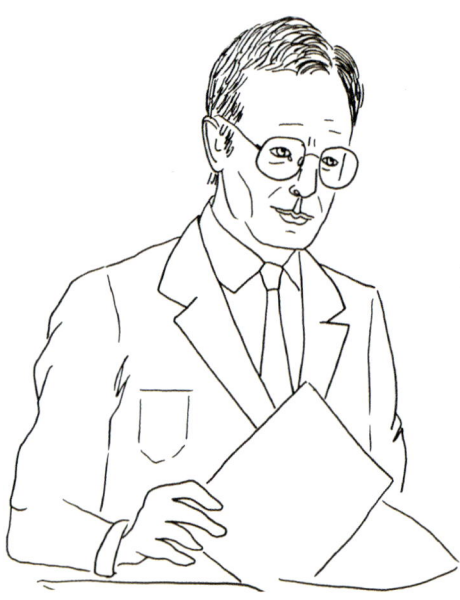

Jacobo Zabludovsky

In the 1970s, she became a theatre director and worked in film, while getting gradually more involved in politics. She also became a more prominent figure in feminist and LGBTQI+ struggles in Mexico and regularly addressed issues about homosexuality in the media. At the age of thirty-nine, she came out during a television interview on the popular show *24 Horas* hosted by journalist Jacobo Zabludovsky. This was prompted by a discussion about the firing of a gay man and the lack of rights for the queer community in Mexico.

It was the first time in Mexico's history that a woman had declared herself to be a lesbian in public. Moreover, she became the first person to come out as queer on Mexican television.

Nancy Cárdenas

As a feminist, Nancy Cárdenas wanted to help in the struggles of lesbians to be treated equally, so she spoke at many national and international conferences on this subject. She helped to increase LGBTQI+ visibility through her many works. She adapted the hit American film *The Boys in the Band* for the stage as a play titled, *Los Chicos de la Banda*, and translated and adapted many lesbian works for Mexican audiences.

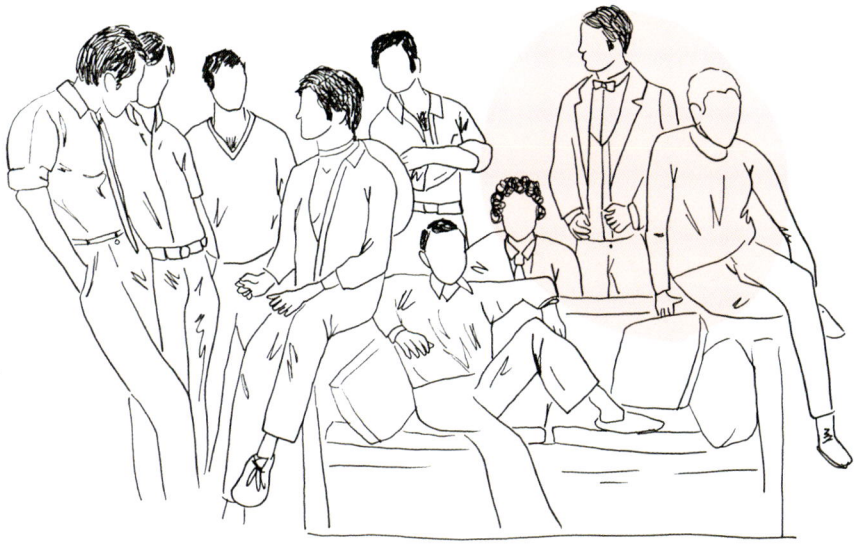

In 1974, she founded the first Mexican association for gay rights: the Frente de Liberación Homosexual (FLH). During this period, she co-wrote *Manifesto in Defence of Homosexuals in Mexico* and, in 1978, participated in the organization of the first Pride March in the country's capital.

In 1992, she founded the Ser Humana association to help people affected by HIV/AIDS. Although she sadly died of breast cancer at the age of fifty-nine, a lesbian archive centre now bears her name (Centro de Documentación y Archivo Histórico Lésbico de México, América Latina y el Caribe Nancy Cárdenas), keeping her memory alive. Today, same-sex marriage is legal in many states in Mexico.

Larry Kramer
1935 – 2020

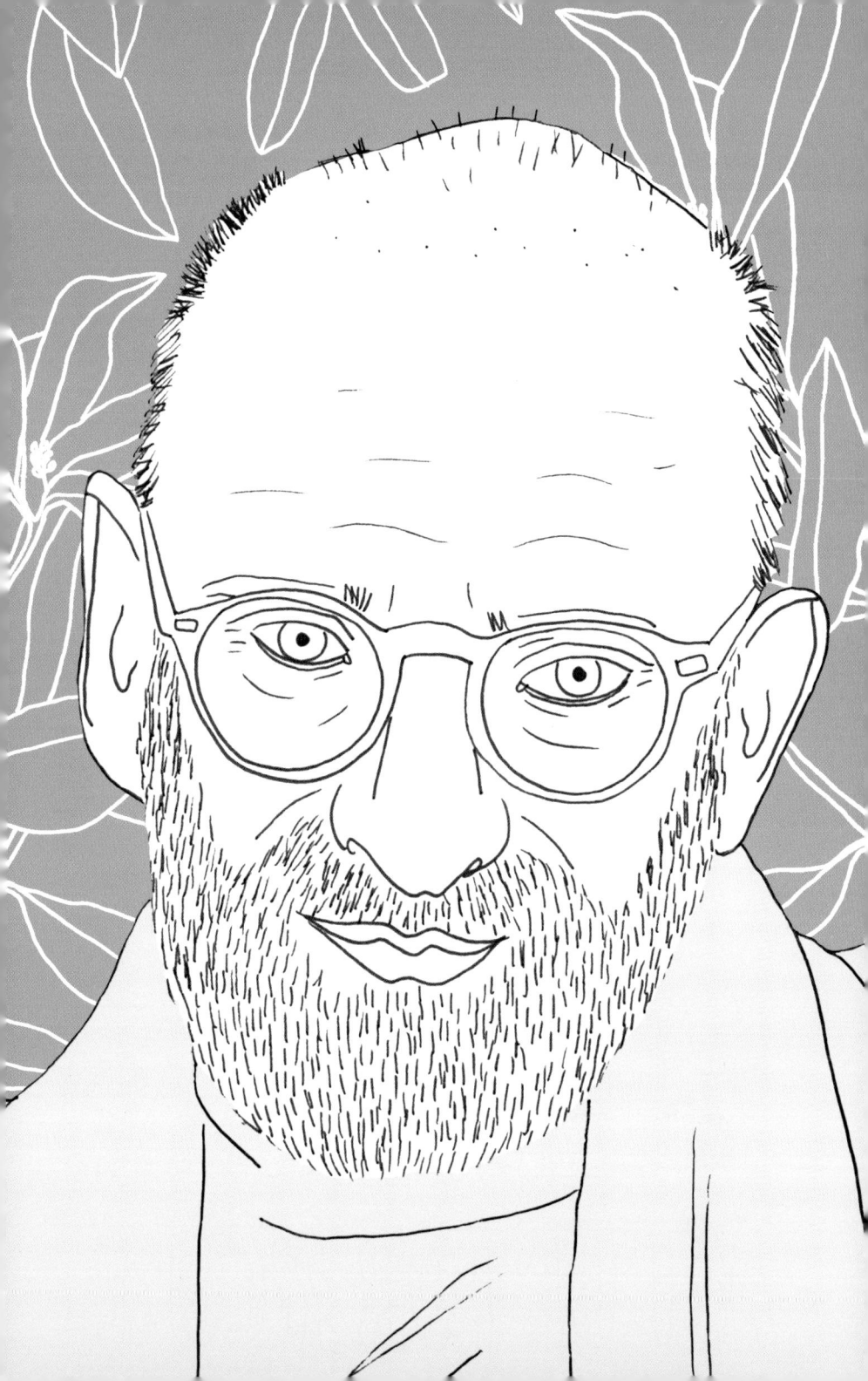

THE DOCUMENTARY FILM *LARRY KRAMER: IN LOVE & ANGER* WAS BROADCAST ON HBO IN 2015. THE TITLE SUMS UP THE WRITER'S LIFE IN BOTH HIS FIGHT FOR GAY RIGHTS AND IN HIS WRITING.

Writer, screenwriter, and award-winning producer, Larry Kramer was also the founder of Gay Men's Health Crisis in 1981 (GMHC – an organization fighting against HIV/AIDS and supporting people with the virus). He later founded ACT UP (AIDS Coalition to Unleash Power) in 1987.

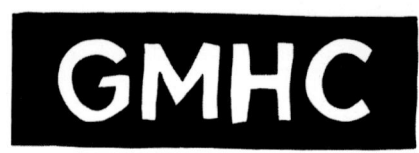

He is famous for having written and published many books and plays on AIDS and the history of the gay community at a time when few people ventured to deal with these subjects: *Faggots*, *The Normal Heart*, *Just Say No*, *The Destiny of Me*, *The American People*.

In *Faggots*, a book published in 1978, he depicts the lives and sexuality of gay people in the 1970s and portrays a community in the midst of a sexual and political revolution.

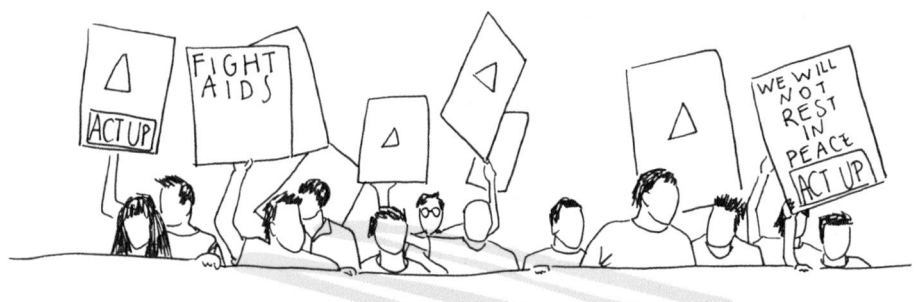

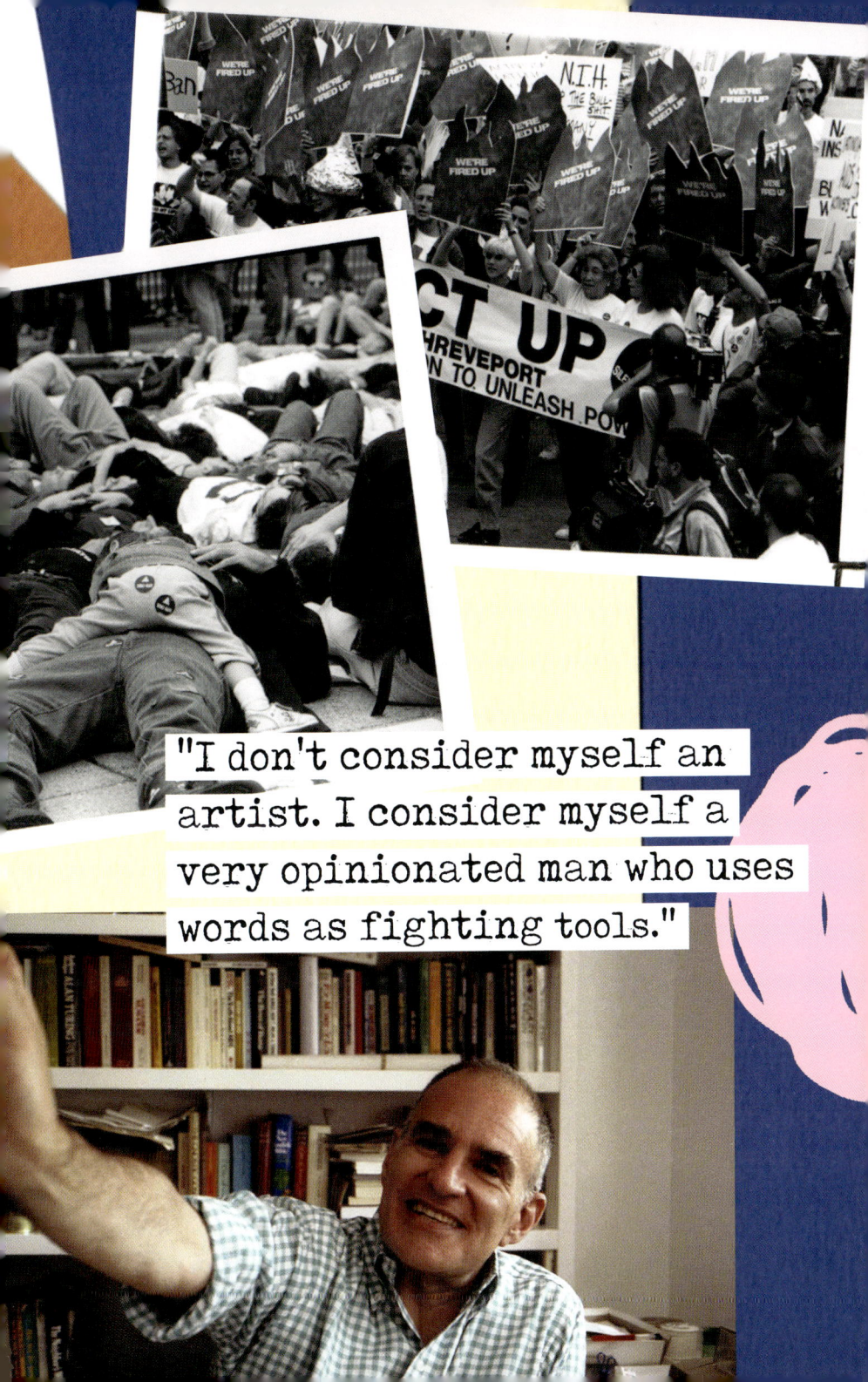

"I don't consider myself an artist. I consider myself a very opinionated man who uses words as fighting tools."

Faggots was seen as controversial as soon as it was released and was withdrawn from many bookstores before reappearing ten years later, when AIDS began to change public perception. He also wrote the play *The Normal Heart*, an autobiography that looked back at the beginnings of the AIDS epidemic, first performed in 1985, and adapted for the screen in 2014 by Ryan Murphy with a five-star Hollywood cast: Julia Roberts, Mark Ruffalo, Matt Bomer and Jim Parsons.

Whilst not widely known outside of America, Larry Kramer was one of the main leaders in successful legal actions that resulted in better treatment for patients with AIDS. While alerting the public and pointing the finger at inept bureaucracies and politicians who were slow to take action in the 1980s, he achieved considerable progress on care, the acceleration of procedures, as well as drug testing. He advocated for civil disobedience, and made it the trademark of ACT UP.

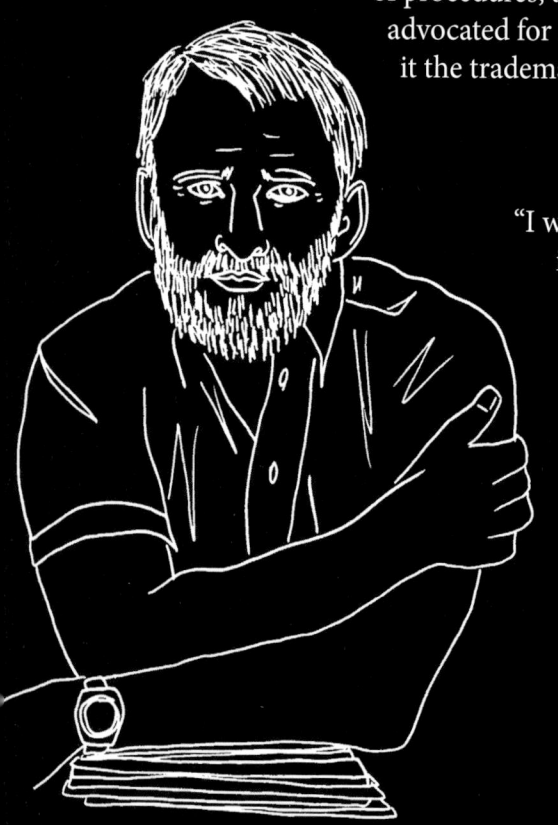

"I was known as the angriest man in the world, mainly because I discovered that anger got you further than being nice. And when we started to break through in the media, I was better TV than someone who was nice."

Larry Kramer

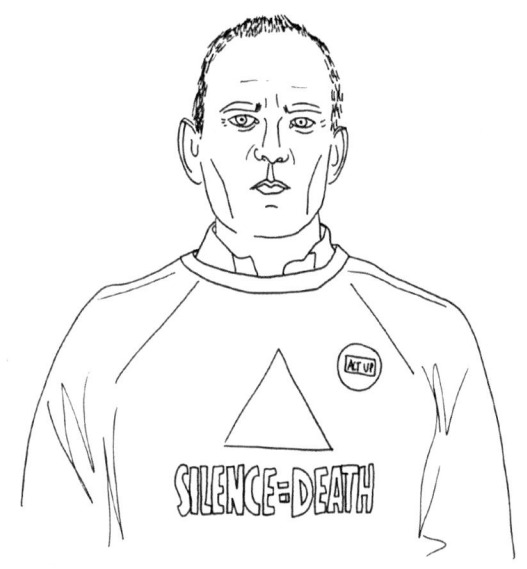

Militant, often described as radical, and living with HIV, his lively personality and energy ensured that his campaigning on behalf of ACT UP or the GMHC gained publicity. You only need to watch his many interventions to recognize his public speaking skills.

Didier Lestrade, founder of Act Up-Paris and *Têtu* magazine, commented "...All his life, he stopped at nothing, despite the unpopularity of his remarks. By personifying the hard wing of the associated movement, he changed the minds of thousands of people, throughout the United States and the world."

More than thirty years after the creation of ACT UP, Larry Kramer remains a major figure in LGBTQI+ struggles. He witnessed and was involved in all the changes within the gay community in recent decades, and agreed to shoot a documentary about his life to tell the LGBTQI+ community about his journey. He died in 2020, but the film lives on as a reminder that change can be achieved through collective action and political activism.

Miss Major
Griffin-Gracy
1940

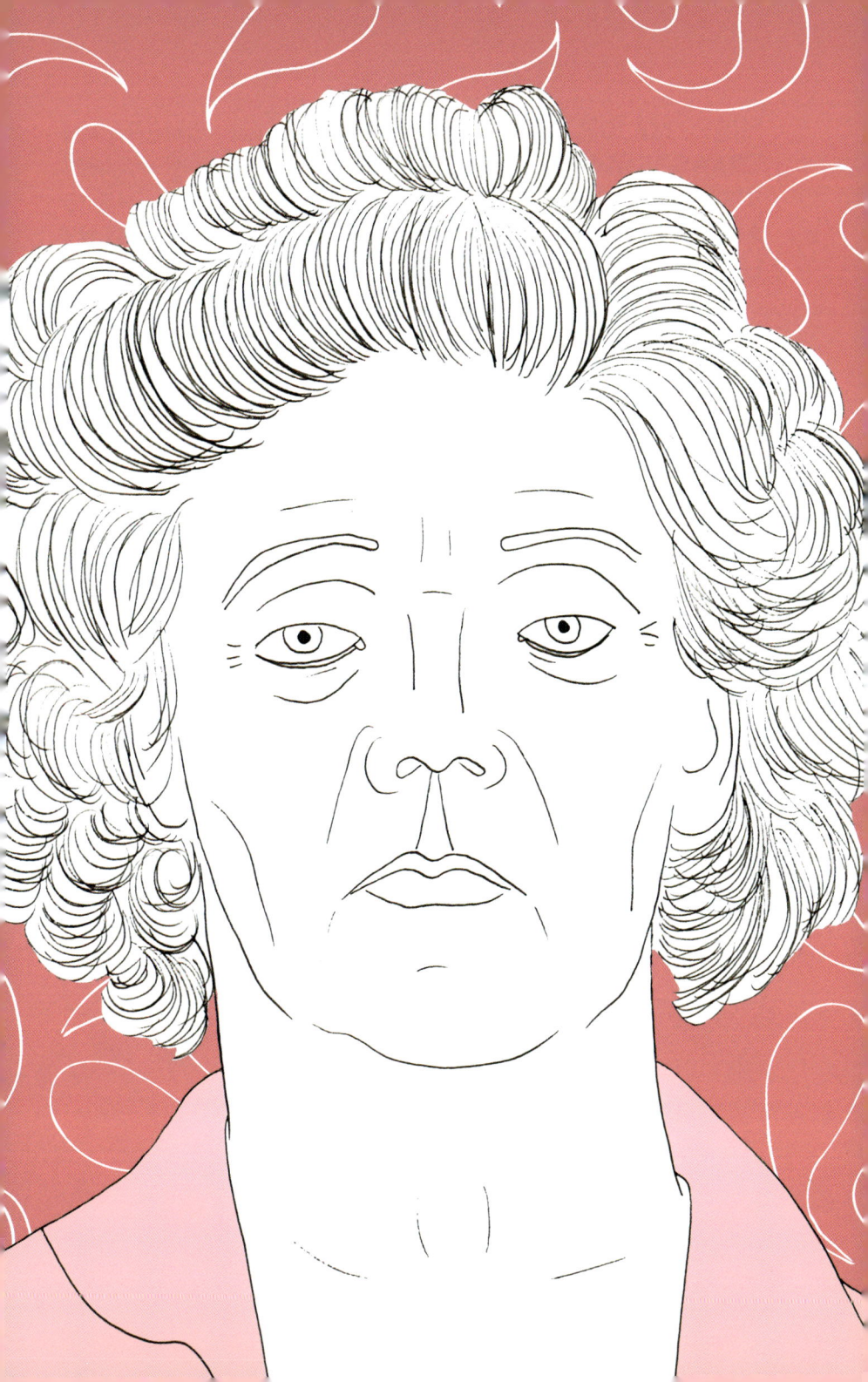

MISS MAJOR GRIFFIN-GRACY IS AN AMERICAN TRANSGENDER ACTIVIST WHO SHAPED THE TRANS RIGHTS MOVEMENT AS WE KNOW IT TODAY. SHE IS A WARRIOR AND SURVIVOR, WHO INSPIRES MANY LGBTQI+ ACTIVISTS AROUND THE WORLD.

She moved to New York in the early 1960s, at a time when police raids on queer bars were legal and commonplace. She became a sex worker and met Sylvia Rivera and Marsha P. Johnson, two Black transgender women, who played a major role in the 1969 Stonewall riots in which Miss Major was arrested.

In the years following the riots, she was imprisoned for five years. She denounced the injustices and discrimination faced by transgender people at the hands of the courts. She has also regularly spoken out against the exclusion of transgender people from the movement, especially those of colour.

After a few years in San Diego, where she worked in various organizations supporting transgender women and people living with HIV/AIDS, she moved to San Francisco where she joined the Transgender Gender-variant and Intersex Justice Project (TGIJP) in 2005.

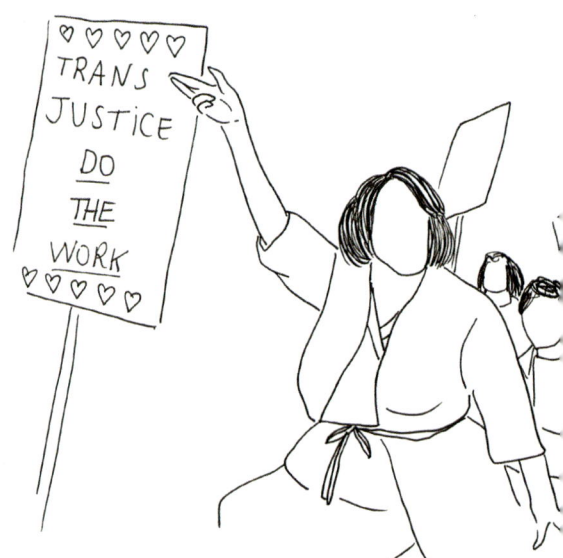

Miss Major Griffin-Gracy

The TGIJP is a non-profit organization that supports trans, non-binary and intersex people inside and outside prisons and detention centres and aims to end the violations of their rights. Miss Major was its Executive Director until 2015.

"We are entitled to be loved, to seek happiness and share that with the people we care about. Blood isn't the only connection that we can have to one another. I want the younger members to understand that things haven't always been like this," she told *Vice* magazine.

A documentary entitled *MAJOR!*, released in 2015, traces the journey of this activist, who spent forty years of her life fighting in the United States against the prison system, racism, and transphobia.

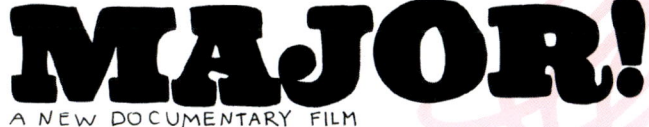

In 2019, she founded the Griffin-Gracy Educational Retreat and Historical Center (House of GG) in Little Rock, Arizona: a place that organizes retreats for transgender women to heal their physical, mental, emotional, and spiritual wounds "from the trauma resulting from generations of transphobia, racism, sexism, poverty, ableism and violence," according to its website. "It's a respite, an oasis, giving my people an opportunity to relax and learn what they need to negotiate through society," said Miss Major Griffin-Gracy.

Craig Rodwell
1940 – 1993

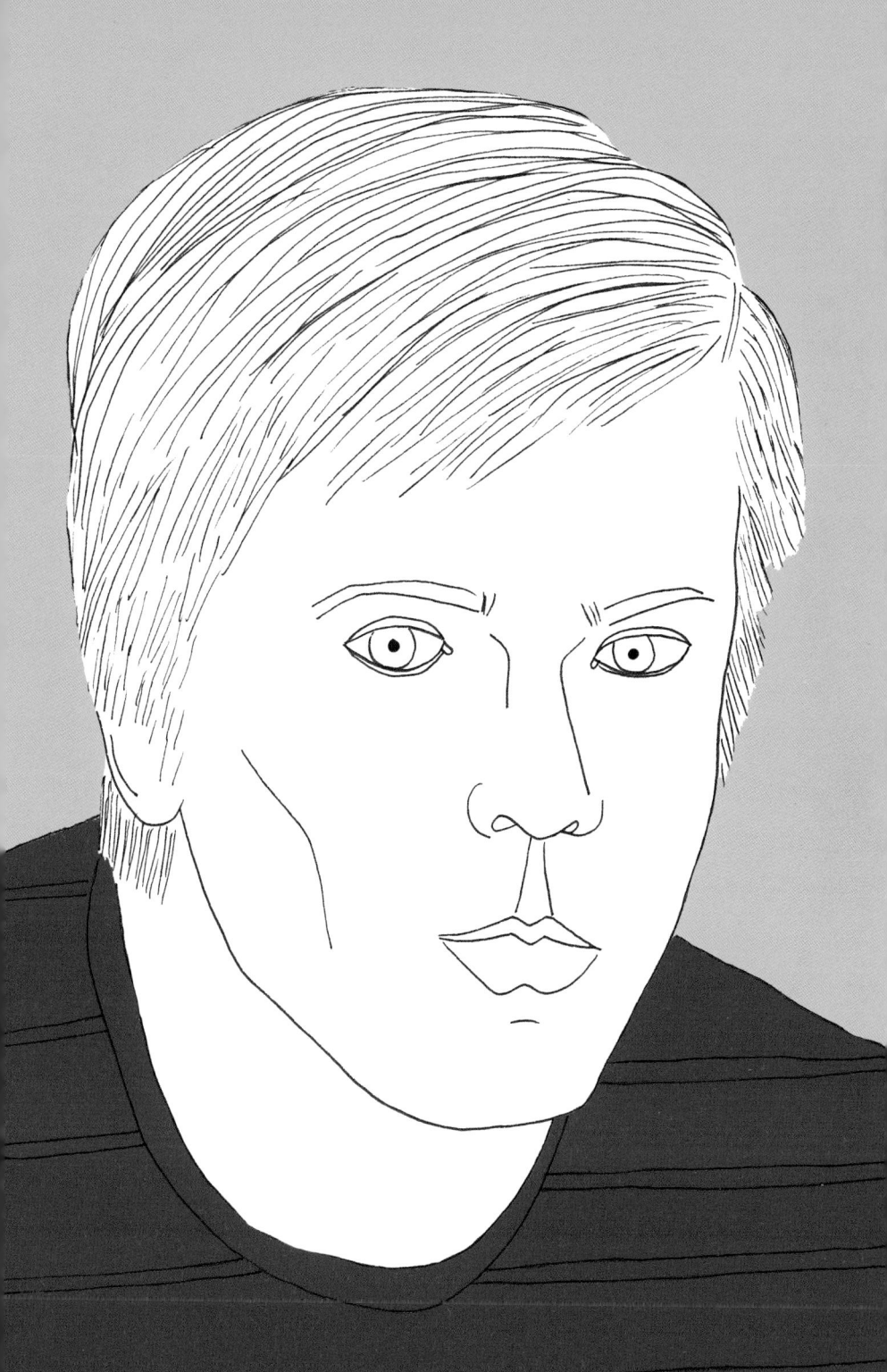

SOMETIMES LEFT OUT OF THE BOOKS AND DOCUMENTS ON LGBTQI+ HISTORY, CRAIG RODWELL WAS AN IMPORTANT ACTIVIST FOR THE GAY CAUSE IN THE UNITED STATES FROM THE 1960S TO THE 1980S.

At the age of eighteen, he moved to New York, where he had a relationship with the famous activist, Harvey Milk. He was arrested by the police several times in cruising spots. A few years later, he joined the New York branch of the Mattachine Society, an association founded in 1950 at the start of the gay liberation movement. He then created the Mattachine Young Adults association in 1964 and was involved, early on, in the East Coast Homophile Organizations (ECHO).

He organized numerous demonstrations and marches with his friend Randy Wicker to protest against the exclusion of gay people from the U.S. army. In 1965, he led a protest in the United Nations Plaza, against the detention of homosexual Cubans in labour camps. For him, visibility was the lever that would put an end to the stigmatization and discrimination.

In 1966, he was part of the group of men, all activists of the Mattachine Society, who participated in the "sip-in" at Julius Bar in Greenwich Village.

Inspired by the "sit-ins" of the civil rights movement, this involved entering a bar and ordering a drink, openly posing as gay. The aim of the "sip-in" was to protest a rule of

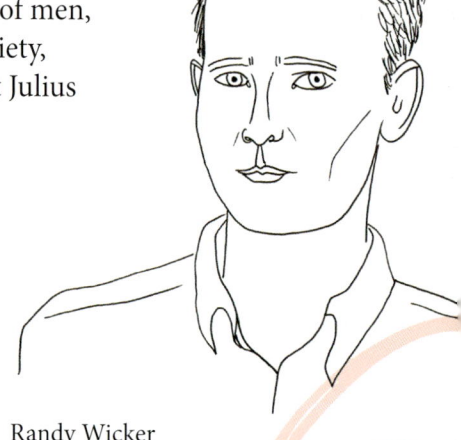

Randy Wicker

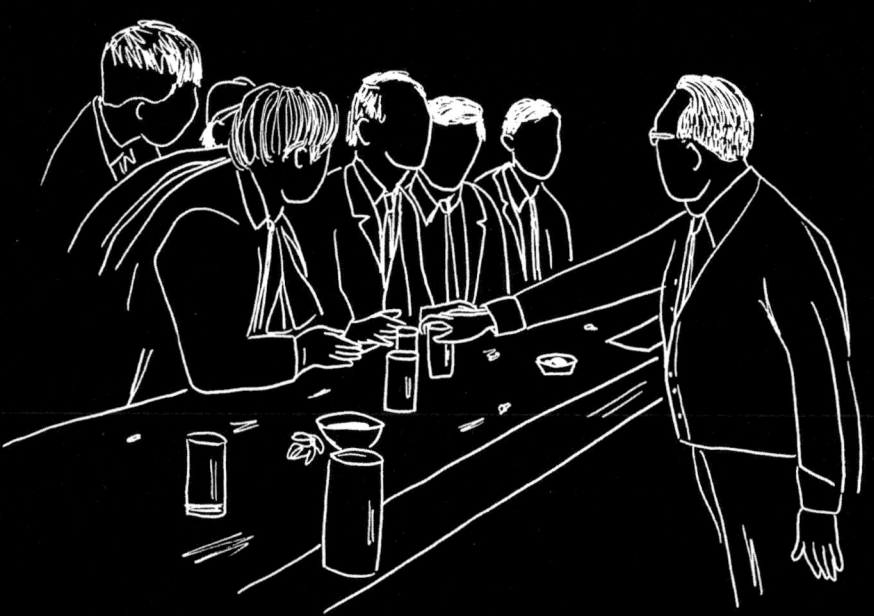

"Sip-in" at Julius Bar

the State Liquor Authority of New York prohibiting establishments from allowing the congregation of known or suspected gay men and lesbians in bars. Bars that did not comply with this rule could lose their license and see large numbers of police officers descend on their premises.

During this period, he also created the Homophile Youth Movement in Neighborhoods (HYMN) and published the newsletter *HYMNAL* to encourage LGBTQI+ people to get involved in activism and defend their rights.

In 1967, he opened the Oscar Wilde Memorial Bookshop: the first gay and lesbian bookstore in the United States (which closed in 2009). For Craig Rodwell, opening this bookstore was a way to "have a shop where gay people would not feel exploited both sexually and economically."

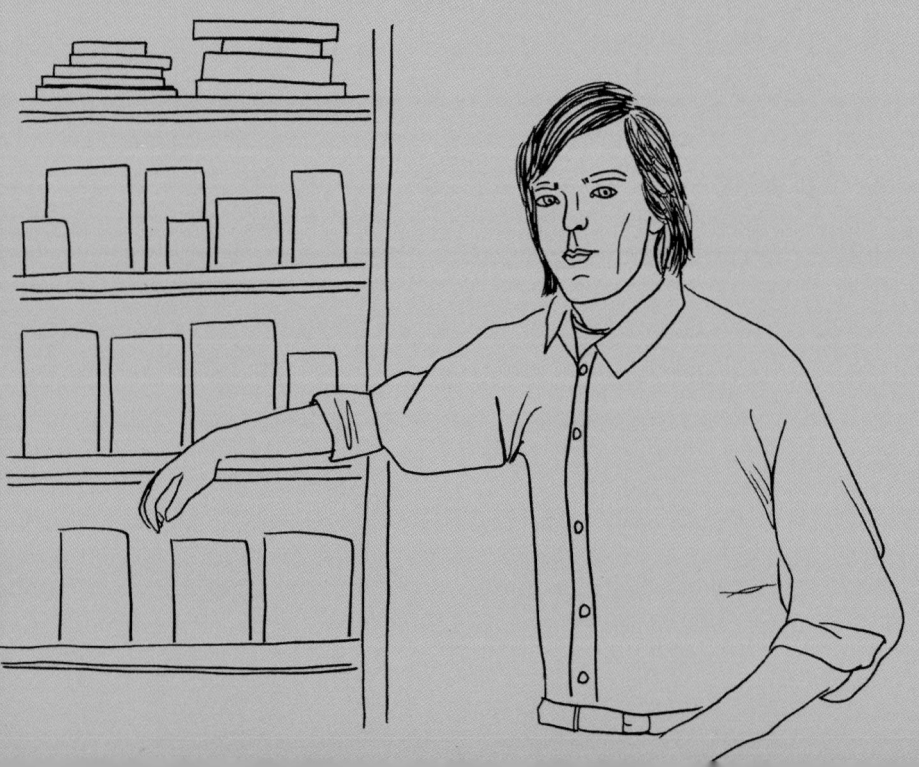

Craig Rodwell

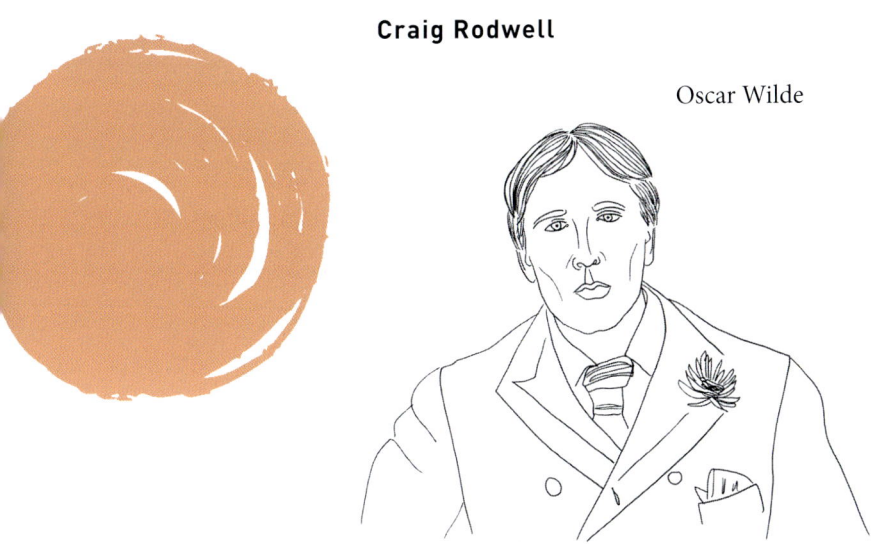

Oscar Wilde

He eventually left the Mattachine Society following several disagreements with its members, but was still an advocate for minority groups and played an active role in the Stonewall riots of 1969. He is also credited with being the first person to shout out "Gay Power!" at the police on the night of the riots.

A year after these events, he co-organized the Christopher Street Liberation Day March, named after the street where the Stonewall Inn was located. This became the very first Pride March that has since been replicated all around the world.

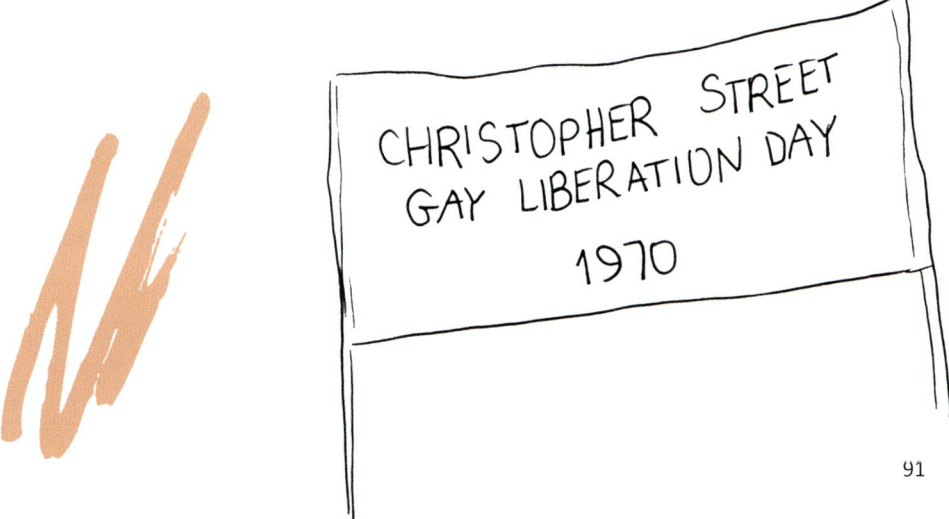

Armistead Maupin
1944

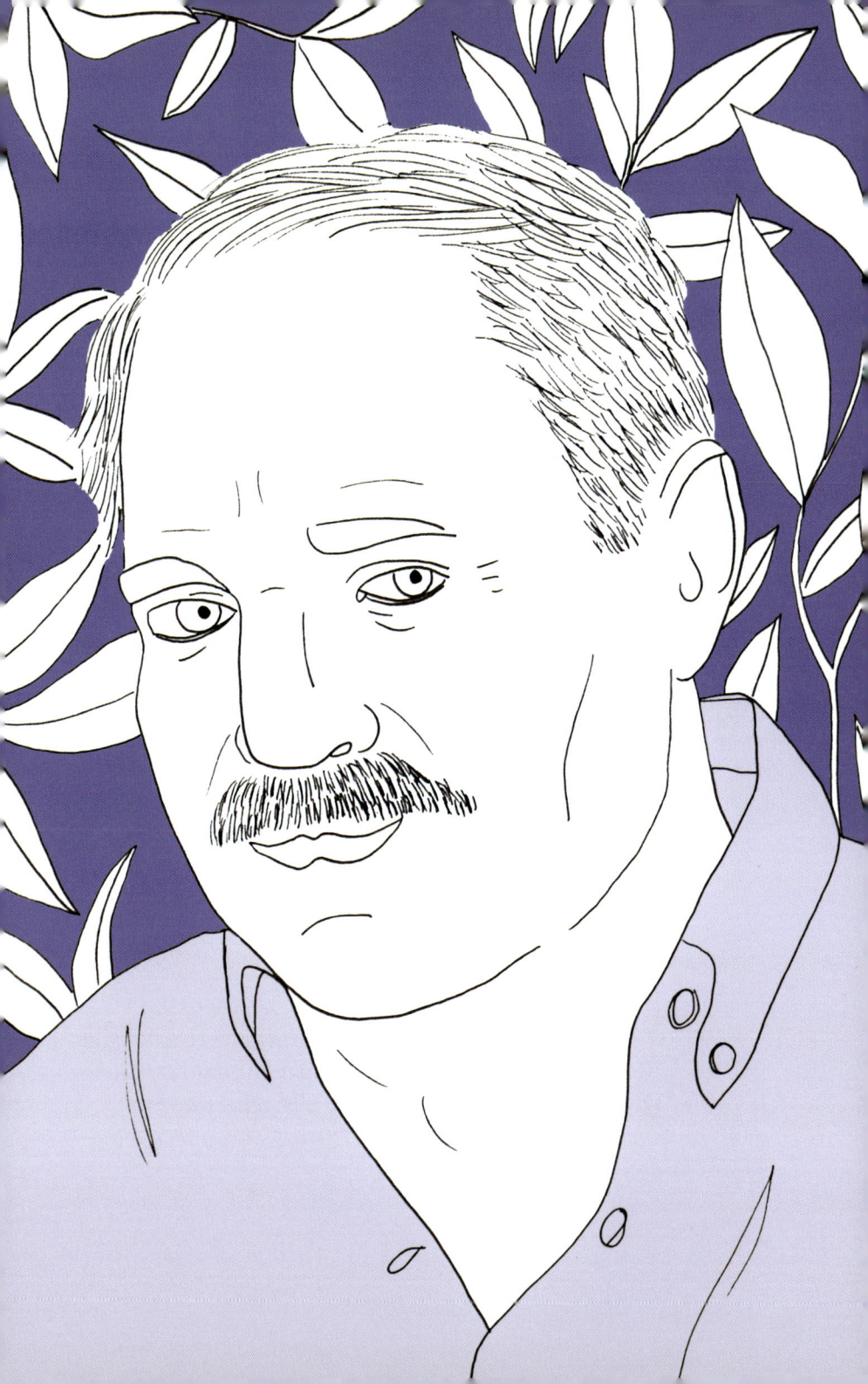

> "THERE ARE TIMES WHEN YOU FEEL THAT YOU ARE GOING TO CHANGE YOUR LIFE, WHEN YOU ALMOST FEEL LIKE YOU HEAR THE HEAVY MECHANICS OF FATE CLICKING," WROTE ARMISTEAD MAUPIN IN HIS BOOK *THE NIGHT LISTENER*.

After growing up in a conservative environment in North Carolina and spending a few years in the military, Armistead Maupin became a reporter for a Charleston newspaper. He moved to San Francisco and was assigned to the press office of *The Associated Press* in 1971. He also began writing short stories which were published in instalments in local newspapers such as the *San Francisco Chronicle*.

San Francisco Chronicle

The stories feature openly gay, lesbian, bisexual and transgender characters, who live a free life in and around the liberated San Francisco of the 1970s, when it was at the centre of the countercultural movement. The stories follow characters through to the 2000s, depicting the suffering of the gay community during the HIV/AIDS epidemic of the 1980s and 90s, reflecting the author's experiences when many of his friends were affected by the illness.

Armistead Maupin

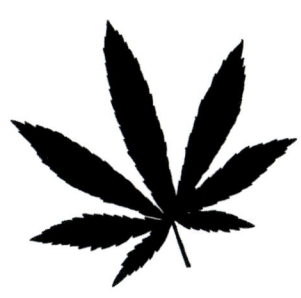

We follow the adventures of Anna Madrigal, a fascinating landlady and inveterate weed smoker, who lets out rooms at the mythical 28 Barbary Lane to two other characters: Michael Tolliver and Mary Ann Singleton. The stories were an immediate hit.

The series of nine novels titled *Tales of the City* became a worldwide success. The series has since been adapted for television by the UK's Channel 4 (1993) and by Netflix in 2019, as well as being adapted for the radio by BBC Radio 4. In addition, several musical adaptations of the stories have been produced on stage.

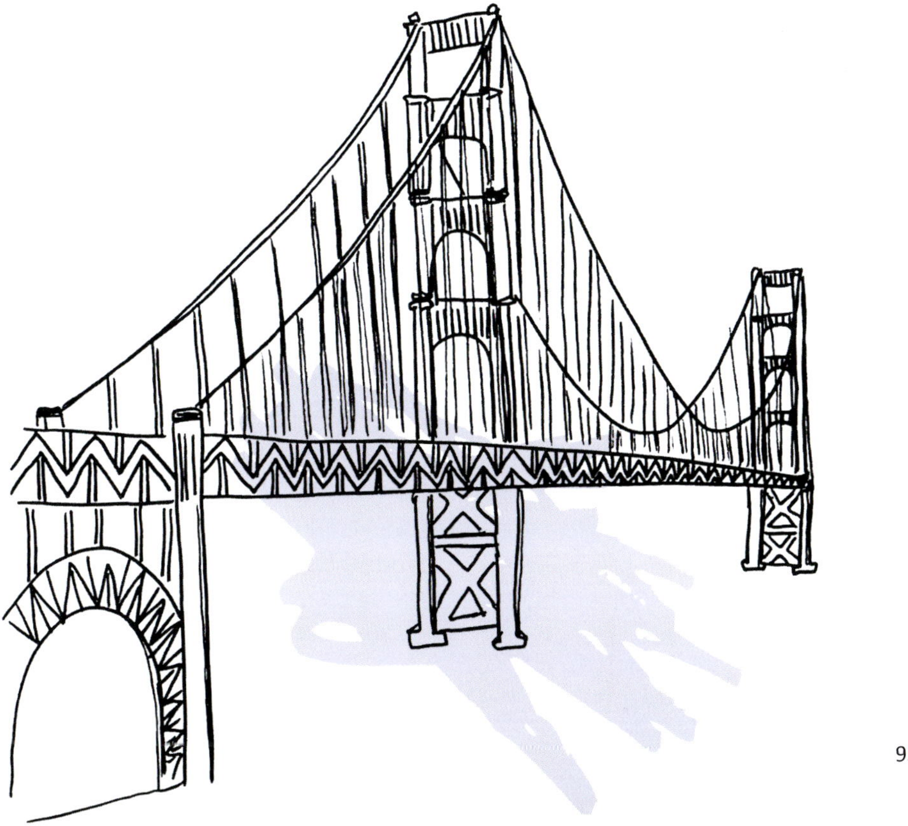

But behind the apparent lightness of these stories, Armistead Maupin tackled more serious topics, such as the HIV/AIDS epidemic, transphobia, and homophobia. Above all, he created characters that have everything working against them, but who found their tribe, and acceptance within their chosen family. There is a large autobiographical element to the stories, which the author does not hide.

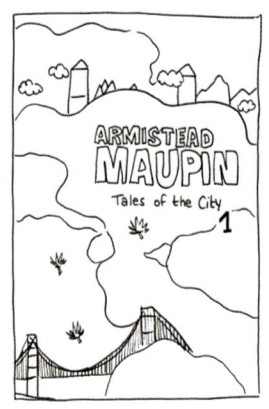

> "I THINK MANY WRITERS WRITE BECAUSE IT'S A CONVENIENT WAY TO EXPLAIN THEMSELVES TO THEMSELVES. WE TAKE THE CHAOS AND THE TURMOIL AND THE BULLSHIT OF OUR LIVES, AND WE MAKE IT INTO SOMETHING THAT HAS A HARMONIOUS SHAPE AND SOUND."

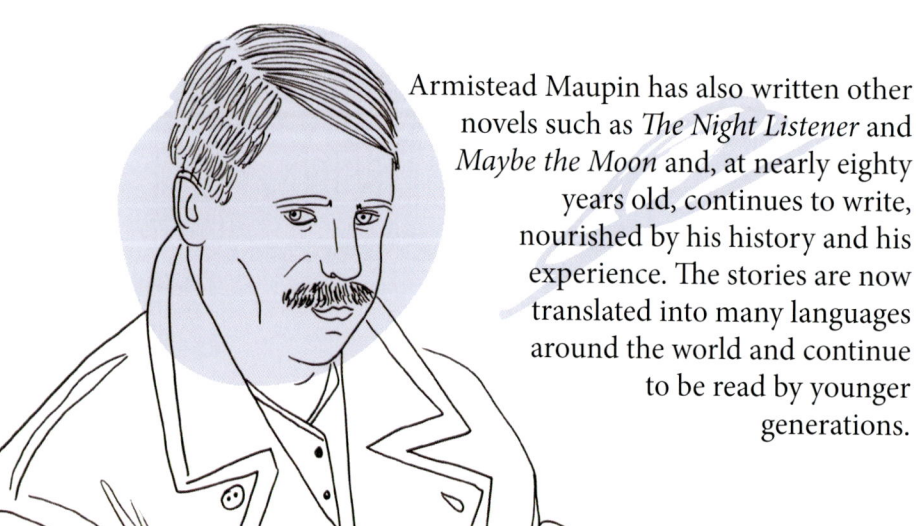

Armistead Maupin has also written other novels such as *The Night Listener* and *Maybe the Moon* and, at nearly eighty years old, continues to write, nourished by his history and his experience. The stories are now translated into many languages around the world and continue to be read by younger generations.

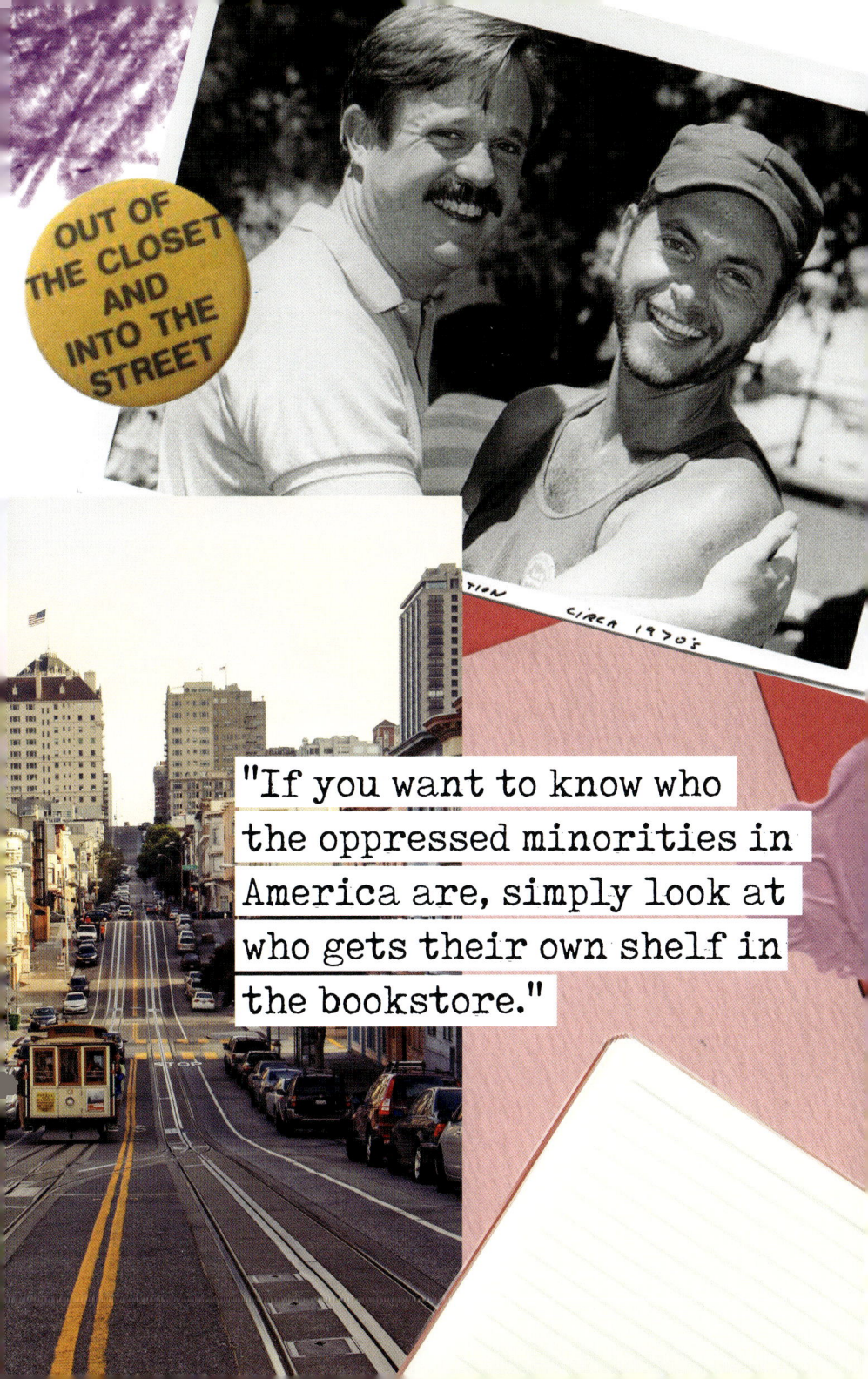

Marsha P. Johnson
1945 – 1992

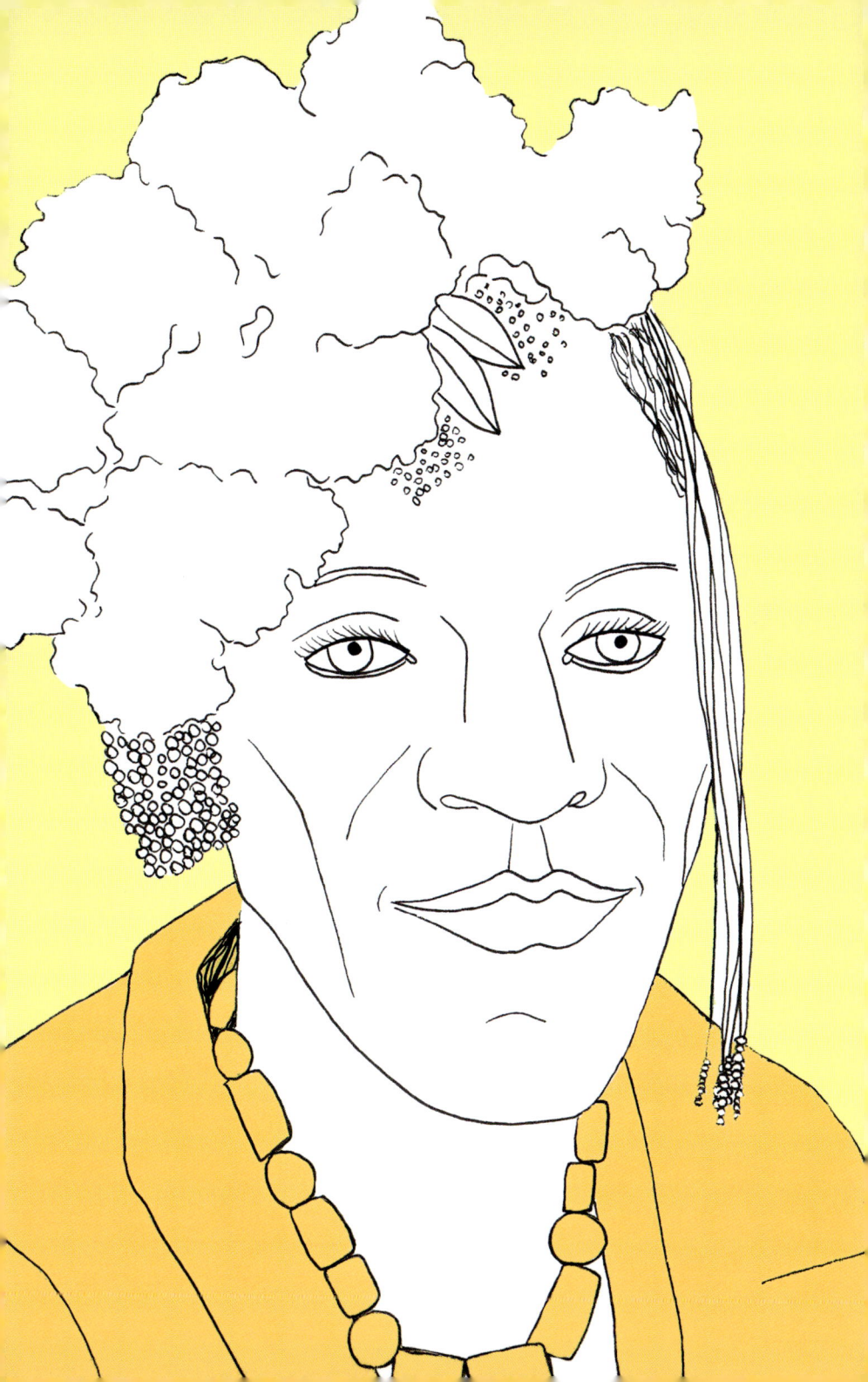

AN AFRICAN AMERICAN TRANSGENDER ACTIVIST AND SEX WORKER, MARSHA P. JOHNSON IS ONE OF THE LEADING FIGURES IN THE LGBTQI+ MOVEMENT. A TRUE PIONEER, SHE IS BEST KNOWN FOR BEING ONE OF THE FIRST PEOPLE TO RETALIATE AGAINST THE POLICE DURING THE STONEWALL RIOTS ON THE NIGHT OF JUNE 28, 1969.

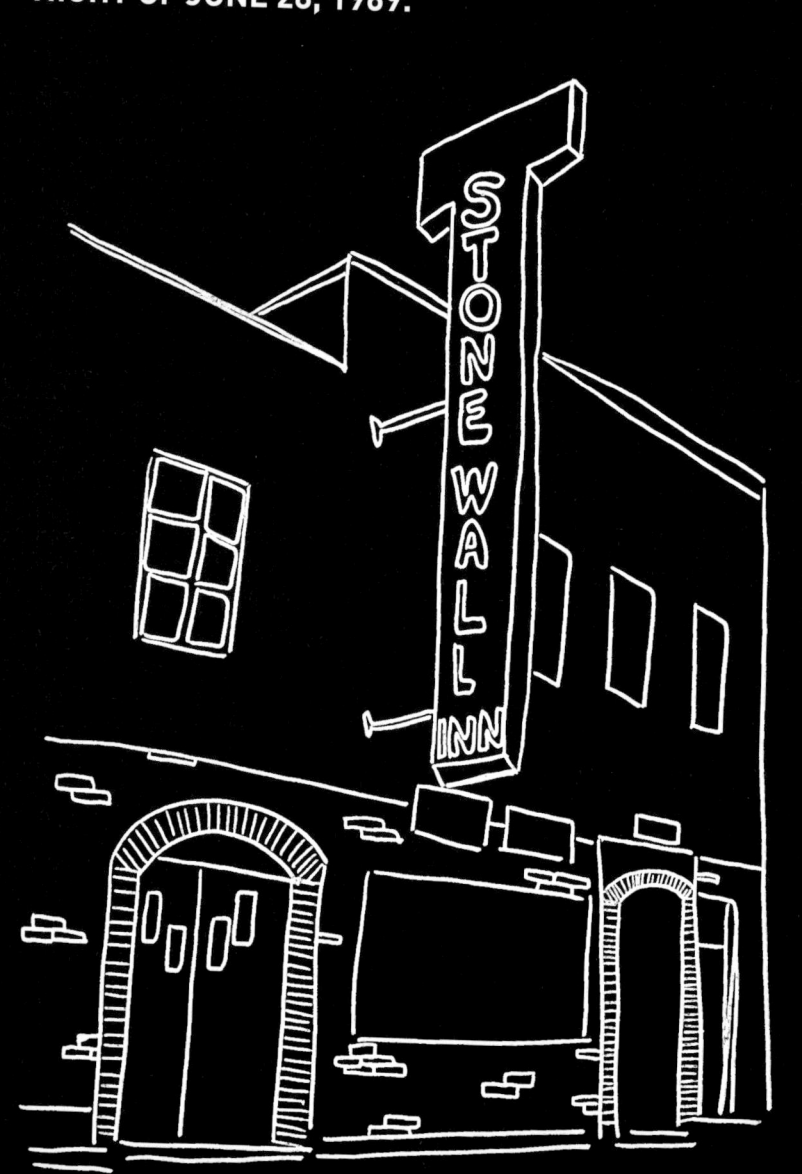

Marsha P. Johnson

Following a string of police raids on the gay bar at the Stonewall Inn, located at 51-53 Christopher Street in New York City, the customers decided to fight back against the police. Their retaliation sparked several days of riots and marked the beginning of the gay liberation movement. Marsha P. Johnson later became involved in the Gay Liberation Front and various lesbian movements.

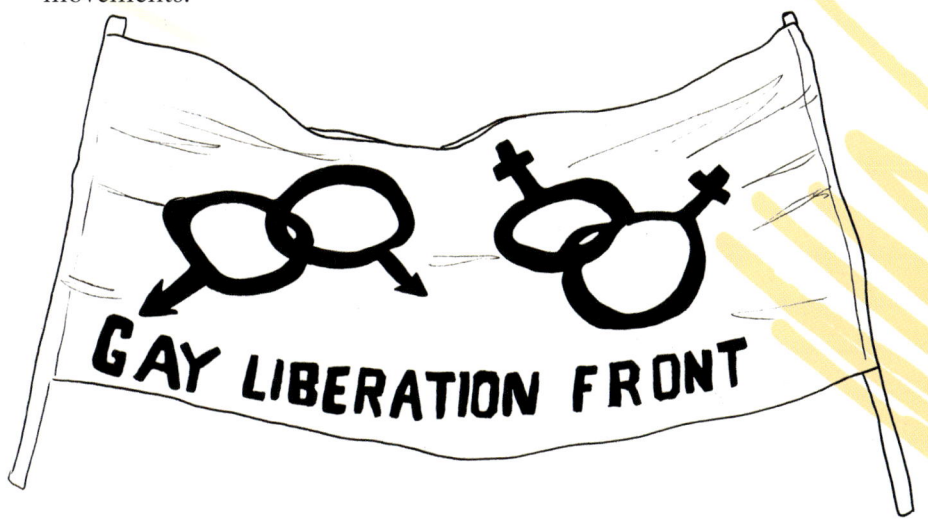

In 1970, with her friend Sylvia Rivera, she founded STAR (Street Transvestite [now Transgender] Action Revolutionaries) and STAR Houses, to house young transgender and queer people living on the streets of New York City. Although they were in demand during the early 1970s, the STAR Houses eventually closed down. During her years of struggle and activism, Marsha never stopped denouncing the transphobia present within the gay community.

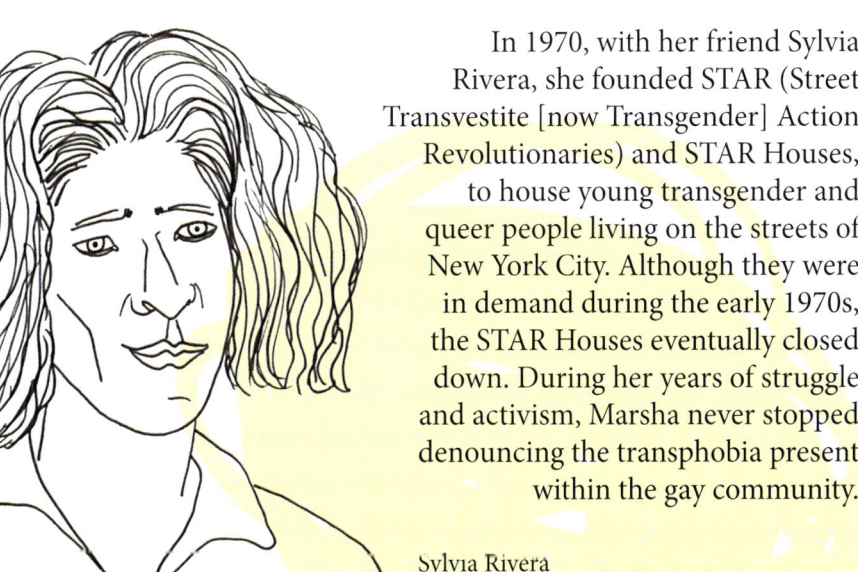

Sylvia Rivera

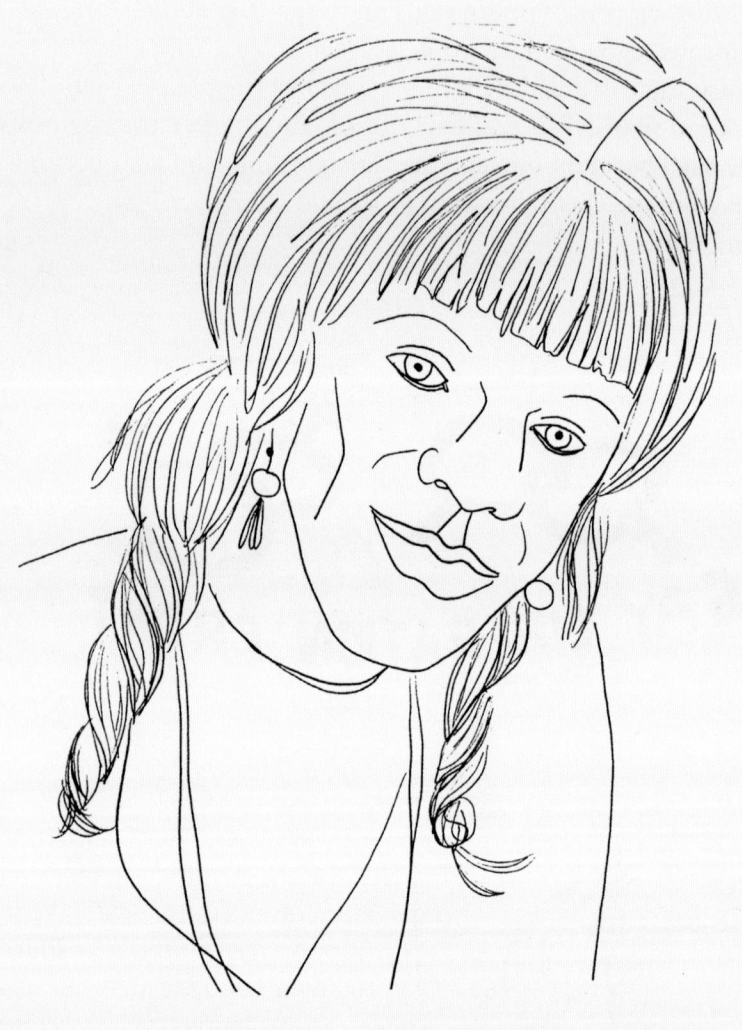

"HOW MANY YEARS HAS IT TAKEN PEOPLE TO REALIZE THAT WE ARE ALL BROTHERS AND SISTERS AND HUMAN BEINGS IN THE HUMAN RACE?"

Marsha P. Johnson

Her flamboyant outfits and hairstyles made Marsha a must-see figure in New York's gay community, and she became popular with the general public too. Photographed by Andy Warhol in 1975 in his series *Ladies and Gentlemen,* she was also a member of the queer theatre company Hot Peaches for a time.

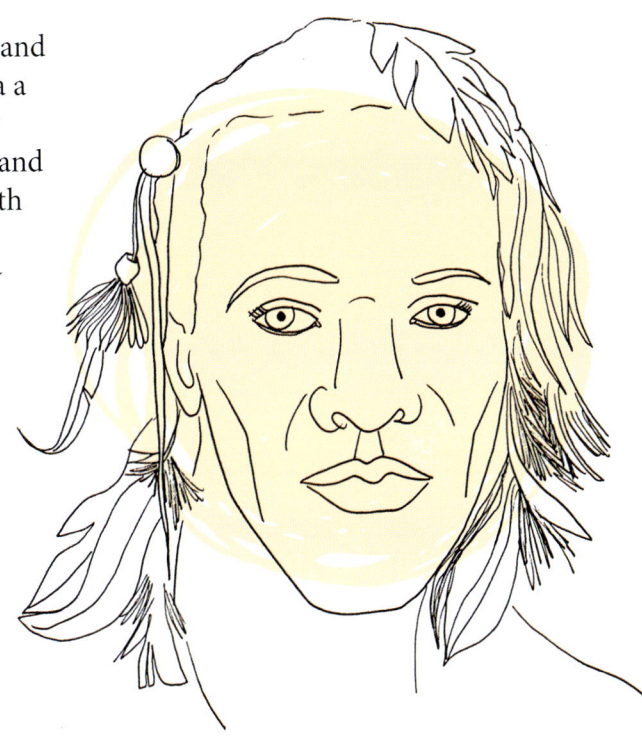

POWER TO THE PEOPLE

Marsha P. Johnson was also recognized by the art scene of the 1970s and used her notoriety for the benefit of her campaigning. An activist on all fronts, she was the organizer of many demonstrations, meetings, and marches. During the 1980s, much of her energy was devoted to the fight for better treatment for those living with HIV/AIDS alongside ACT UP.

In July 1992, Marsha's body was found in the Hudson River. She was forty-six years old. The whole community was shocked by the news. While the police concluded that she committed suicide, her relatives and friends tended to believe that she was murdered.

The documentary *The Death and Life of Marsha P. Johnson*, directed by David France and released in 2017 on Netflix, traces the journey of trans activist Victoria Cruz, who reopens the investigation and sheds light on the death of the "Rosa Parks of the LGBT movement".

An institute now bears her name: The Marsha P. Johnson Institute. Its vision is to "elevate, support, and nourish the voices of Black trans people."

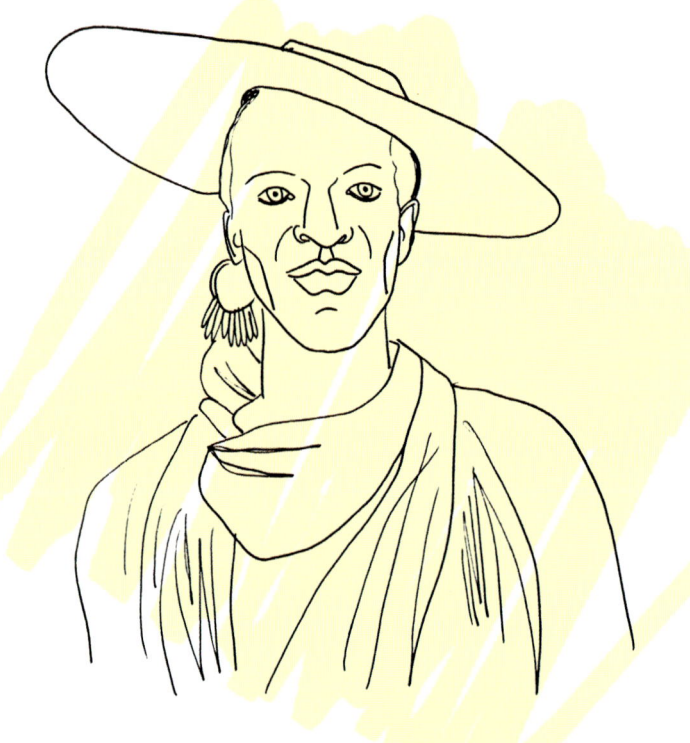

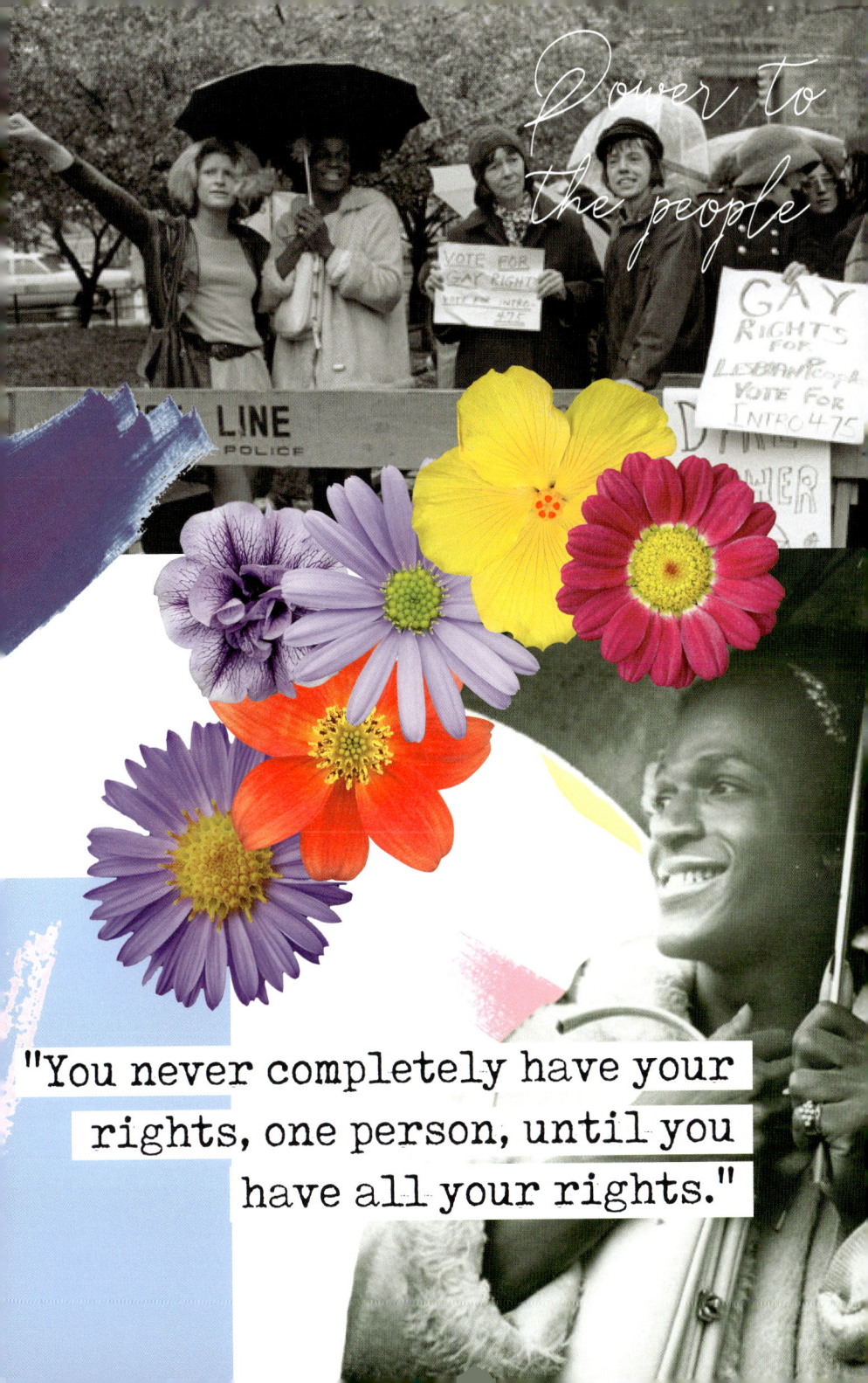

Brenda Howard
1946 – 2005

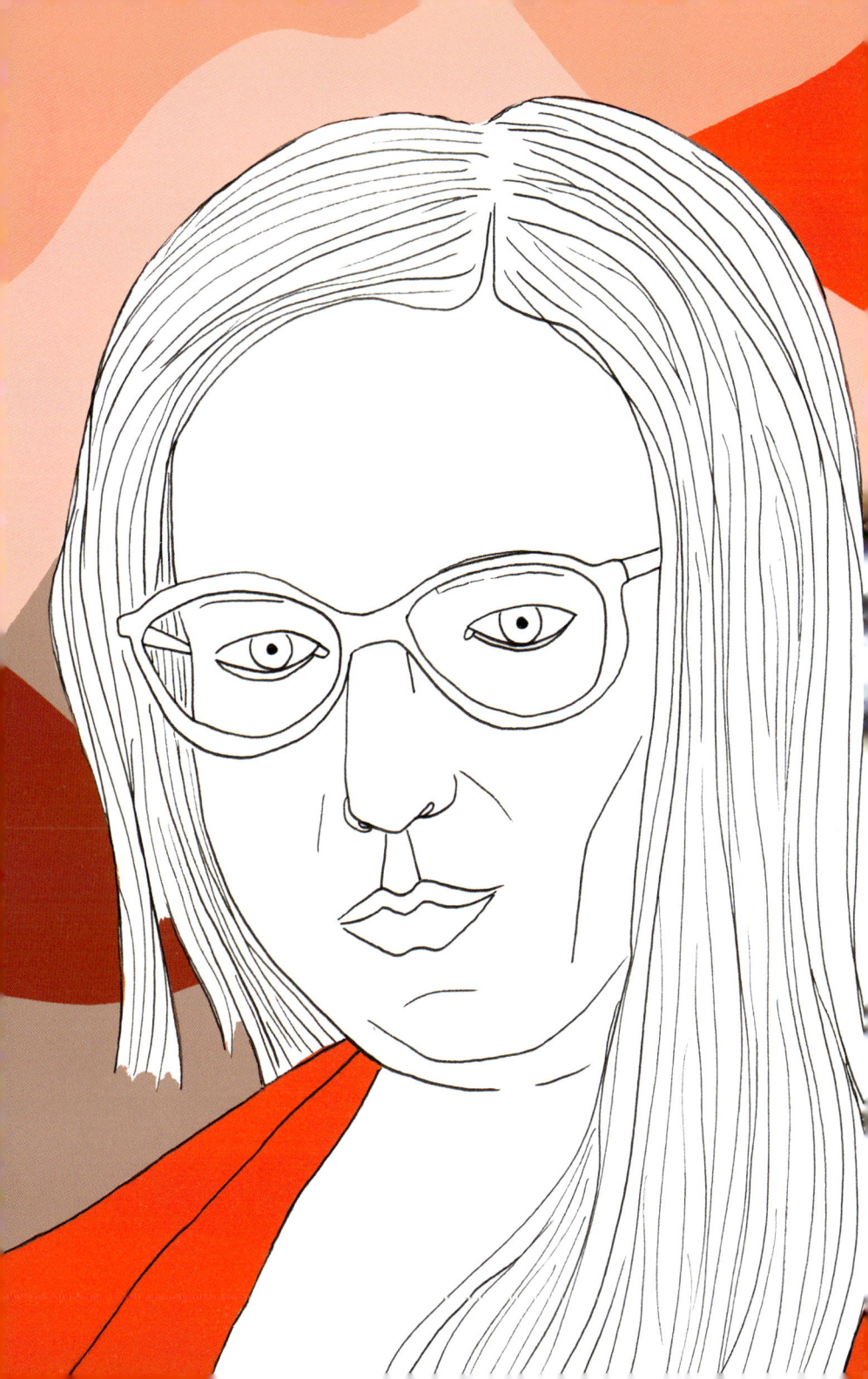

BRENDA HOWARD WAS A BISEXUAL, SEX-POSITIVE FEMINIST, AND ANTI-WAR ACTIVIST, WHO IS OFTEN REFERRED TO AS "THE MOTHER OF PRIDE".

Brenda Howard organized the first Stonewall memorial march just one month after the riots, before setting up the Christopher Street Liberation Day March with other activists. This became the first Pride March as we know it today. She also widened the scope of the march by coming up with events to hold alongside it.

During the 1970s, she became involved in the Gay Activists Alliance (GAA) and the Gay Liberation Front (GLF), two associations fighting for gay and lesbian rights. She was also part of the coalition in 1986 that led New York City to pass a law that would "prohibit discrimination based on sexual orientation in housing, employment, and public places."

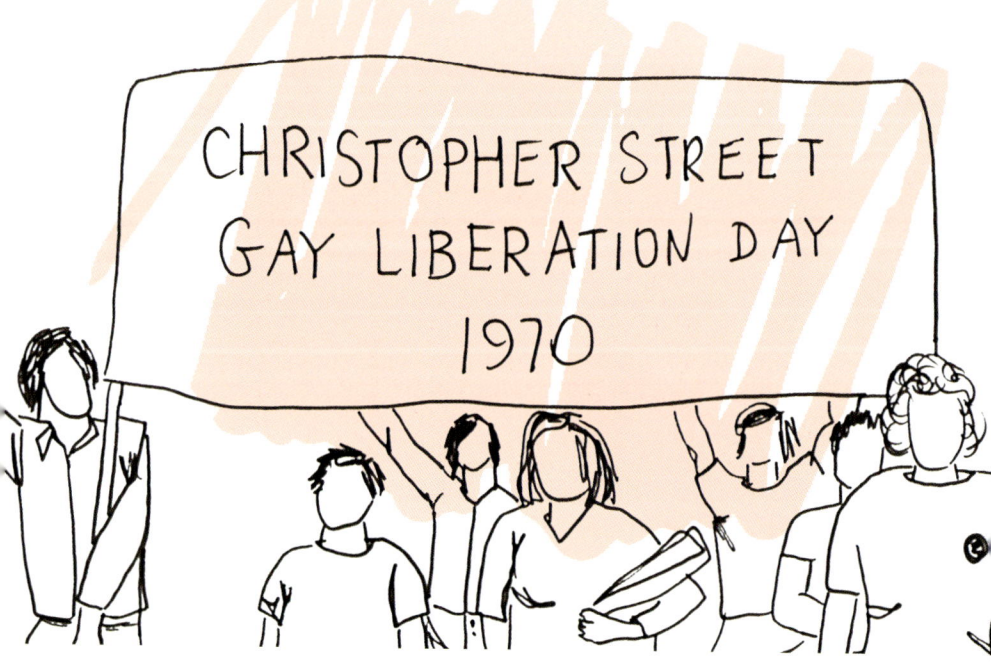

Brenda Howard

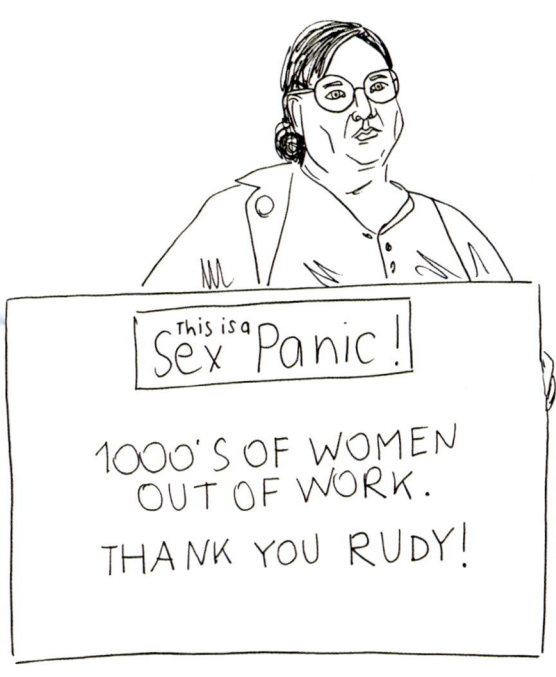

A determined and resolute activist, she was arrested in 1988 in Chicago during a protest for national health insurance and equal treatment for women, Black and Latino people, and people living with HIV. This was just one of the many times that she was arrested, but she carried on her fight for equal rights, regardless of the difficulties.

Determined to give more visibility to bisexual people, she created the New York Area Bisexual Network, an association that informs and serves as a communication network for bisexual or bi-friendly organizations in the region. She became an active member of BIPAC, an association for information exchange around bisexual issues and the fight against biphobia. She also founded the bisexual section of Alcoholics Anonymous.

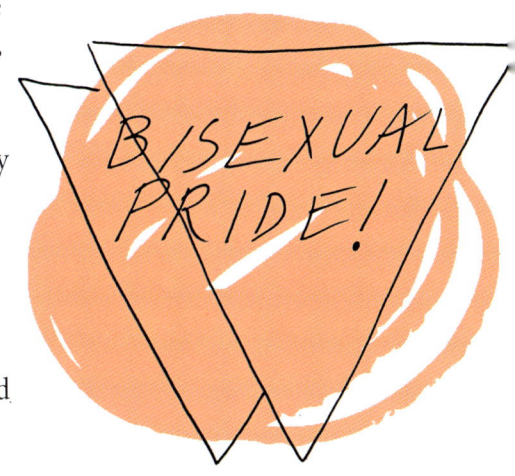

While the early LGBTQI+ movement focused primarily on the rights of gay men (and largely ignored lesbian, bisexual, intersex, and transgender people), Howard argued with the organizers of the 1993 March on Washington for the inclusion of bisexuals at this event, which would eventually be called the "March on Washington for Lesbian, Gay and Bi Equal Rights and Liberation".

She protested with ACT UP in the 1980s and continued her activism up until the last years of her life. Thanks to her struggles and determination, Brenda Howard remains a major figure in the fight against LGBTQI+phobia to this day.

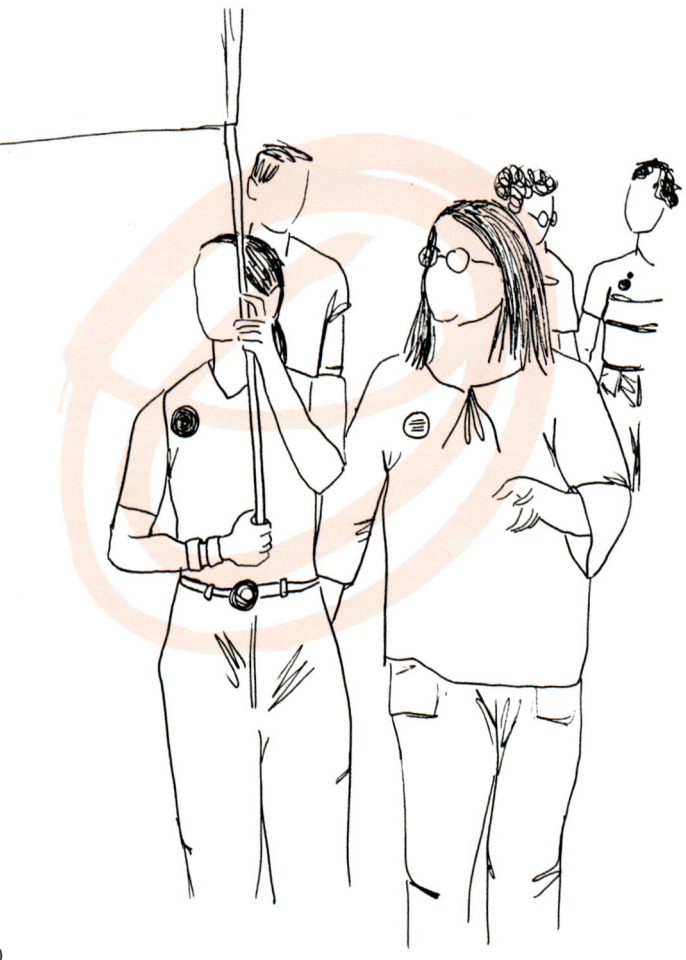

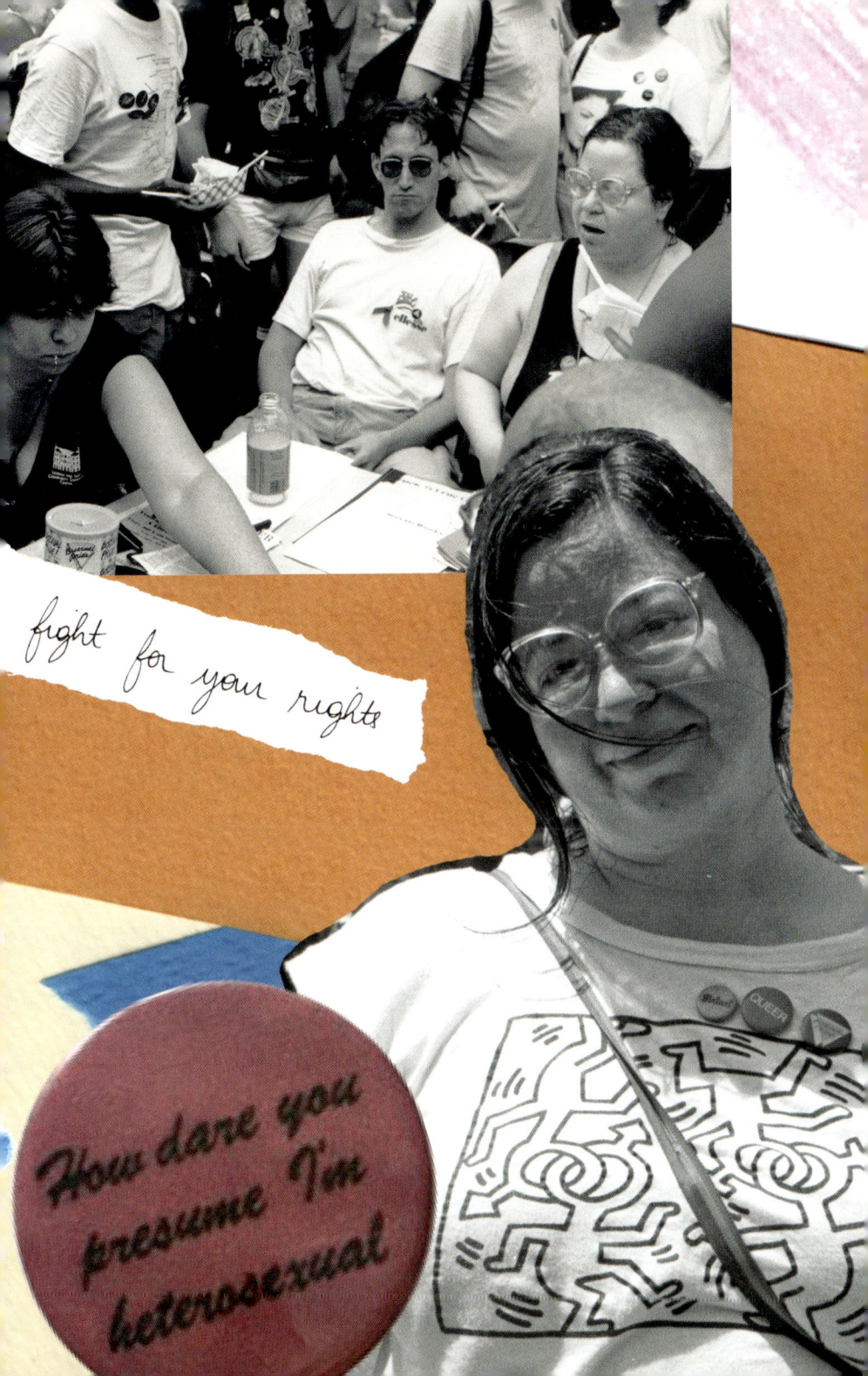

Jean Le Bitoux
1948 – 2010

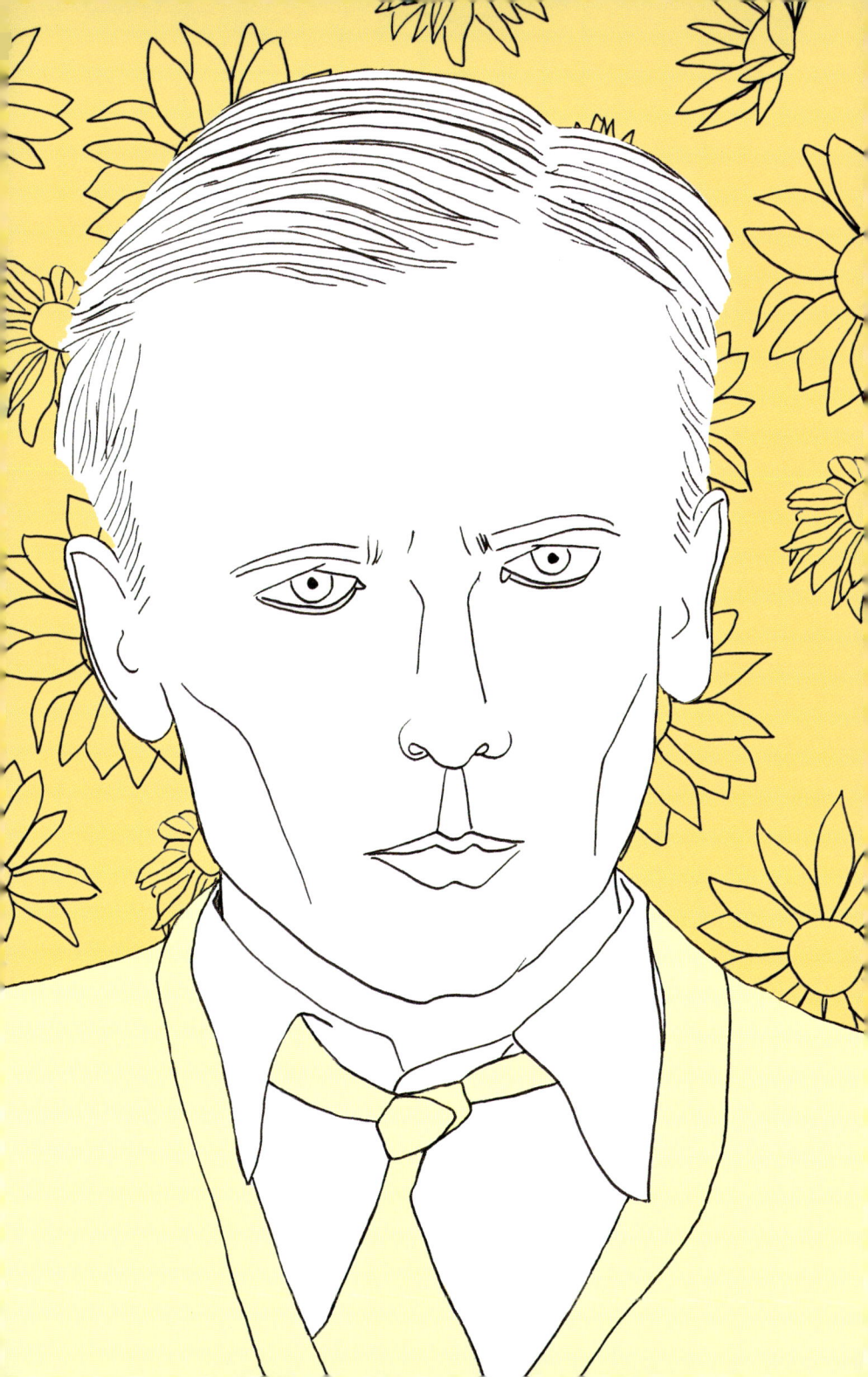

THE SON OF AN ADMIRAL, JEAN LE BITOUX WAS ACTIVE DURING HIS YOUTH IN THE FHAR (HOMOSEXUAL FRONT FOR REVOLUTIONARY ACTION) AND IN RADICAL GAY CIRCLES. FROM CHALLENGING THE PRESS, TO PRESERVING THE MEMORY OF GAY VICTIMS OF THE HOLOCAUST, THROUGH TO THE FIGHT AGAINST AIDS AND THE PRIDE MARCH, HIS VARIOUS STRUGGLES HAVE MADE HIM ONE OF THE LEADING GAY ACTIVISTS IN FRANCE.

It was after the attack on the audience by a far-right group during a gay film festival that Jean Le Bitoux decided to push for concrete changes to be made in the law. This was why he ran in the 1978 general elections with Guy Hocquenghem. His goal? To repeal Article 331, paragraph 2 of the French Penal Code, an Article inherited from the Vichy regime penalizing homosexual relations for those under twenty-one years of age. It was finally repealed in 1982 by Robert Badinter, Minister of Justice in the Pierre Mauroy government.

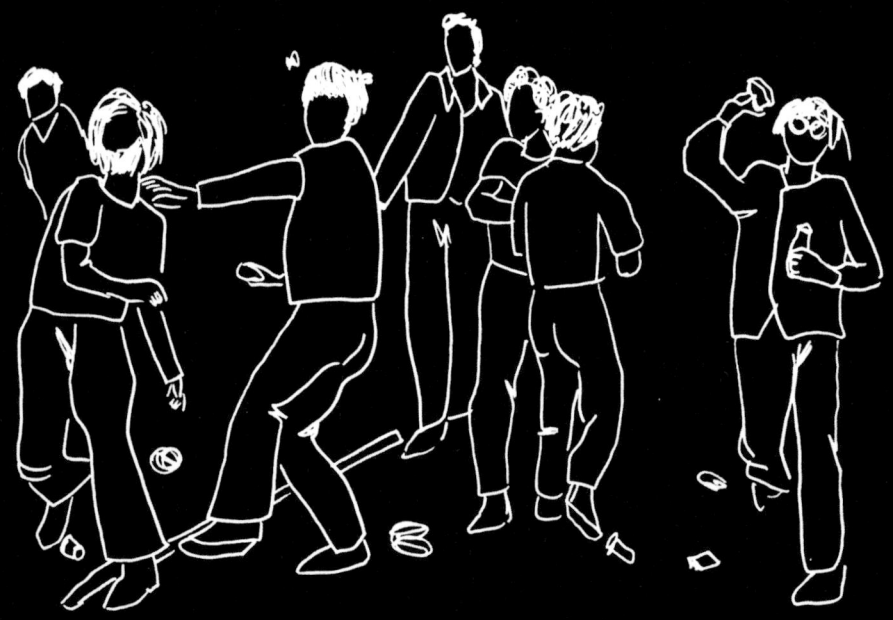

Jean Le Bitoux

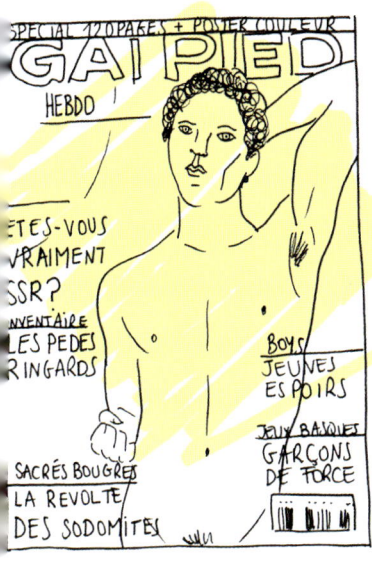

In 1979, Jean Le Bitoux co-founded *Gai Pied* with Gérard Vappereau, a gay magazine sold on news-stands, with distribution reaching 50,000 copies at the height of its popularity. It was a hit with its readers, and the magazine paved the way for other LGBTQI+ newspapers and media, celebrating the gay culture of the 1980s. Despite the success of the magazine, Jean Le Bitoux left the editorial staff of *Gai Pied* in 1983 because, according to him, the magazine had "lost its social purpose". *Gai Pied* ceased publication in 1992.

In 1985, he joined the AIDES association, an HIV/AIDS awareness organization founded by Daniel Defert. HIV-positive, Le Bitoux was one of the first activists to speak about AIDS in public, to demonstrate, promote prevention, and organize marches.

He helped to organize the first Pride Marches in Paris, which brought together a few thousand people at the beginning, and which led to the Pride celebrations that we know today.

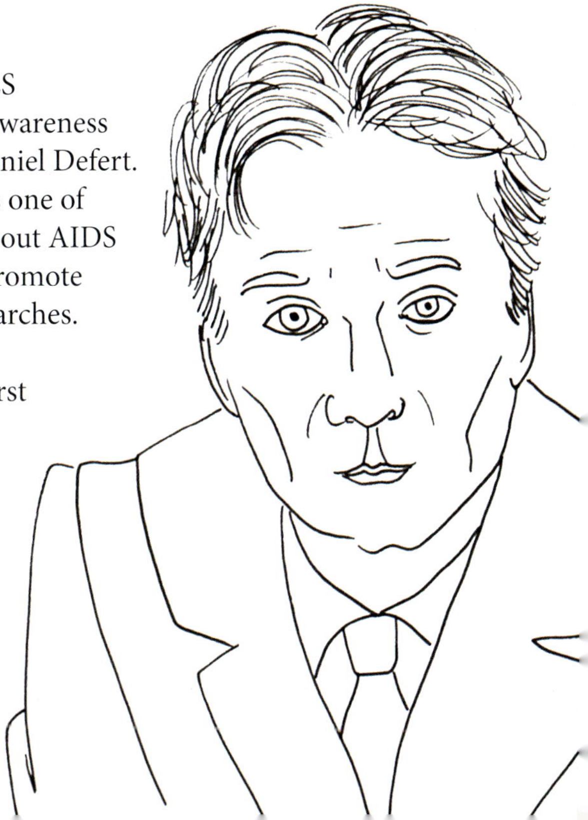

Daniel Defert

His last campaign was for the remembrance of gay victims of the Holocaust who were deported to concentration camps during the Second World War. He succeeded in creating the non-profit organization called the Memorial of the Homosexual Deportation (MDH). Their objective is "to defend the memory of the victims of intolerance regarding sexual orientation and gender identity and particularly of homosexuals persecuted or murdered in Europe as part of Nazi racial policy." Thousands of LGBTQI+ people were deported to concentration camps between 1939 and 1945 and later killed.

The new LGBTQI+ archives in Paris will act as a memorial so that the names of those LGBTQI+ victims of the Holocaust will not be forgotten. Since the 1980s, cities around the world have erected memorials to LGBTQI+ victims of the Second World War.

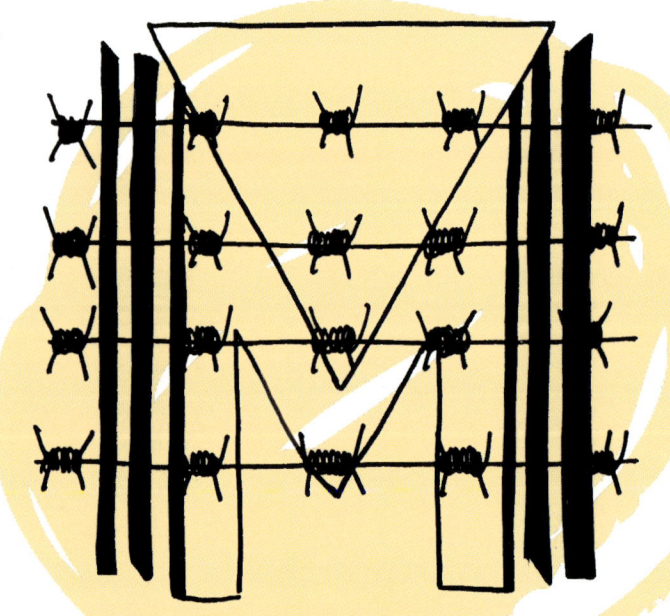

Logo for the Memorial of the Homosexual Deportation

"SEXUALITY IS SOMETHING THAT WE HAVE INSIDE OURSELVES, A KIND OF DYNAMIC, A MOVEMENT, A PERPETUAL IMPULSE THAT IS ORIENTED TOWARDS A BASIC PLEASURE WHICH IS THE PLEASURE OF OUR OWN BODY."

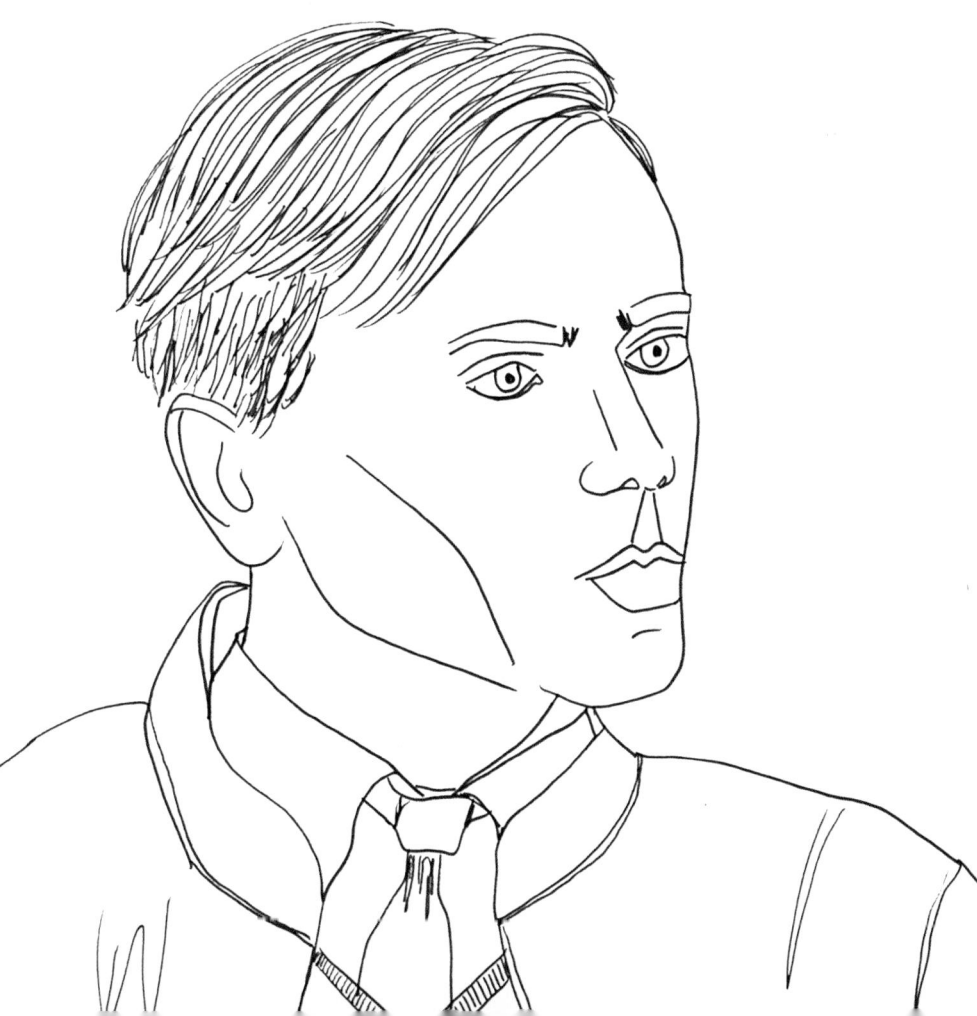

Pedro Almodóvar
1949

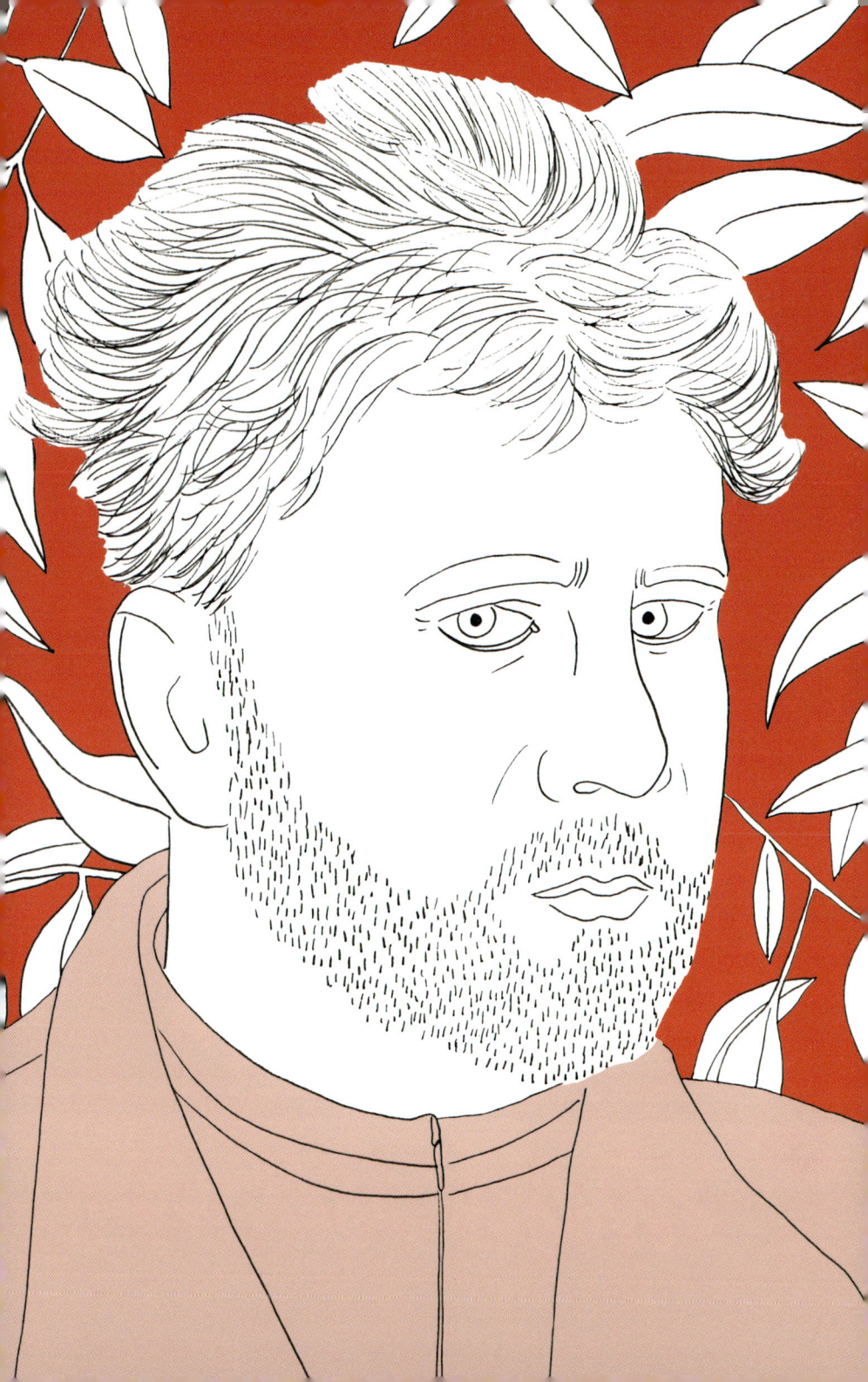

***WOMEN ON THE VERGE OF A NERVOUS BREAKDOWN, VOLVER, ALL ABOUT MY MOTHER, BAD EDUCATION, KIKA, BROKEN EMBRACES*... MORE THAN TWENTY FEATURE FILMS CAN BE CREDITED TO ALMODOVAR.**

He grew up during la Movida Madrileña – a post-Franco countercultural movement – which was galvanizing for a whole generation suffocated by years of repression.

Born in 1949 in a region south of Madrid, Pedro Almodóvar directed his first film, *Pepi, Luci, Bom and Other Girls Like Mom*, in 1980, when he had just moved to the Spanish capital. At that time, Madrid was a city full of creativity that saw the birth of an underground punk scene. An openly gay director, many of Pedro Almodóvar's works are considered queer by critics. Often provocative, they depict a range of free and flamboyant characters.

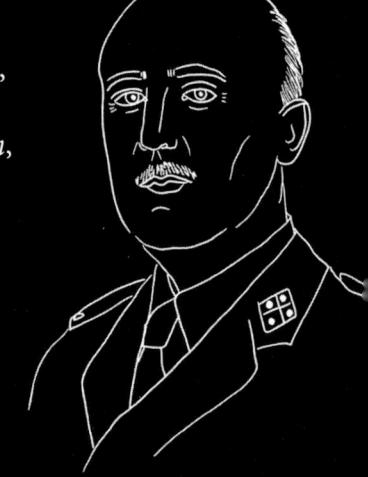

Francisco Franco

PEPI, LUCI, BOM
y otras chicas del montón

Pedro Almodóvar

A few years after his first feature film, he founded his own production company with his brother: El Deseo.

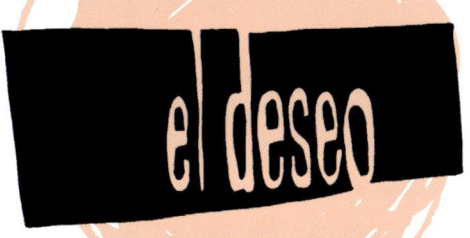

If desire is a recurring theme in his works, questions of gender and sexuality also occupy an important, even central, place in his creations. With his keen eye and characters with assumed sexualities and fluid genders, Almodóvar explores lives, sometimes tormented journeys, in which being LGBTQI+ is not regarded as a disadvantage.

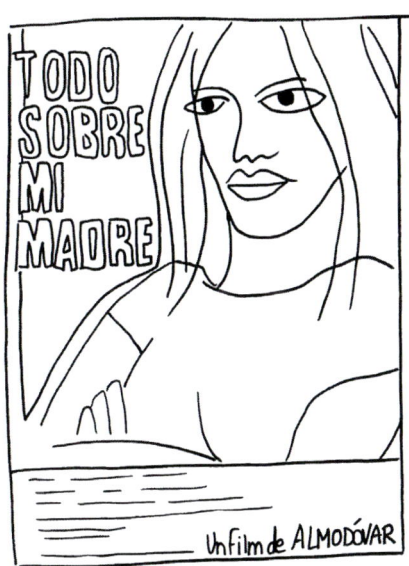

His protagonists are strong, combative, deeply alive and often have a scathing sense of humour. The representation of LGBTQI+ people in his films differs from the usual LGBTQI+ stereotypes seen in cinema.

The Celluloid Closet, first released as a book and then a documentary, broadcast in 1995, explains very clearly how Hollywood cinema has stereotyped gay people and lesbians on screen (sometimes depicting them as killers, sometimes as suicidal, but often as characters with tragic fates) and this has influenced the public perception of LGBTQI+ people over time, highlighting the power of this popular art and the importance of positive LGBTQI+ representation.

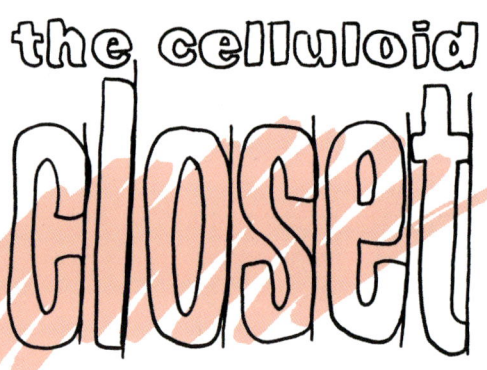

But Pedro Almodóvar's films are bold and bright with a strong sense of colour (especially red), portraying people with powerful emotions. Spain, and Spanish folklore and its symbols play a part too. All with a touch of spectacle and melodrama.

For the director, the question of love is always at the heart of things: "To love, to desire, is also to suffer, and to be ready to start again…"

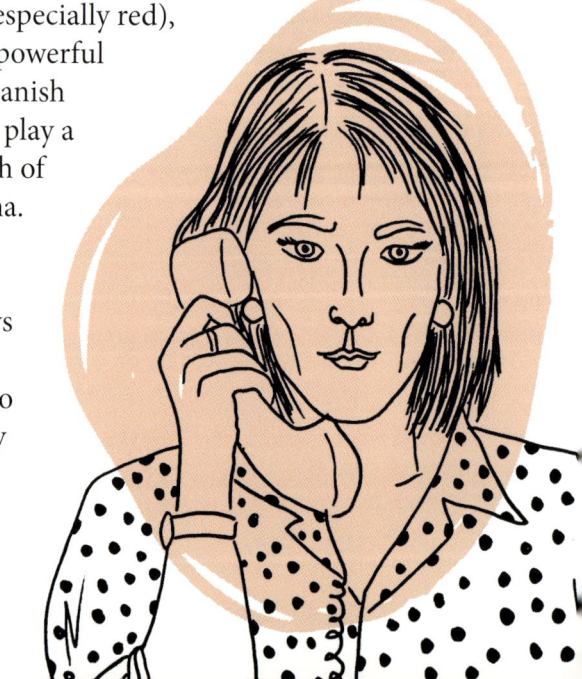

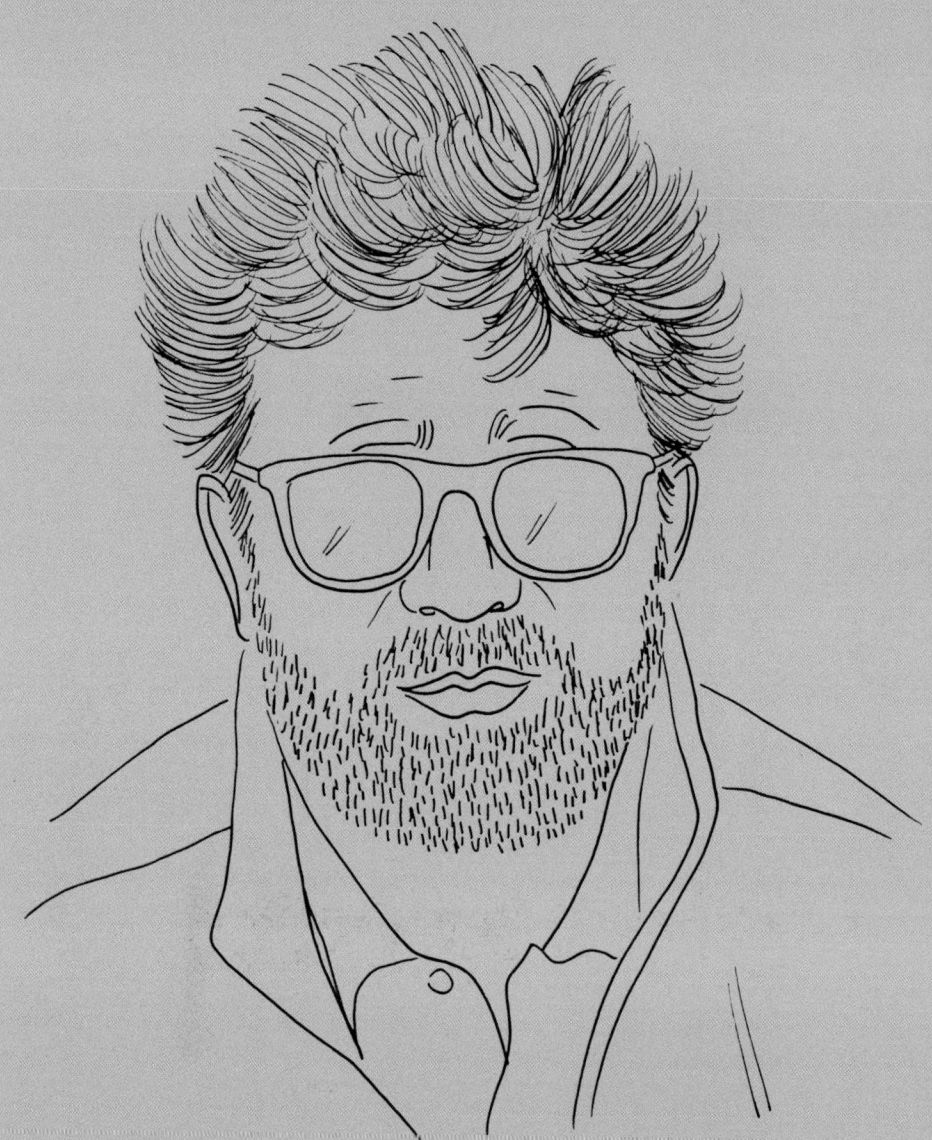

His themes are well expressed through his complex female characters, as is his love for his actresses (particularly Victoria Abril, Carmen Maura, Marisa Paredes, and Penélope Cruz) who give stand out performances in each of his works.

With their beautiful and luminous characters, Pedro Almodóvar's films shine a light on people who are often poorly represented on the big screen.

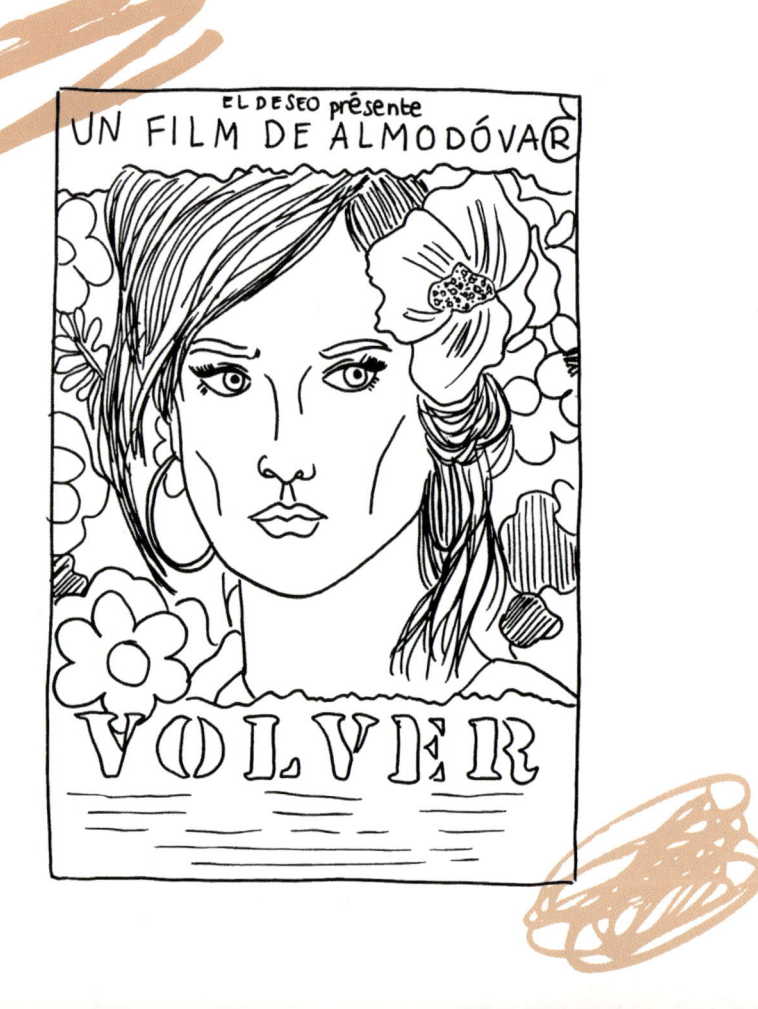

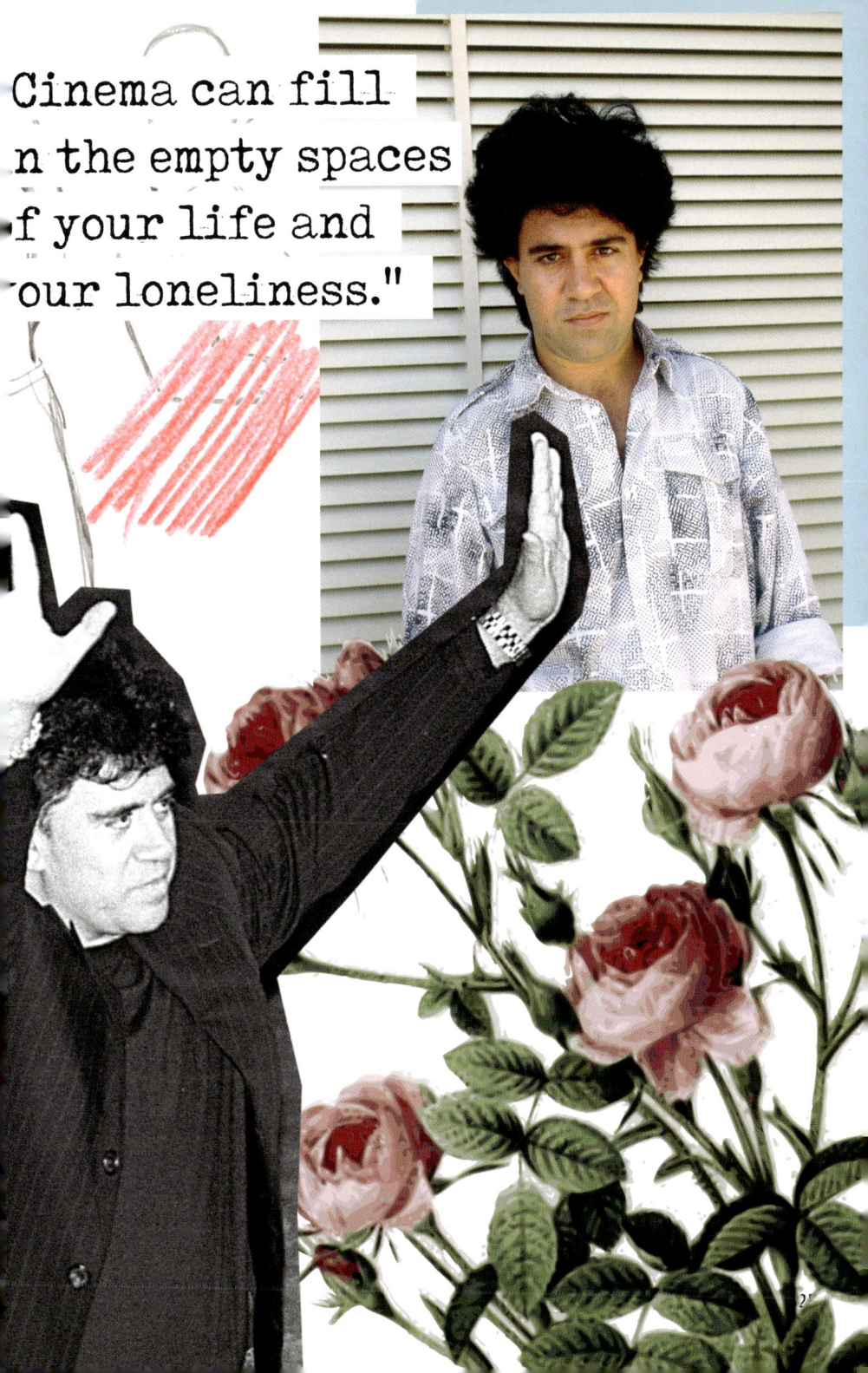

Michael Cashman
1950

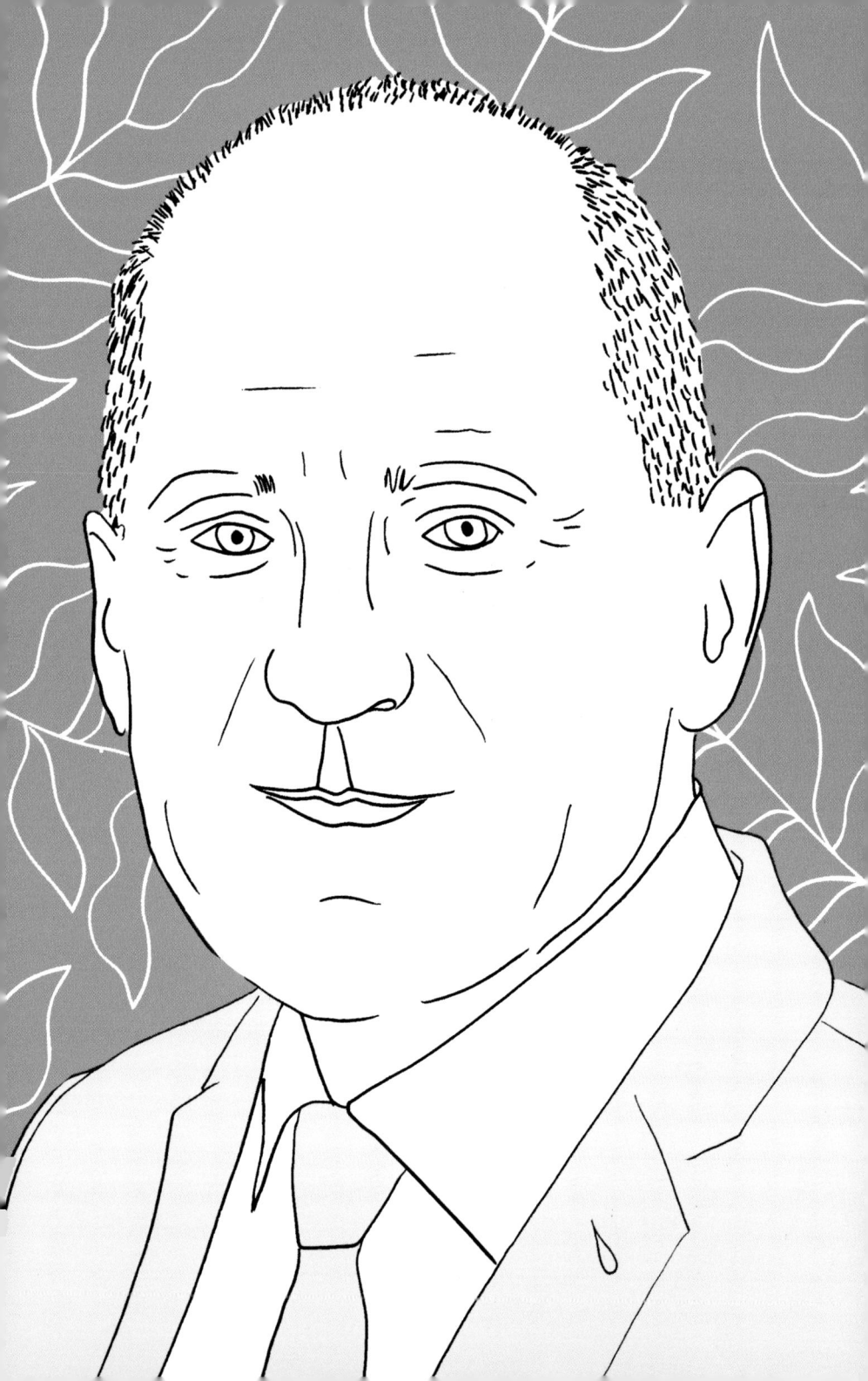

MICHAEL CASHMAN HAS HAD A HIGHLY SUCCESSFUL CAREER AS AN ACTOR, SINGER, WRITER, DIRECTOR AND POLITICIAN. HE IS A CO-FOUNDER AND FOUNDING CHAIR OF THE STONEWALL GROUP IN THE UK.

His most recognisable acting role is that of Colin Russell in the BBC's long-running television soap opera *EastEnders*. In 1989, the character had the first gay kiss in a British soap, with over seventeen million people tuning in to watch the moment. It was a ground-breaking scene, and was so controversial at the time that some MPs called for the programme to be cancelled.

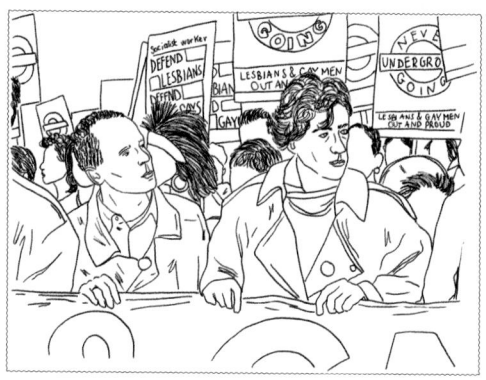

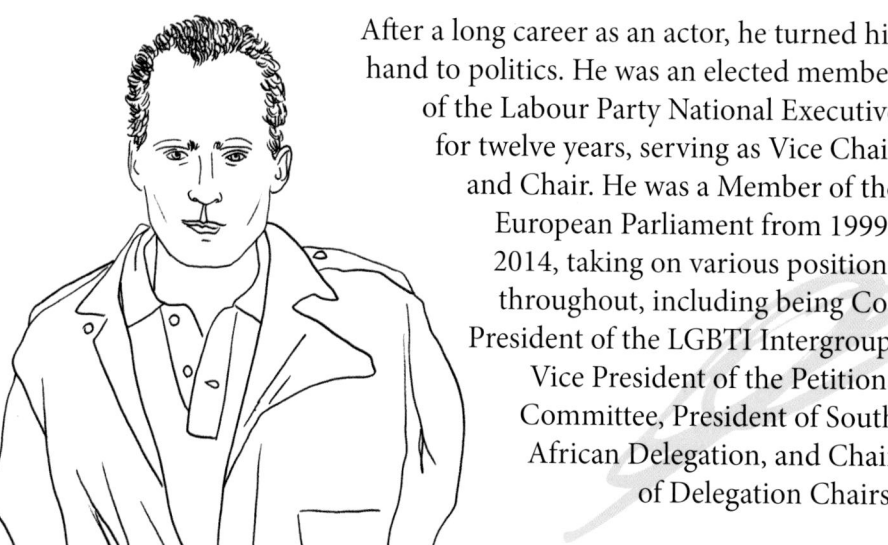

After a long career as an actor, he turned his hand to politics. He was an elected member of the Labour Party National Executive for twelve years, serving as Vice Chair and Chair. He was a Member of the European Parliament from 1999-2014, taking on various positions throughout, including being Co-President of the LGBTI Intergroup, Vice President of the Petitions Committee, President of South African Delegation, and Chair of Delegation Chairs.

Michael Cashman

After more than forty-five years of continuous membership, Lord Cashman publicly resigned from the Labour Party (over anti-Semitism and the Party's stance on the EU) on 22 May 2019 on the eve of the European elections. He rejoined the Labour Party in 2022 and now sits as a Labour peer in the House of Lords.

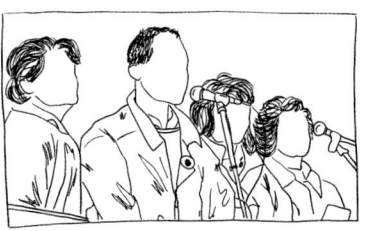

He has been a firm supporter of human rights, with a focus on LGBTQI+ rights throughout his life. He is a co-founder and founding Chair of the Stonewall Group, the largest LGBTQ+ rights organization in Europe. He was also the Labour Party's LGBT Global Envoy from 2014-2016.

He was awarded an honorary doctorate from the University of Staffordshire for his human rights work in 2007. That same year he was elected MEP of the Year for Justice and Fundamental Rights by his peers. He has received numerous awards and recognition for his advocacy work including a CBE, Lifetime Achievement Award and British LGBT Awards 2020.

In 1983, he met Paul Cottingham (1964-2014), and they were together for thirty-one years celebrating their civil partnership in 2006. Paul was a fellow actor and human rights activist, also working for the Labour Party. In 2014, Michael was raised to the Peerage, taking the title "Baron Cashman of Limehouse". Paul died four days before Michael's entry into the House, but he remains his inspiration and the love of his life.

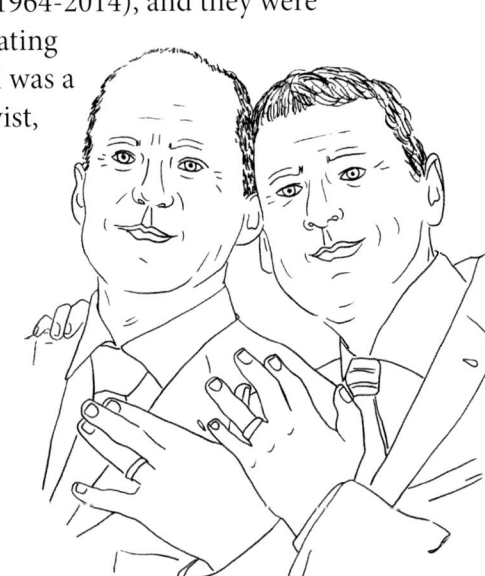

Sylvia Rivera
1951 – 2002

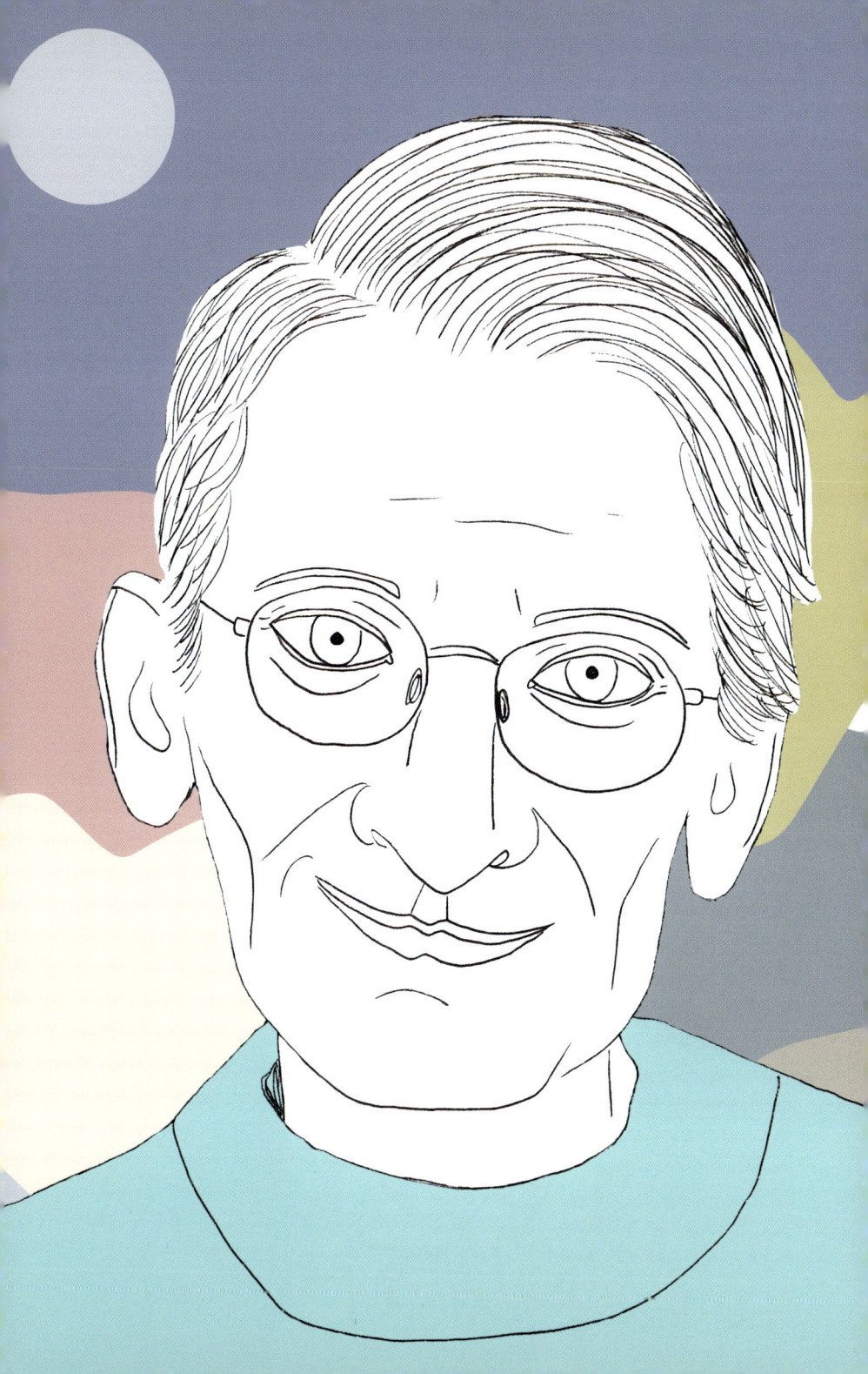

AFTER A DIFFICULT CHILDHOOD, SYLVIA RIVERA WAS KICKED OUT BY HER GRANDMOTHER AND LEFT TO FEND FOR HERSELF AT THE AGE OF ONLY TEN.

She found refuge with a group of drag queens and transgender women and, a few years later, became a sex worker in the Times Square neighbourhood of New York. It was there that she met her sister in arms: Marsha P. Johnson.

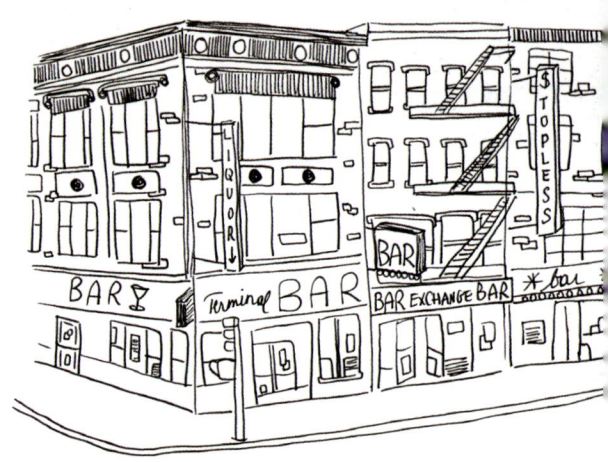

Times Square

A tireless, radical activist, determined to break the cycle of precariousness, police violence and discrimination suffered by many transgender women, she was one of the first people to retaliate against the police during the Stonewall riots. She was one of the most active protesters on the night of June 28, 1969, which forever changed the history of the LGBTQI+ movement.

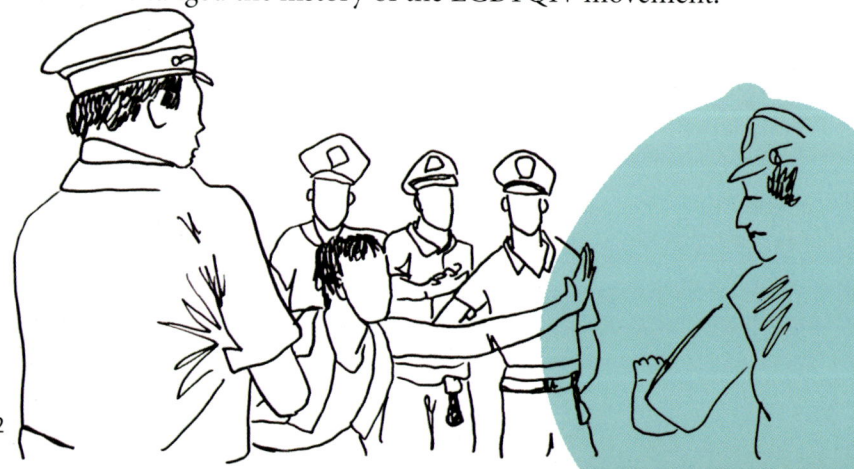

About the Stonewall riots, she said several times in interviews "We were the front liners… we had nothing to lose." She also took part in the very first post-Stonewall movements: Gay Liberation Front and the Gay Activists Alliance, although these organizations gradually turned away from Sylvia Rivera, whom they considered to be a troublemaker.

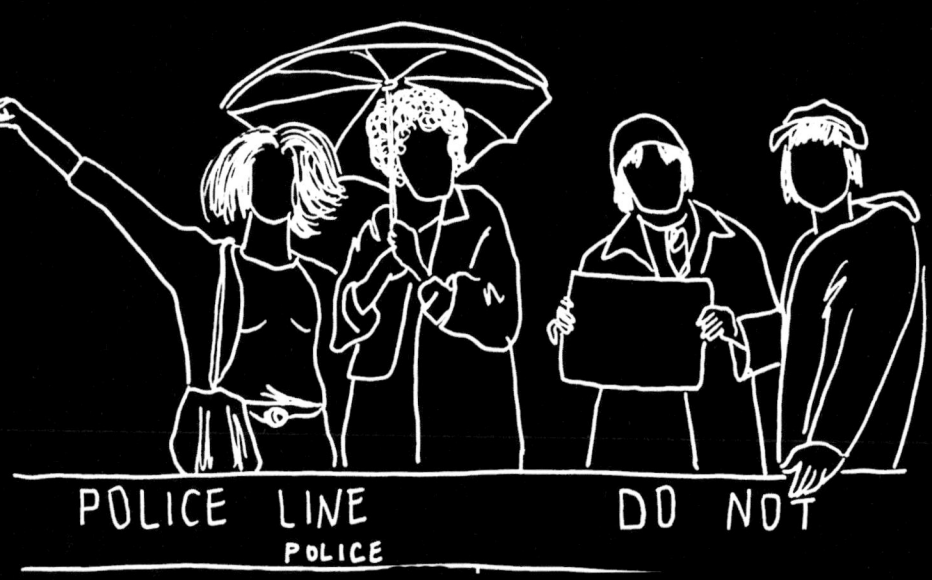

It was also at this time that she became the voice of marginalized and excluded people from the gay liberation movement: lesbian and bisexual women, transgender and non-binary people, the homeless, and people of colour.

In 1970, with Marsha P. Johnson, she created STAR (Street Transvestite [now Transgender] Action Revolutionaries) and provided shelter, food and clothing to homeless transgender and queer people. At that time, she also joined the Young Lords, a far-left Puerto Rican nationalist group who were close to the Black Panthers.

Marsha P. Johnson

Tired of gay men ignoring the violence against transgender people, she spoke on stage in 1973 at a gay rally in Washington Square Park and delivered these poignant words: "I will no longer put up with this shit. I have been beaten. I have had my nose broken. I have been thrown in jail. I have lost my job. I have lost my apartment, for gay liberation – and you all treat me this way?" She ended her speech with the words "Gay Power!"

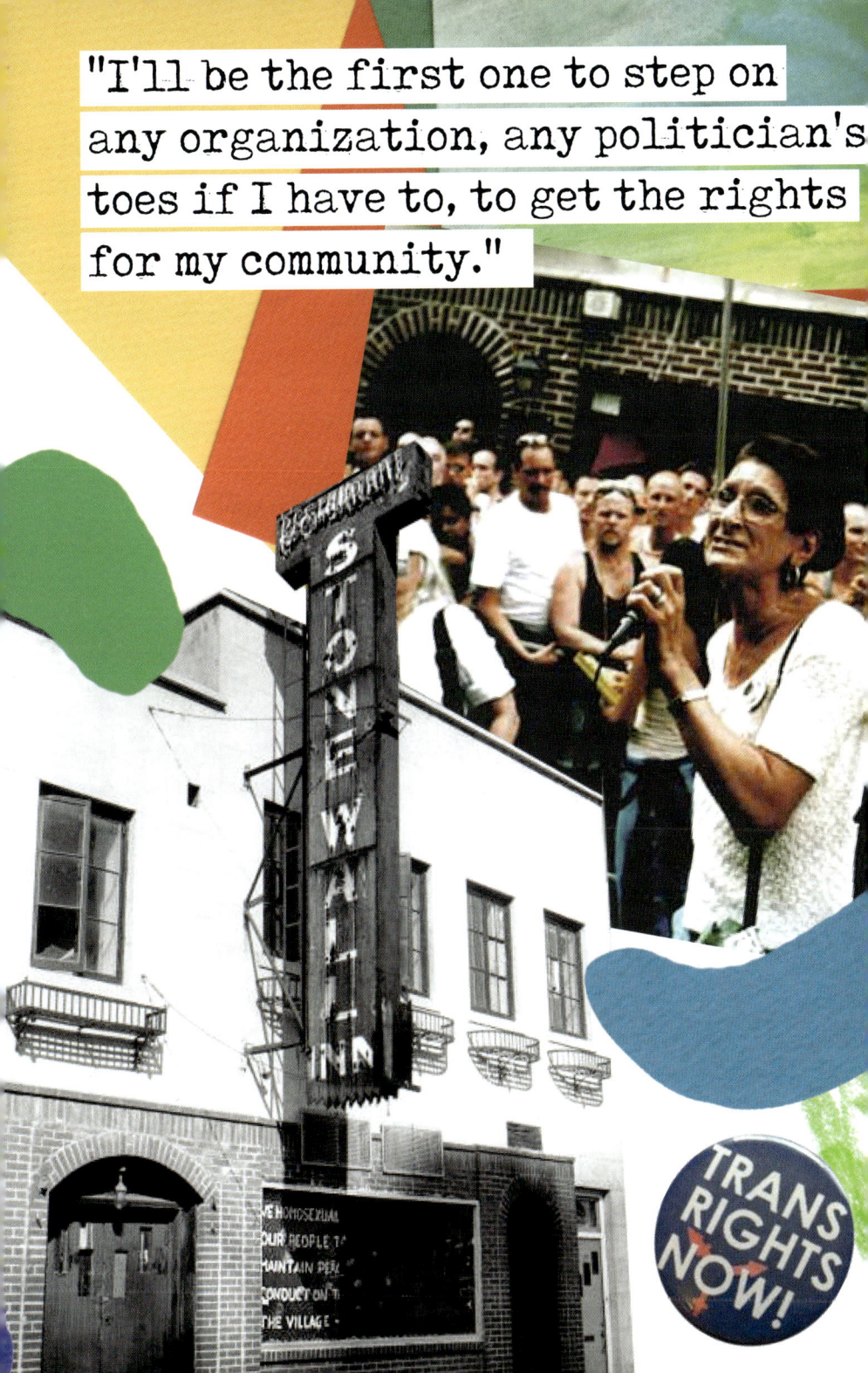

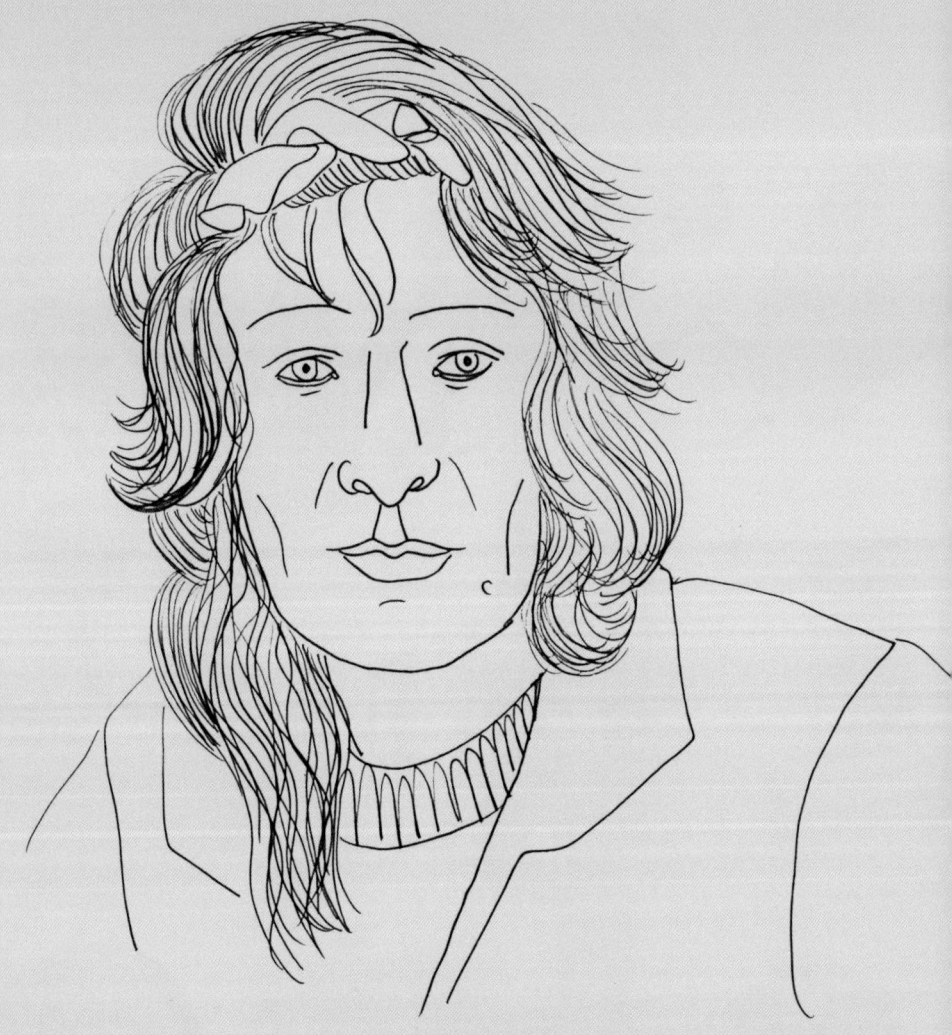

Sylvia Rivera

Arrested and imprisoned several times by the police, she is, according to several activists, the person who argued for the presence of the "T" in the acronym "LGBT" and challenged the lack of inclusivity in the community.

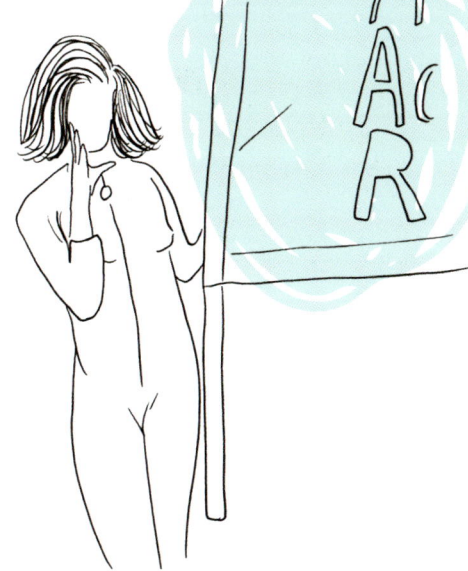

After a life marked by homelessness, drugs, and depression, she advocated for those people who were homeless and poor and whom she felt were ignored by the wider movement. She continued during the last years of her life to spread the messages that had always engaged her: those regarding the freedom to live and be true to oneself.

One organization now bears her name, the Sylvia Rivera Law Project, which, according to its website, aims to "guarantee that all people are free to self-determine gender identity and expression, regardless of income or race, and without facing harassment, discrimination or violence."

On the 50th anniversary of the Stonewall Riots in 2019, Rivera was one of the inaugural fifty American "pioneers, trailblazers, and heroes" inducted on the National LGBTQ Wall of Honor within the Stonewall National Monument (SNM) in New York City's Stonewall Inn.

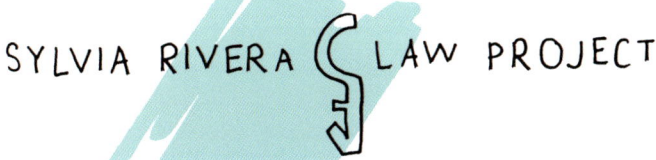

Peter Tatchell
1952

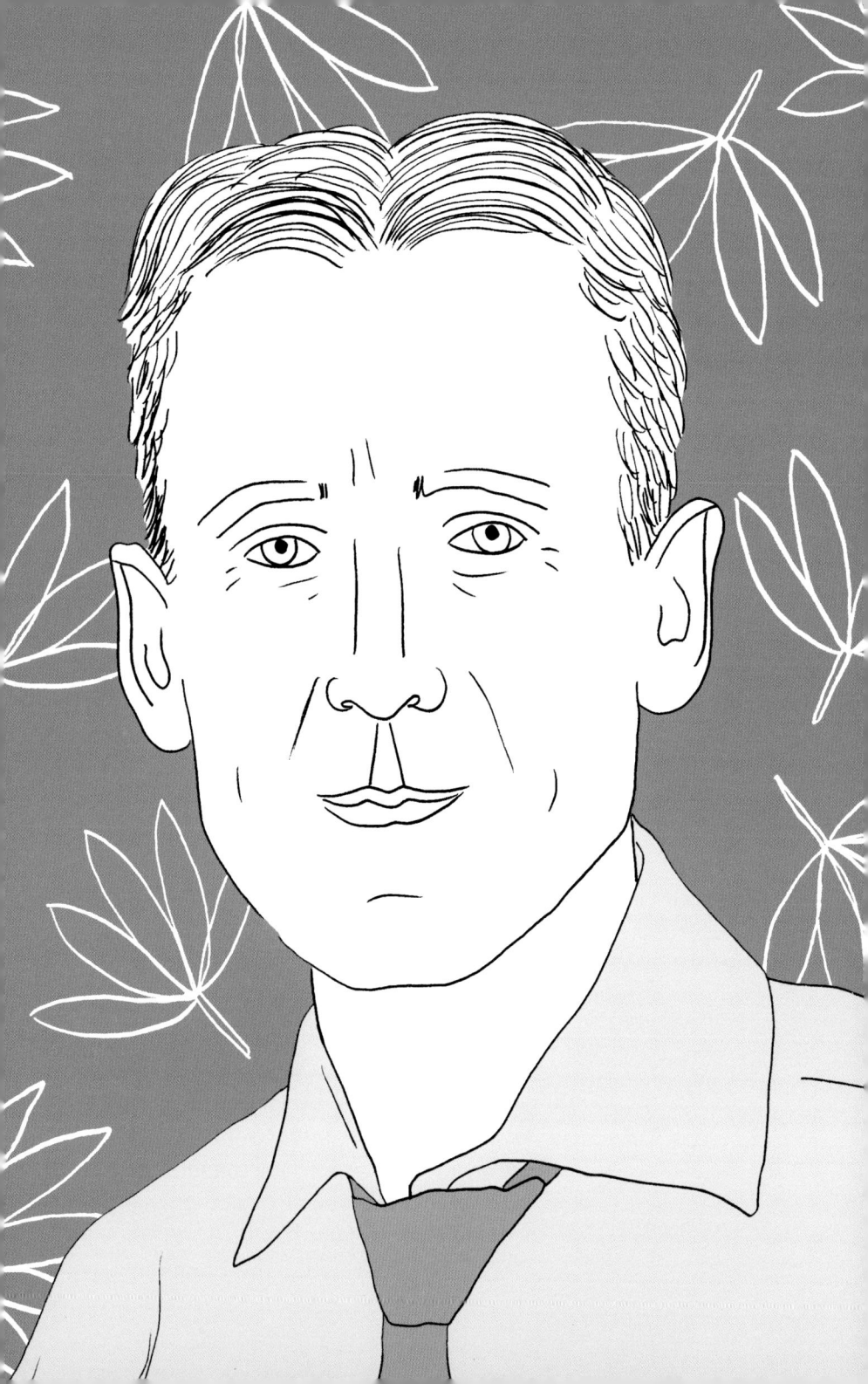

PETER TATCHELL HAS BEEN CAMPAIGNING FOR HUMAN RIGHTS FOR OVER 55 YEARS, ON ISSUES OF DEMOCRACY, CIVIL LIBERTIES, SOCIAL EQUALITY, GAY RIGHTS, ENVIRONMENTAL PROTECTION, PEACE, AND GLOBAL JUSTICE.

He began campaigning for human rights in 1967, primarily fighting against the death penalty and the Vietnam War, and for Aboriginal rights in his homeland of Australia. Moving to the UK, from 1971, he was a leading activist in the Gay Liberation Front in London. Two years later, he staged the first LGBTQI+ rights protest in a communist state – East Germany – which resulted in his detention and interrogation by the Stasi.

In 1983, he ran for election as the Labour candidate for Bermondsey but was defeated in one of the dirtiest, most homophobic elections in Britain. He received death threats, was assaulted in the street, and members of the opposition party wore homophobic badges without shame.

In 1990, he co-founded the direct action group OutRage! In a campaign against the Church of England, they targeted ten Anglican bishops in 1994, accusing them of hypocrisy for publicly endorsing the church's homophobic stance, whilst being gay in private. Four years later, Peter interrupted the Easter Sermon of the Archbishop of Canterbury in protest at Dr Carey's support for laws that discriminate against queer people. In 1999, in London, he ambushed the motorcade of the Zimbabwean President, Robert Mugabe (left), attempting a citizen's arrest on charges of torture. A repeat attempt in Brussels in 2001 resulted in him being beaten unconscious by Mugabe's bodyguards, which left him with permanent, minor brain injuries.

Peter Tatchell

Two years later, he ran in front of, and halted, Tony Blair's motorcade in protest of the Iraq War. In 2007, he was bashed by neo-Nazis and arrested at the attempted Moscow Gay Pride parade.

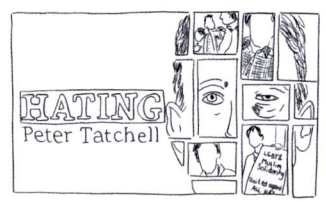

Over two decades ago, he warned of the dangers of global warming, resource depletion, species extinction and environmental degradation. In 2021, a documentary about his life, *Hating Peter Tatchell*, began streaming on Netflix. The same year, he coordinated the first Reclaim Pride March, which sought to get Pride back to its roots, with corporate sponsorship being replaced by a grassroots community and a human rights' focus.

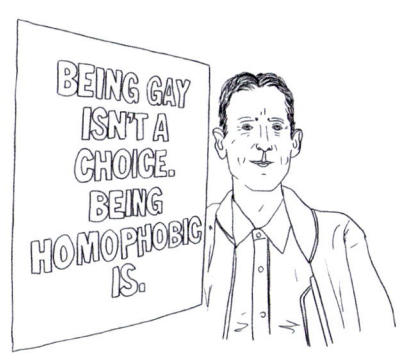

He was voted the sixth greatest "Hero of our Time" by readers of the *New Statesman* in 2006, and in the same year *The Independent* listed him as one of the top fifty "Good" people in Britain. In 2009, he won Campaigner of the Year at the *Observer* Ethical Awards.

He is Director of the Peter Tatchell Foundation.

"WOMEN AND GAY PEOPLE ARE THE LITMUS TEST OF WHETHER A SOCIETY IS DEMOCRATIC AND RESPECTING HUMAN RIGHTS. WE ARE THE CANARIES IN THE MINE."

Judith Butler
1956

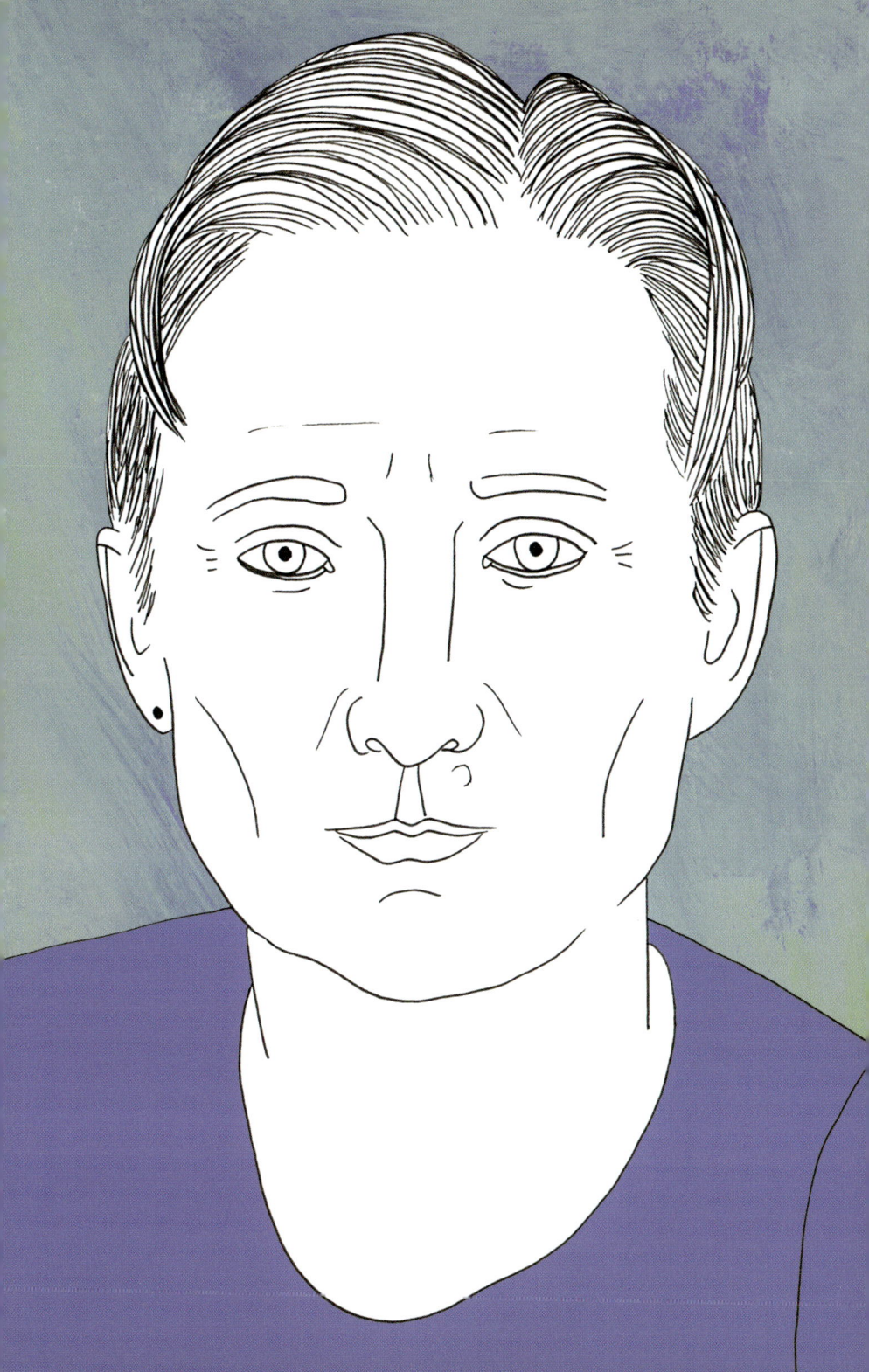

JUDITH BUTLER'S WORK HAS LEFT ITS MARK ON QUEER THINKING, GENDER, AND CULTURAL STUDIES. HER DETAILED AND RIGOROUS ANALYSIS HAS GREATLY IMPACTED THE LGBTQI+ COMMUNITY.

Judith Butler is an American philosopher, and has been a university professor at Berkeley since 1993. They are best-known as a theorist, whose 1990 book *Gender Trouble: Feminism and the Subversion of Identity* upset the boundaries of gender, sex, and their standard definitions.

Gender Trouble is considered by many as one of the foundations of queer theory and has been a major influence for several third-wave feminists, and on sociological, philosophical, and artistic works. Translated into several languages, and selling thousands of copies worldwide, it received a second edition in 2006, more than fifteen years after its initial publication in the United States. This writing has resonated within queer and LGBTQI+ circles but also among researchers and philosophers who study gender and sexuality. "Performativity must be understood not as a singular or deliberate 'act' but, rather, as the reiterative and citational practice by which discourse produces the effects that it names."

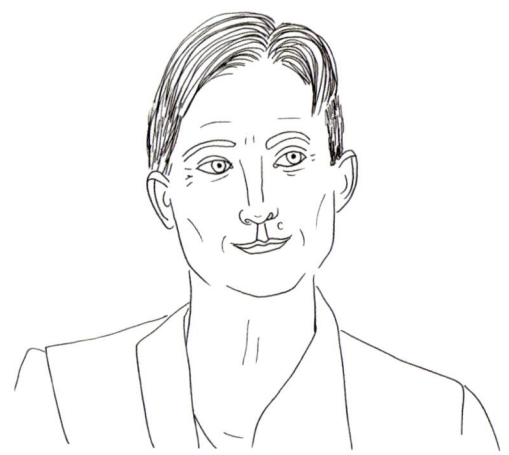

With the theorization of the "performativity of gender" (seeing gender as a social performance that we have learned, that we repeat, and in which we seek a resemblance to an original model), Judith Butler's analysis feeds and reinforces the politics of the feminist and queer movements particularly from 1990 to 2000.

With *Gender Trouble*, Judith Butler seeks to shake up heterosexuality, while examining the writings of Monique Wittig, Sigmund Freud, and Michel Foucault.

Their publications include *Undoing Gender* (2006), *Giving an Account of Oneself* (2005) and *Bodies That Matter: On the Discursive Limits of Sex* (1993). In these works they challenge "essentialist" understandings of gender which define masculinity and femininity as naturally or biologically given, and that desire for the "opposite" gender is the norm.

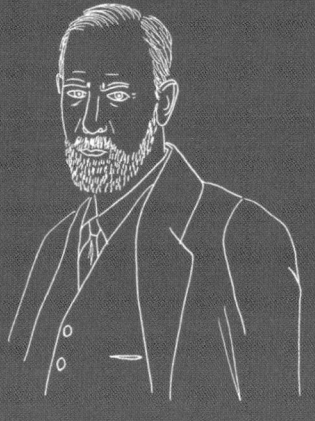

Sigmund Freud

Judith Butler has also actively campaigned for the rights of LGBTQI+ people. They were president of the International Gay and Lesbian Human Rights Commission (now OutRight Action International) from 1994 to 1997, an organization that defends LGBTQI+ people around the world.

Following the tragic events in New York of September 11, 2001, their writing in the early 2000s addressed issues related to racial and social inequalities, mourning, the violence of war and precariousness.

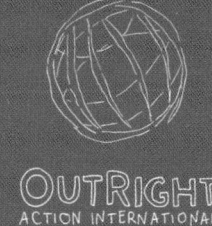

In *Frames of War*, they explain, "Precariousness and precarity are intersecting concepts. Lives are by definition precarious: they can be expunged at will or by accident; their persistence is in no sense guaranteed."

In 2012, they received the Adorno Prize for contributions in the fields of music, philosophy, film, and theatre.

Rosanna
Flamer-Caldera
1956

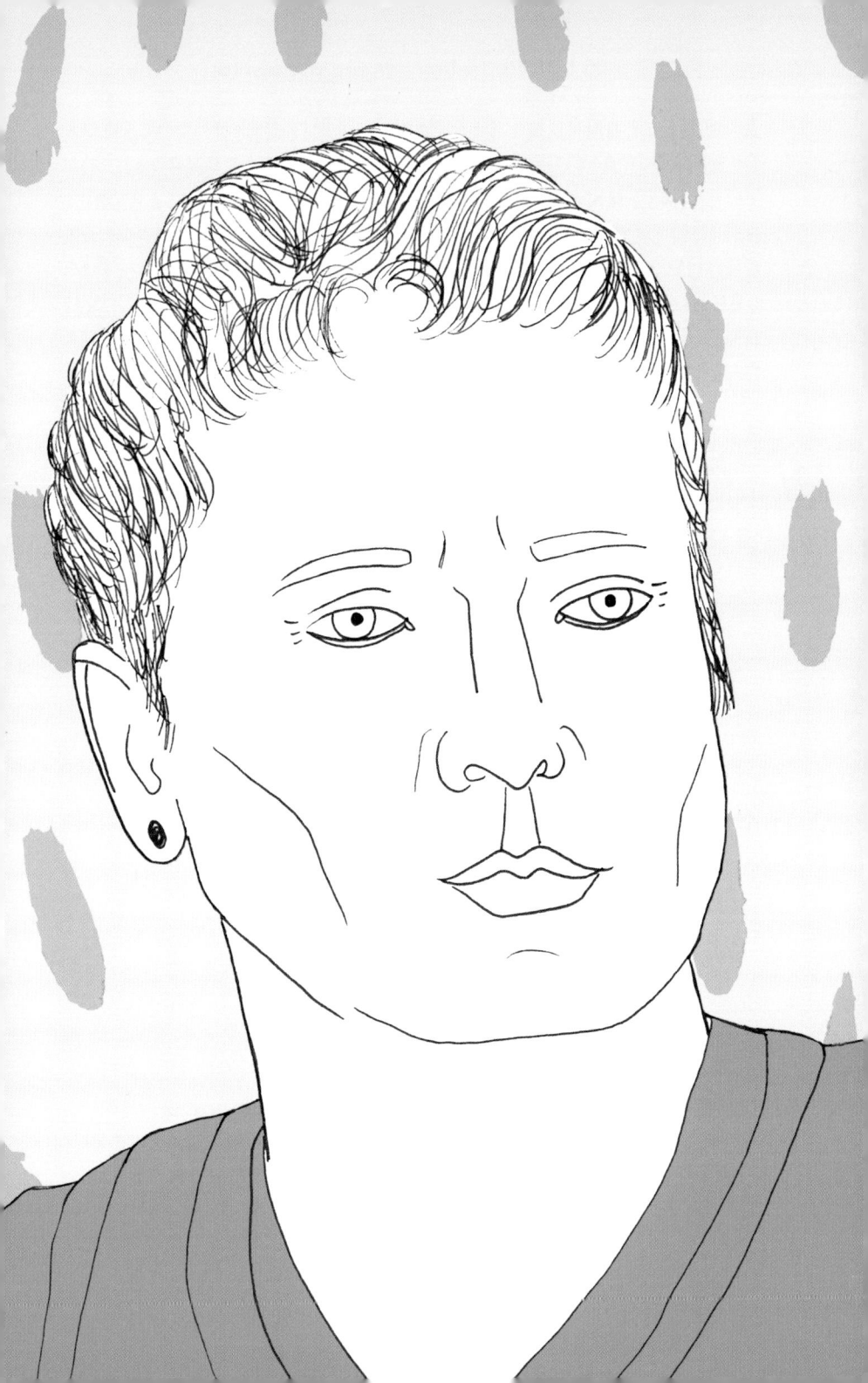

A SRI LANKAN LESBIAN ACTIVIST, ROSANNA FLAMER-CALDERA WAS SECRETARY GENERAL OF THE INTERNATIONAL LESBIAN AND GAY ASSOCIATION (ILGA), FOUNDER OF THE WOMEN'S SUPPORT GROUP IN 1999 (AN ASSOCIATION SUPPORTING LESBIAN, BISEXUAL, AND TRANSGENDER WOMEN) AND IN 2004 CREATED THE EQUAL GROUND, THE ONLY LGBTQI+ RIGHTS ORGANIZATION IN SRI LANKA.

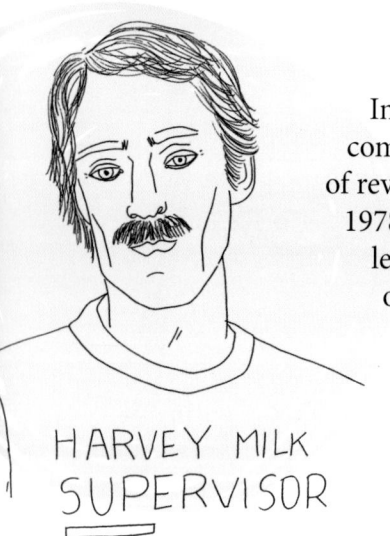

HARVEY MILK SUPERVISOR

In the 1970s, she left her native country after coming out and settled in San Francisco, a city of revolts and nascent LGBTQI+ movements. In 1978, she participated in her first Pride March, led by the well-known activist, Harvey Milk, only a few weeks before his death. She lived in San Francisco for fifteen years before returning to Sri Lanka to campaign for her rights and those of thousands of other LGBTQI+ people.

Since 1883 and up until February 2023, "homosexual acts" in Sri Lanka have been illegal under Article 365 of the country's Penal Code, which dates back to the British colonial era. It criminalizes "carnal intercourse against the order of nature," which can be punished with up to ten years in prison. Article 365A (introduced in 1995) further generalizes by prohibiting "public and private acts of gross indecency between two persons". Section 399, which criminializes cheating by "pretending to be someone else", is regularly used by the police to arrest transgender, gay men and lesbians, whose physical appearance is considered not to conform to the social norm with regard to biological sexual identity.

These laws pave the way for harassment, assault, rape, and stigmatization against LGBTQI+ communities by individuals as well as the police. Psychological and physical violence, and the criminalization of homosexuality are also factors that increase the risk of AIDS infection among LGBTQI+ people, the vast majority of whom do not wish to seek medical care for fear of having to reveal their sexuality.

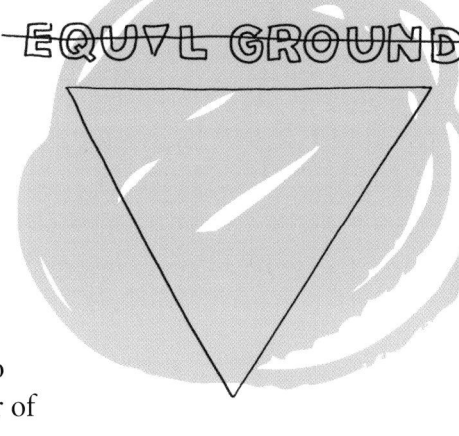

Determined to bring about change, Rosanna Flamer-Caldera campaigned for a total decriminalization of homosexuality in Sri Lanka, stating, "I don't care what I do before I die… but I want to see decriminalization in my country."

In February 2023, the government announced its support for the repeal of Articles 365 and 365A, giving hope for change. Now, the most important thing for Rosanna Flamer-Caldera is to unite the LGBTQI+ community behind the ongoing fight for equality and social justice.

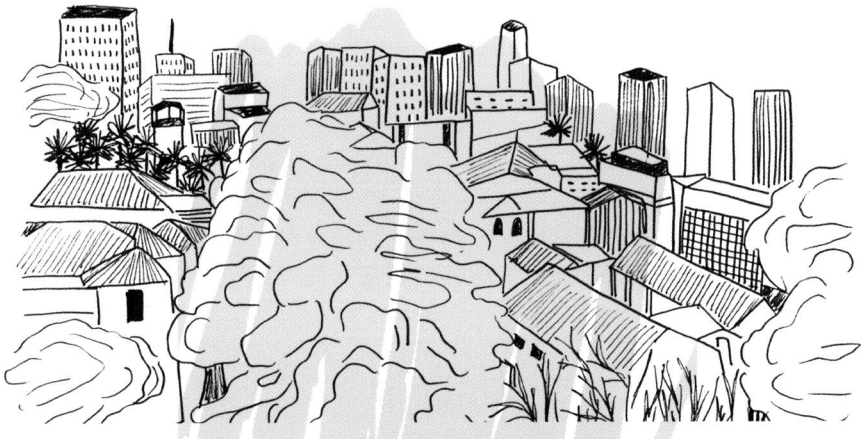

Colombo, Sri Lanka

Martina Navratilova 1956

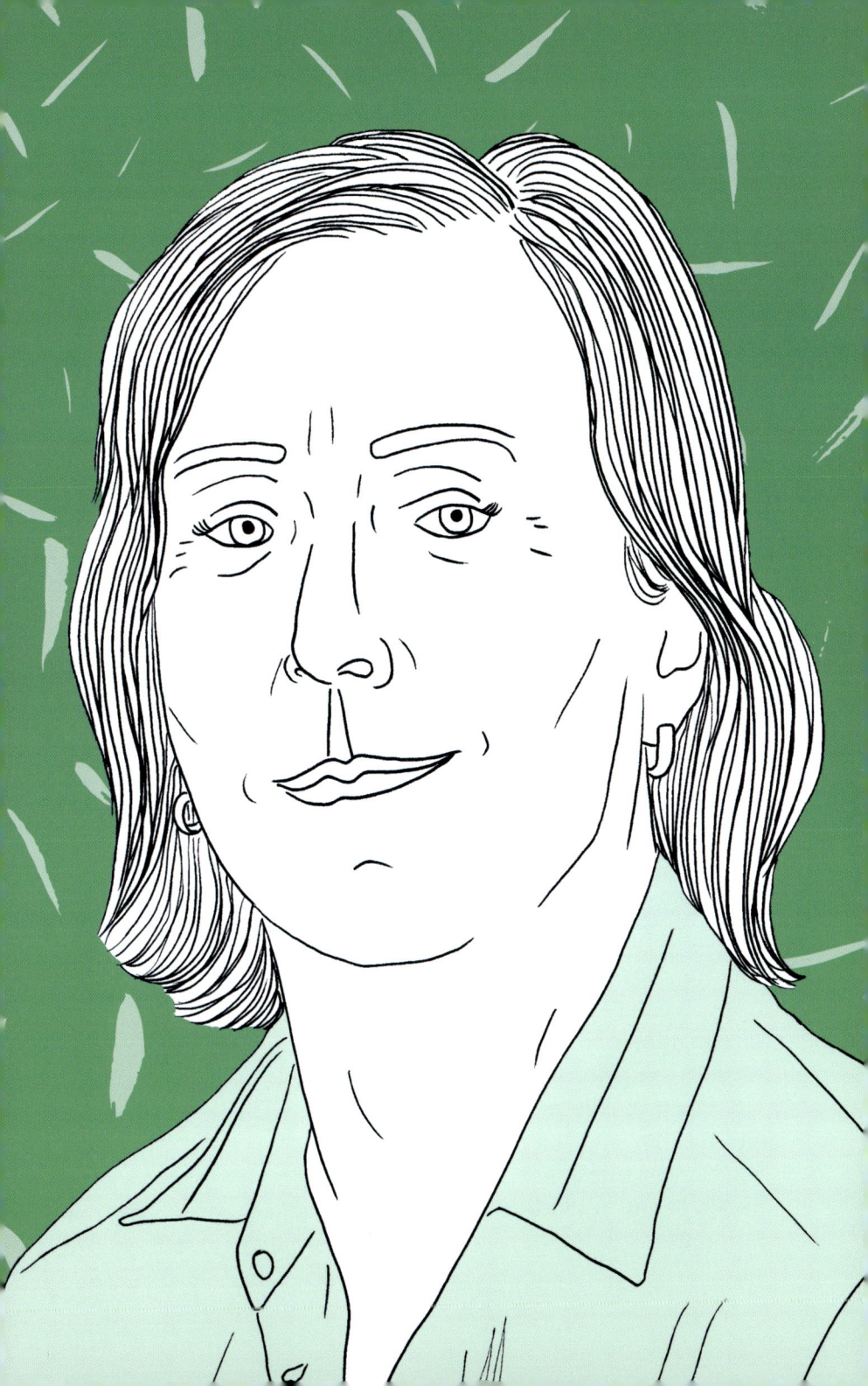

"JUST BY BEING OUT YOU'RE DOING YOUR PART. IT'S LIKE RECYCLING. YOU'RE DOING YOUR PART FOR THE ENVIRONMENT IF YOU RECYCLE; YOU'RE DOING YOUR PART FOR THE GAY MOVEMENT IF YOU'RE OUT."

One of the greatest tennis players of all time, Martina Navratilova took women's tennis to an entirely new level with her skill, speed and aggression.

Born in the Czech Republic, she moved to the United States when she was eighteen, seeking political asylum. She had won her first professional singles title the year before, in Orlando, Florida. Only four years later, in 1978, she won the women's singles title at Wimbledon, defeating the then world number one, and her long-time rival, Chris Evert. In 1985, this rivalry played out again in one of the best women's tennis matches of all time: the final of the French Open. Chris won that match, but over the course of their decade-long competition against each other, Martina ended on top with a 43-37 advantage.

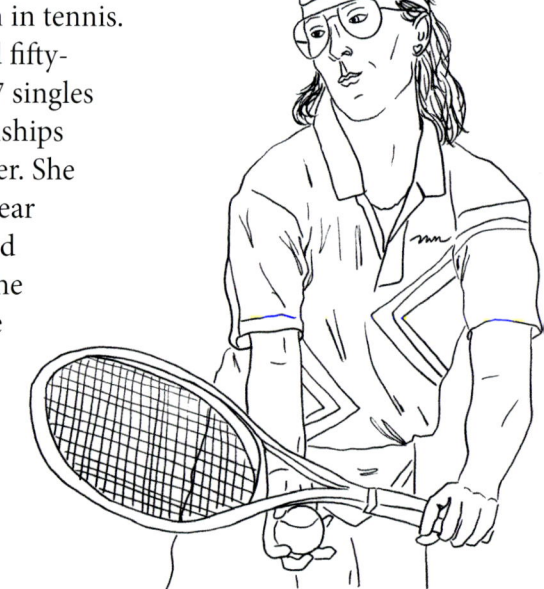

Martina's win at Wimbledon was just the start of her domination in tennis. She won an unprecedented fifty-nine Grand Slam titles, 167 singles and 177 doubles championships over the course of her career. She competed until 2006, the year in which she won the mixed doubles championship at the U.S. Open, and became the oldest player in history to win a major title only a month before her fiftieth birthday.

Martina Navratilova

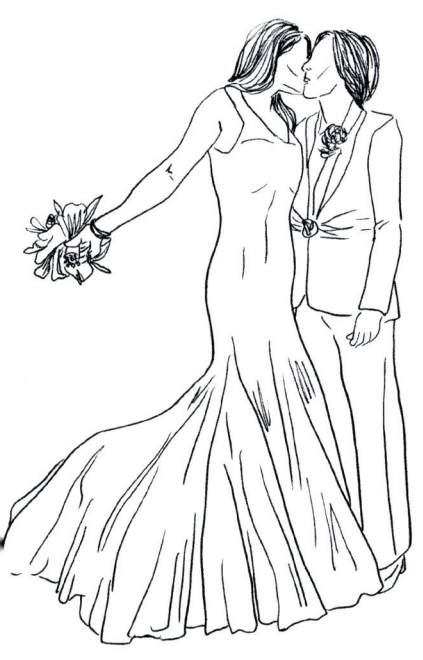

As well as her impact on tennis, Martina has been a long-time advocate for gay rights. She came out as bisexual in 1981, later redefining herself as lesbian, making her one of the first sports superstars to do so. In 1993, she joined the March on Washington for Lesbian, Gay and Bi Equal Rights and Liberation. She was also involved in a landmark lawsuit against Amendment 2 in the U.S., which ensured that sexual orientation remained a protected class.

Holding the world number one spot for a total of 332 weeks, the second longest time in history, Martina brought women's tennis and lesbian rights to a new level of visibility.

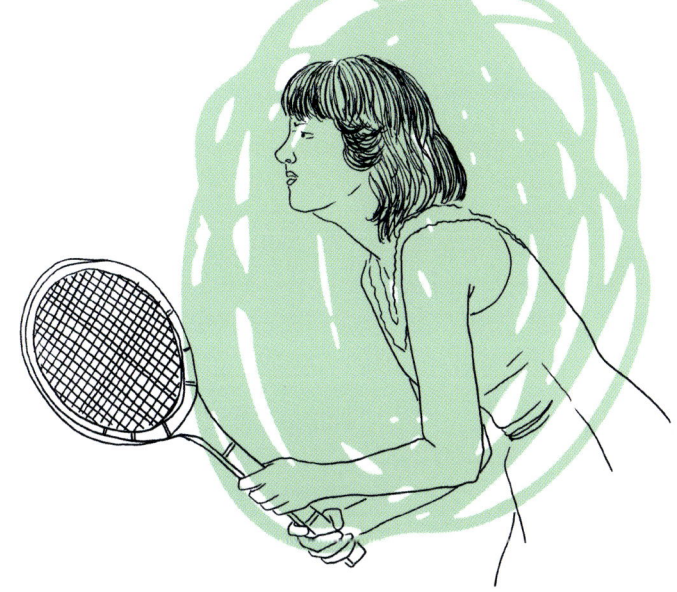

Simon Nkoli
1957 – 1998

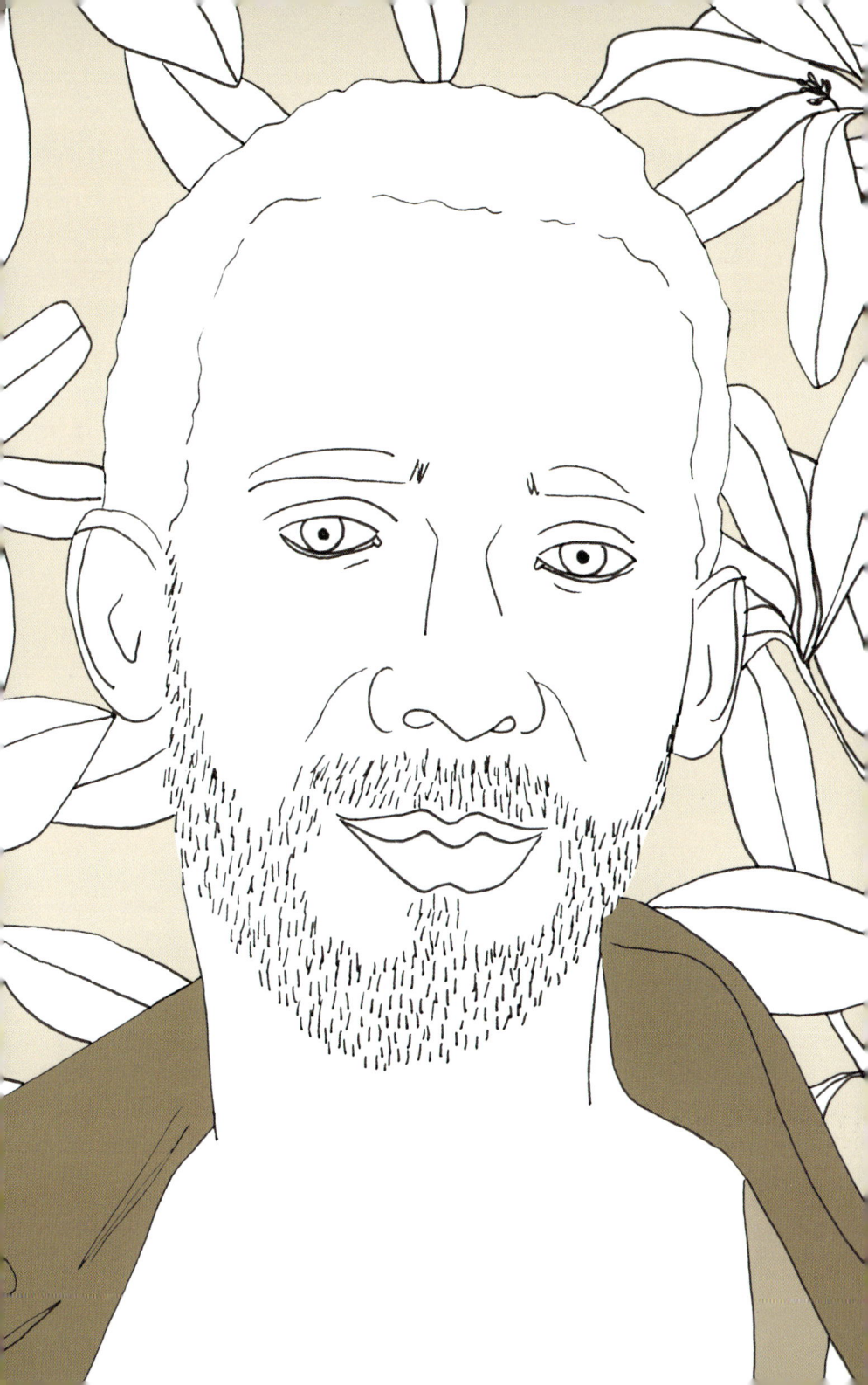

"I AM BLACK AND I AM GAY. I CANNOT SEPARATE THE TWO PARTS OF ME INTO SECONDARY OR PRIMARY STRUGGLES. IN SOUTH AFRICA, I AM OPPRESSED BECAUSE I AM A BLACK MAN AND I AM OPPRESSED BECAUSE I AM A GAY MAN. SO, WHEN I FIGHT FOR MY FREEDOM, I MUST FIGHT AGAINST BOTH OPPRESSIONS."

GAY AND ANTI-APARTHEID ACTIVIST SIMON NKOLI IS PROOF THAT INTERSECTIONALITY IS A CENTRAL ISSUE IN HUMAN RIGHTS STRUGGLES.

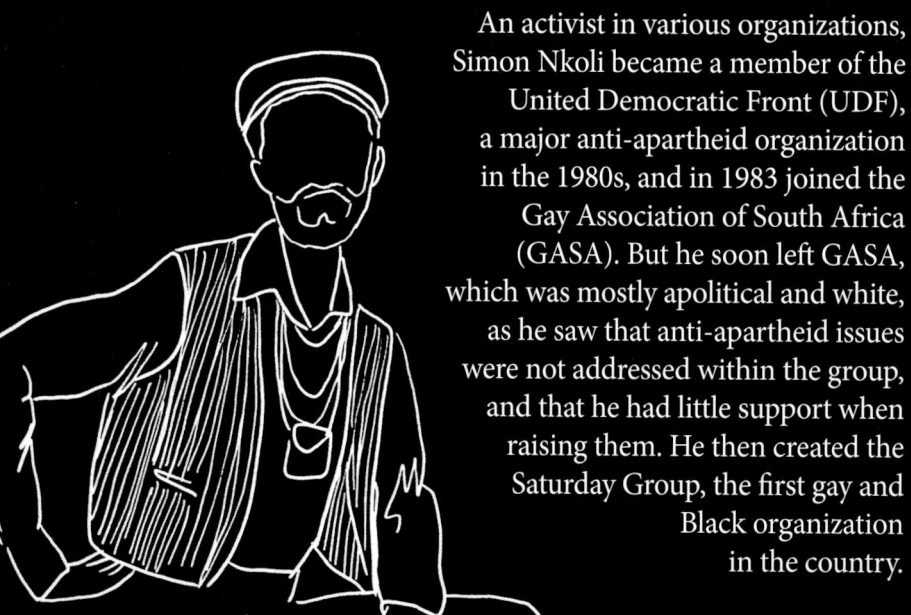

An activist in various organizations, Simon Nkoli became a member of the United Democratic Front (UDF), a major anti-apartheid organization in the 1980s, and in 1983 joined the Gay Association of South Africa (GASA). But he soon left GASA, which was mostly apolitical and white, as he saw that anti-apartheid issues were not addressed within the group, and that he had little support when raising them. He then created the Saturday Group, the first gay and Black organization in the country.

Simon Nkoli

In 1984, for opposing apartheid, Simon Nkoli and twenty-one others were charged with treason in the so-called "Delmas Treason Trial" and faced the death penalty. He was finally imprisoned for four years and decided to come out whilst in prison in order to bring greater awareness of homosexual issues within the UDF.

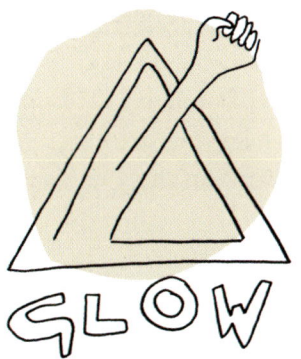

Acquitted in 1988, soon after his release he founded GLOW (Gay and Lesbian Organization of the Witwatersrand). The aim of GLOW was to create spaces for non-homophobic, non-sexist, and non-racist exchanges, and give visibility to gay people in Johannesburg. GLOW set up several working groups, a preventive forum on education and HIV/AIDS, a lesbian forum, and a monthly newsletter: the *Glowletter*

With GLOW, Simon Nkoli, organized the very first Pride March on the African continent in 1990. He came out as HIV positive the same year, at a time when there was great stigma around HIV, and sufferers faced violence and discrimination.

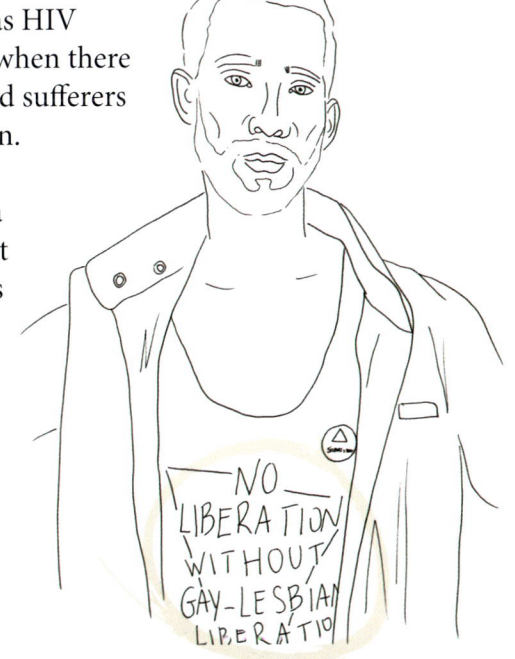

He worked with Nelson Mandela in the 1990s and won the support of the African National Congress (ANC) to include the protection of sexual minorities in the country's constitution, which would become effective in 1996: a historic moment for South Africa and the country's gay liberation movement.

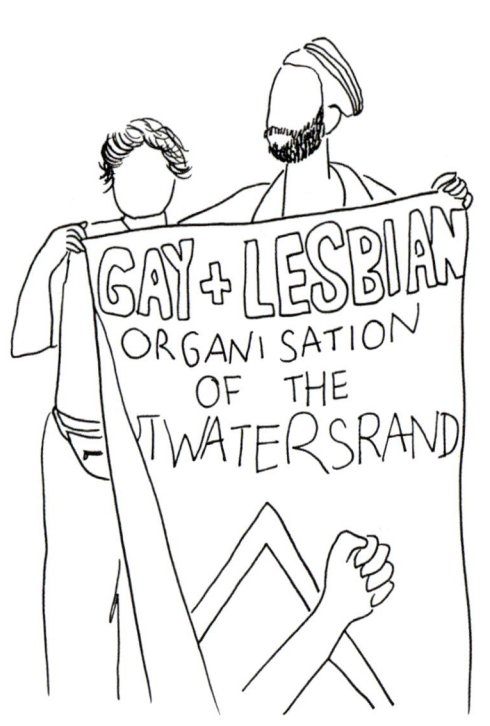

Simon Nkoli focused on HIV/AIDS advocacy in the last years of his life. He established the Township AIDS Project and the Gay Men's Health Forum to raise awareness of HIV/AIDS and address the discrimination faced by HIV-positive people. He died in 1998 from HIV-related complications, leaving behind an indelible mark on the history of LGBTQI+ struggles.

BLACK GAYS ARE BEAUTIFUL

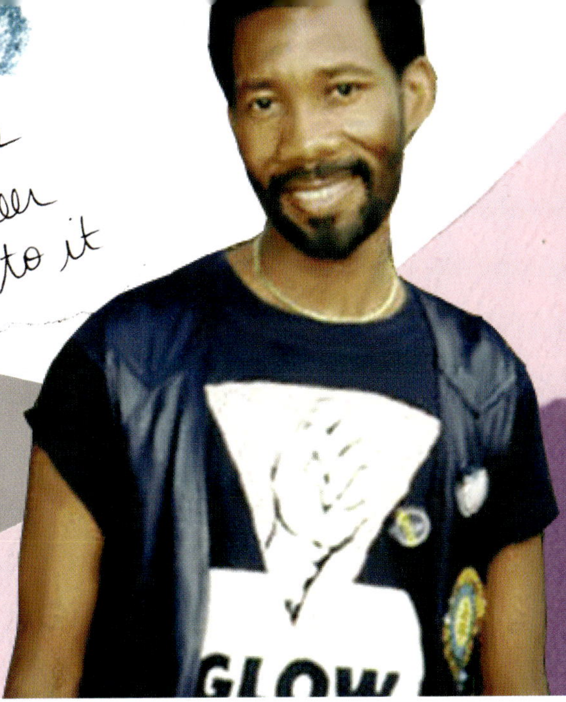

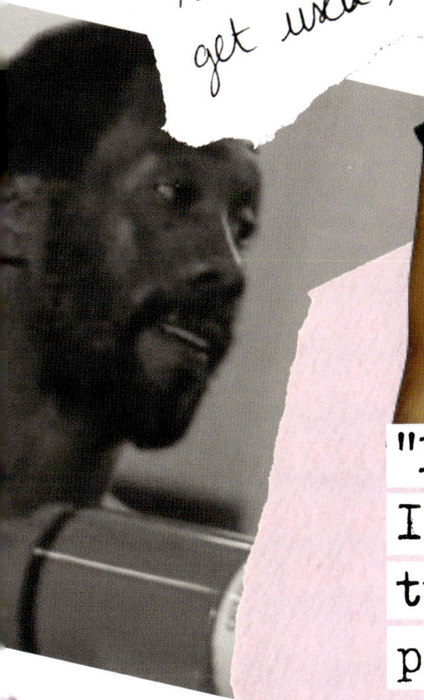

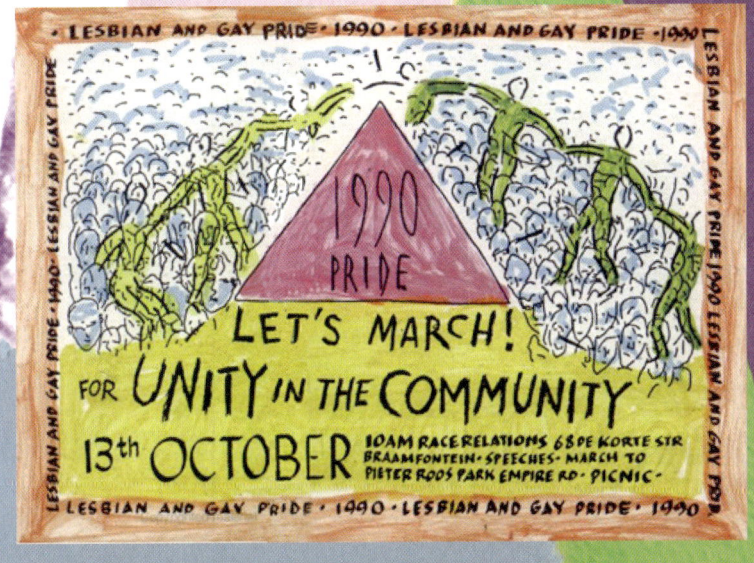

Keith Haring
1958 – 1990

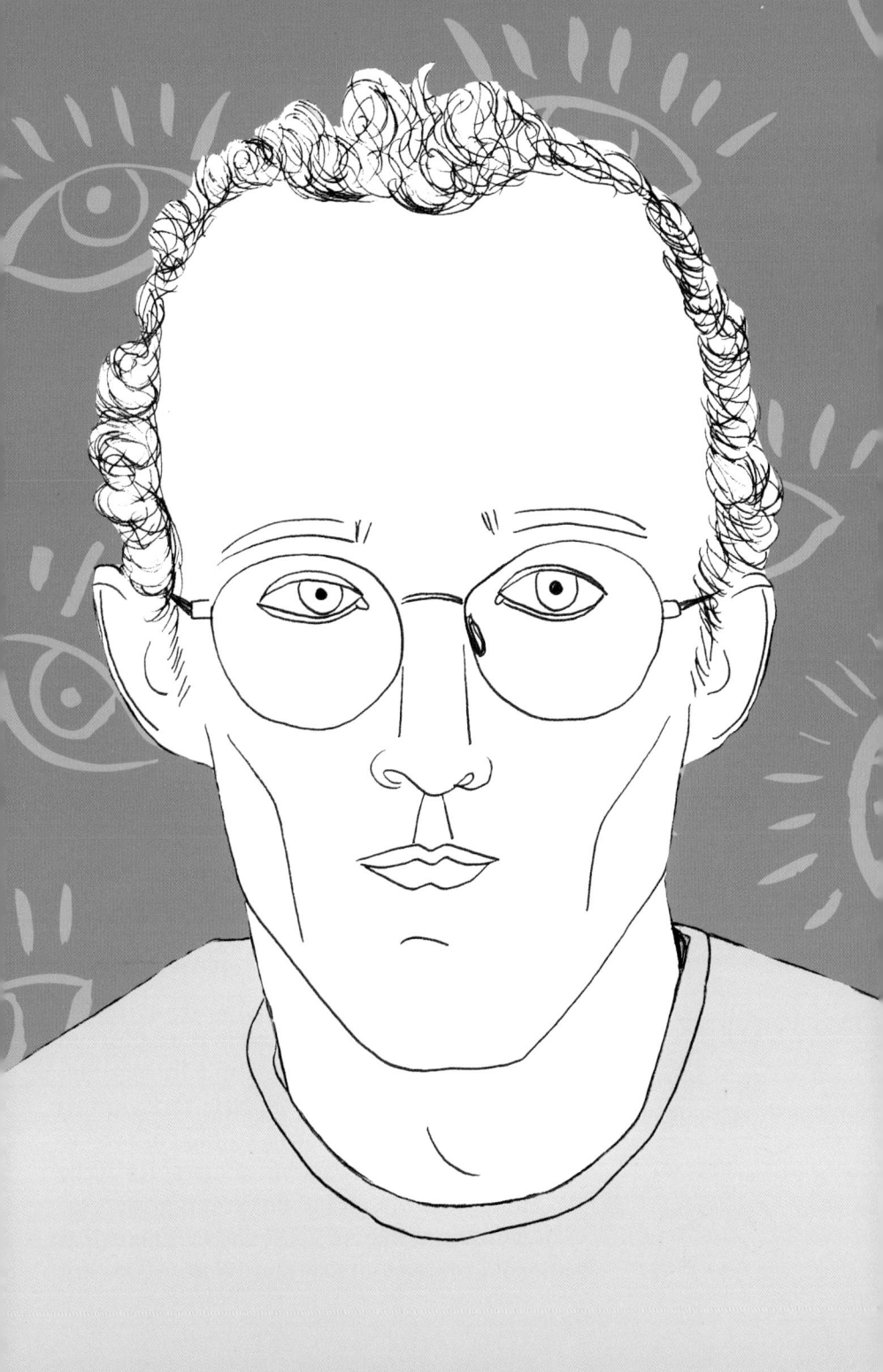

AN ARTIST FAMED FOR HIS SHARP DRAWINGS AND POP STYLE, KEITH HARING TURNED TO DRAWING AFTER GRADUATING FROM THE IVY SCHOOL OF PROFESSIONAL ART IN PITTSBURGH WITH A DEGREE IN COMMERCIAL ART. PAINTING GRAFFITI IN THE NEW YORK SUBWAY EARNED HIM A FEW ARRESTS, BUT REINFORCED A TASTE FOR VIVID, FREEHAND, AND SPONTANEOUS DRAWING.

A protégé of Andy Warhol, he saw his commissions multiply in the early 1980s, and galleries quickly bought up his works. He was even invited to the Paris Biennale in 1985. Wishing for his art to be accessible to all and visible to as many people as possible, he created his "Pop Shop" in 1986, an ephemeral place where he sold products derived from his works.

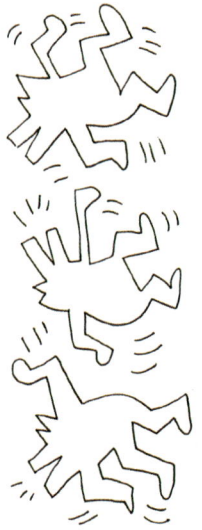

A committed and openly gay artist, Keith Haring painted many canvases, murals and posters to alert and educate the public about war, drugs (e.g. *Crack Is Wack*, 1986), homophobia, AIDS, nuclear power, and religion. Diagnosed with HIV in 1988, Keith Haring created a series of works about the virus. This included a large mural in the bathroom of The Lesbian, Gay, Bisexual and Transgender Community Centre in New York entitled *Once Upon a Time* which he painted in 1989 to celebrate the twentieth anniversary of the Stonewall riots, alongside various posters for organizations like ACT UP, and events such as National Coming Out Day and World AIDS Day.

Keith Haring

He was a generous artist who cared about others, and in 1987 he created a large fresco at the Necker Hospital in Paris.

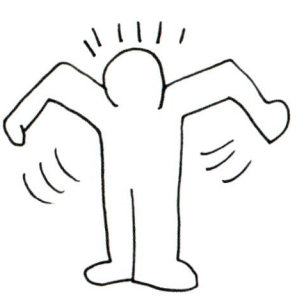

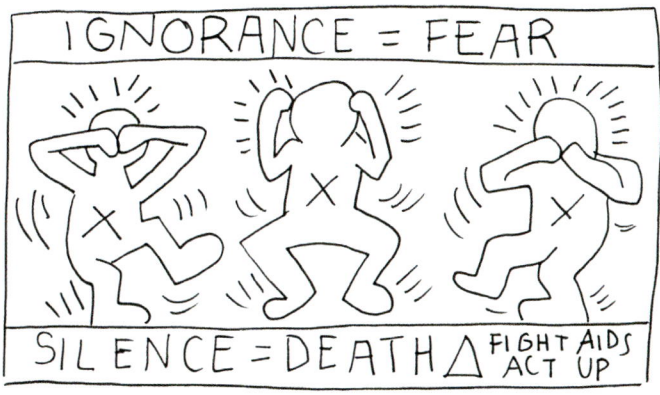

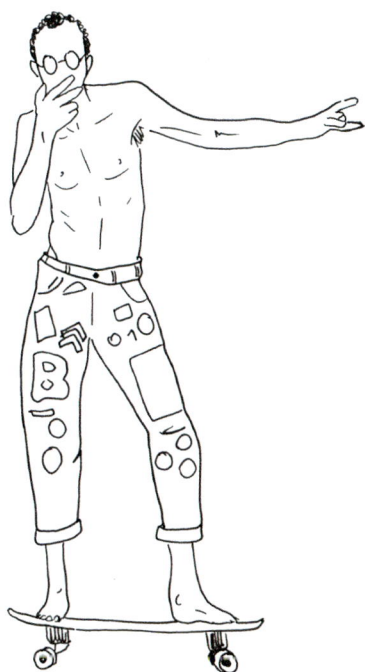

His painting *Untitled*, made in 1985, is one of his most powerful. At a time when AIDS was spoken of as a "gay cancer", and when many people died without understanding the causes, this work is striking in its message and bold composition. The accumulation of bodies on a bright yellow background evokes an almost apocalyptic, orgiastic scene, where the male sexes seem to infuse a patient with a deformed face and wearing a red cross around the neck.

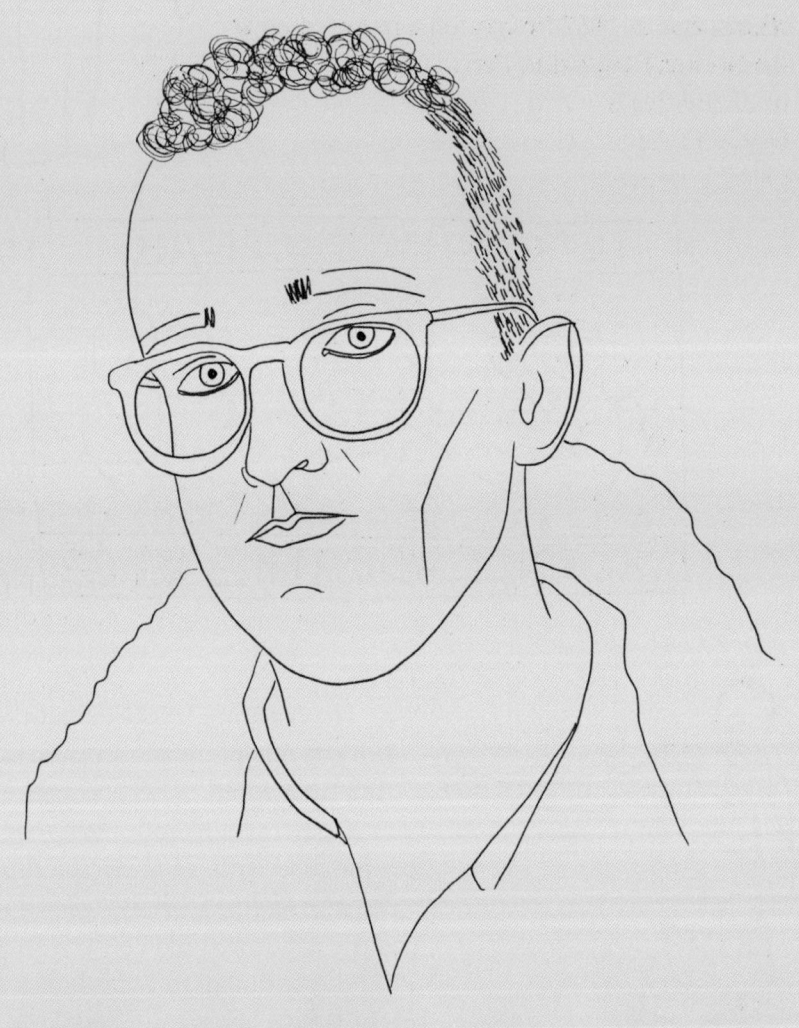

"ART IS NOT AN ELITIST ACTIVITY RESERVED FOR THE APPRECIATION OF A SMALL NUMBER OF AMATEURS, IT IS FOR EVERYONE."

Keith Haring

Keith Haring, who died of AIDS-related complications at the age of thirty-one, left behind thousands of distinctive works that still speak to the public today, and are just as popular as ever.

A foundation now bears his name and honours his memory. It is dedicated to helping disadvantaged children as well as people affected by AIDS.

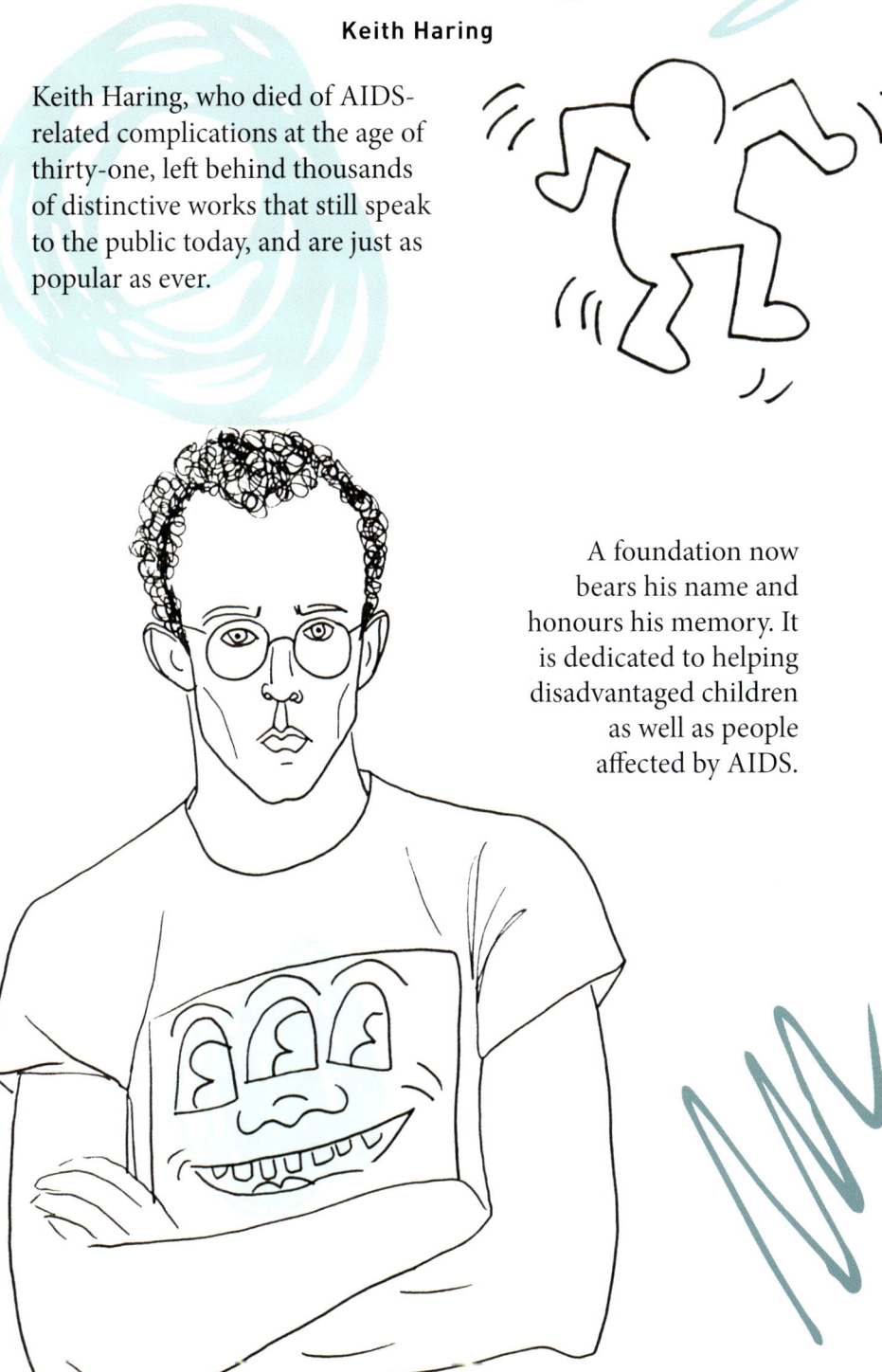

Chi Chia-wei
1958

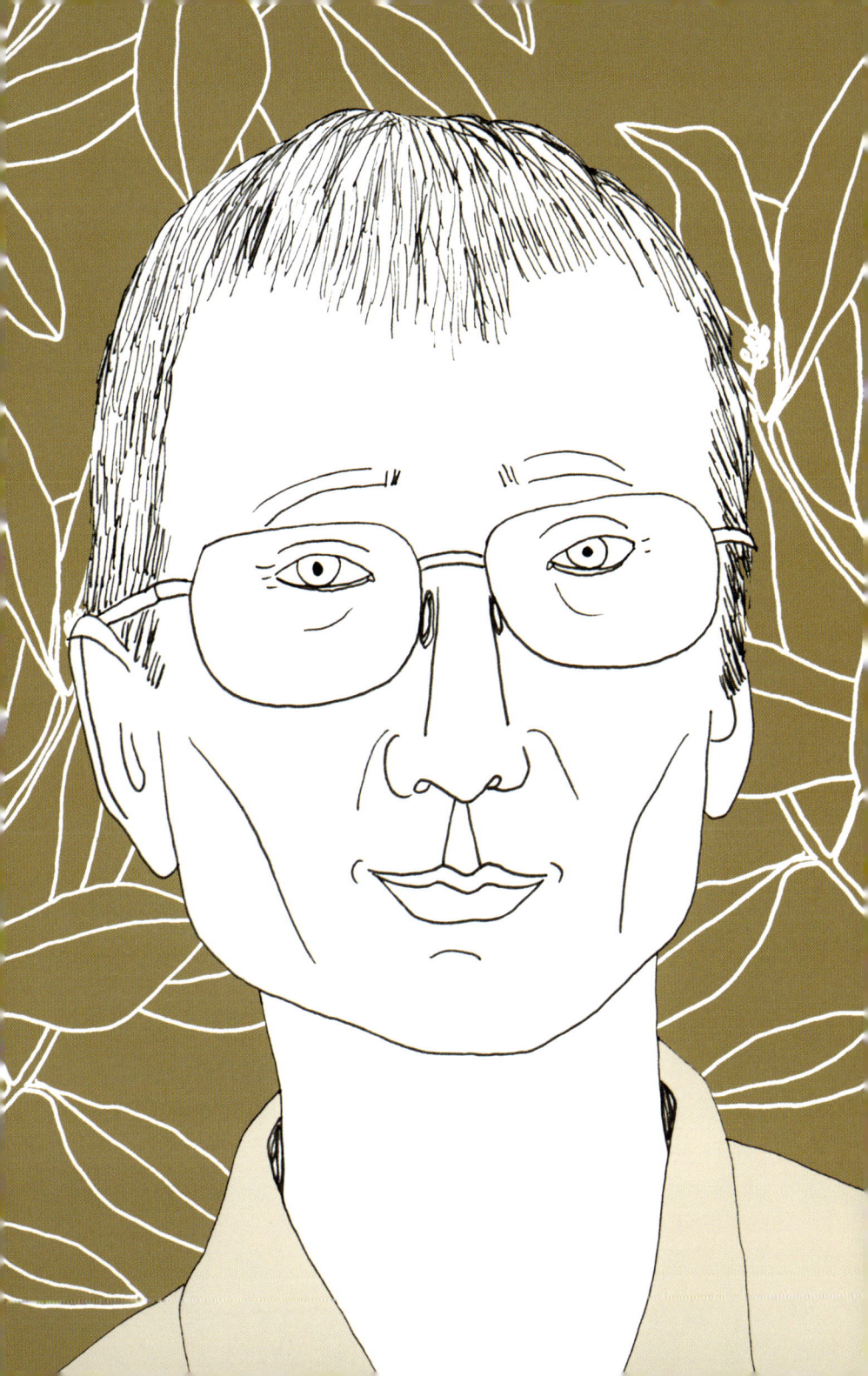

CHI CHIA-WEI IS A TAIWANESE GAY ACTIVIST WHO CAMPAIGNED FOR MORE THAN THIRTY YEARS FOR THE ADOPTION OF MARRIAGE EQUALITY IN HIS COUNTRY.

In 1986, at the age of twenty-eight, he was the first person to come out as gay on national television in Taiwan, a very conservative country. He is a true pioneer, advocating for gay rights and working tirelessly to fight the spread of HIV/AIDS in the 1980s through various prevention campaigns in his country.

In the 1980s, Chi Chia-wei wanted to marry his long-time partner, although this was prohibited by law. In 1986, he filed an application for marriage with his partner, with the Taiwanese authorities. It was refused, so he repeated the application several times, without success. After years of struggle, on May 24, 2017, the country's justice system ruled in his favour, with the Taipei Constitutional Court declaring the current marriage law unconstitutional. Chi Chia-wei could now marry his partner. This was a long fight with a positive ending for all gay rights activists in the country. It gave the government two years to change the law. If they didn't, gay and lesbian couples could de facto marry after May 24, 2019.

On this date, Taiwan became the first country in Asia to legalize same-sex marriage.
Behind this historic decision were two petitions, one of which was Chi Chia-wei's appeal to the Supreme Court after the registration of the union with his partner was once again refused.

Chi Chia-wei

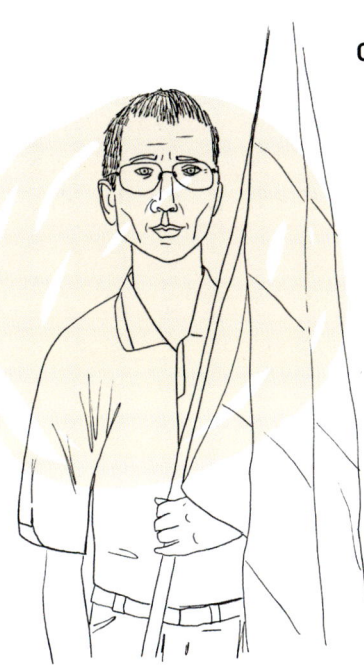

The decision to change the law was a first in Asia. "I'm leaping for joy like a bird," he said at the verdict. At the age of sixty, this committed, long-term campaigner, regained hope that society can change after all.

Many people now look to Taiwan, an island of just 23 million people, as an example of liberalism in Asia. Despite strong Chinese influence, Taiwan's decision is a giant leap for an entire region of the globe, often lagging behind on these issues. Even if this decision leads to opposition, and even if there is still work to be done with regards to transgender rights, the change in law is nonetheless encouraging for the LGBTQI+ community. Some experts predict that this judgement could have repercussions for the rest of Asia, while South Korea and Indonesia are currently hardening their stance towards LGBTQI+ people.

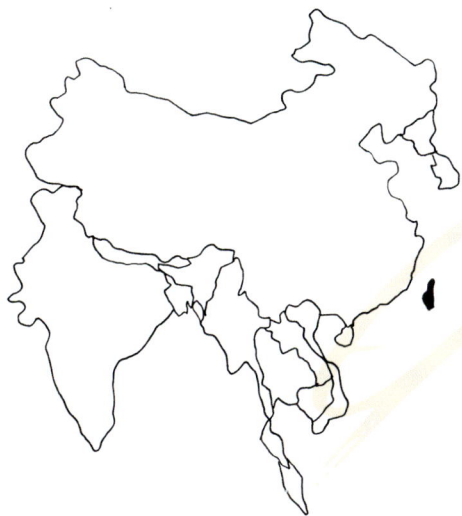

Mark Ashton
1960 – 1987

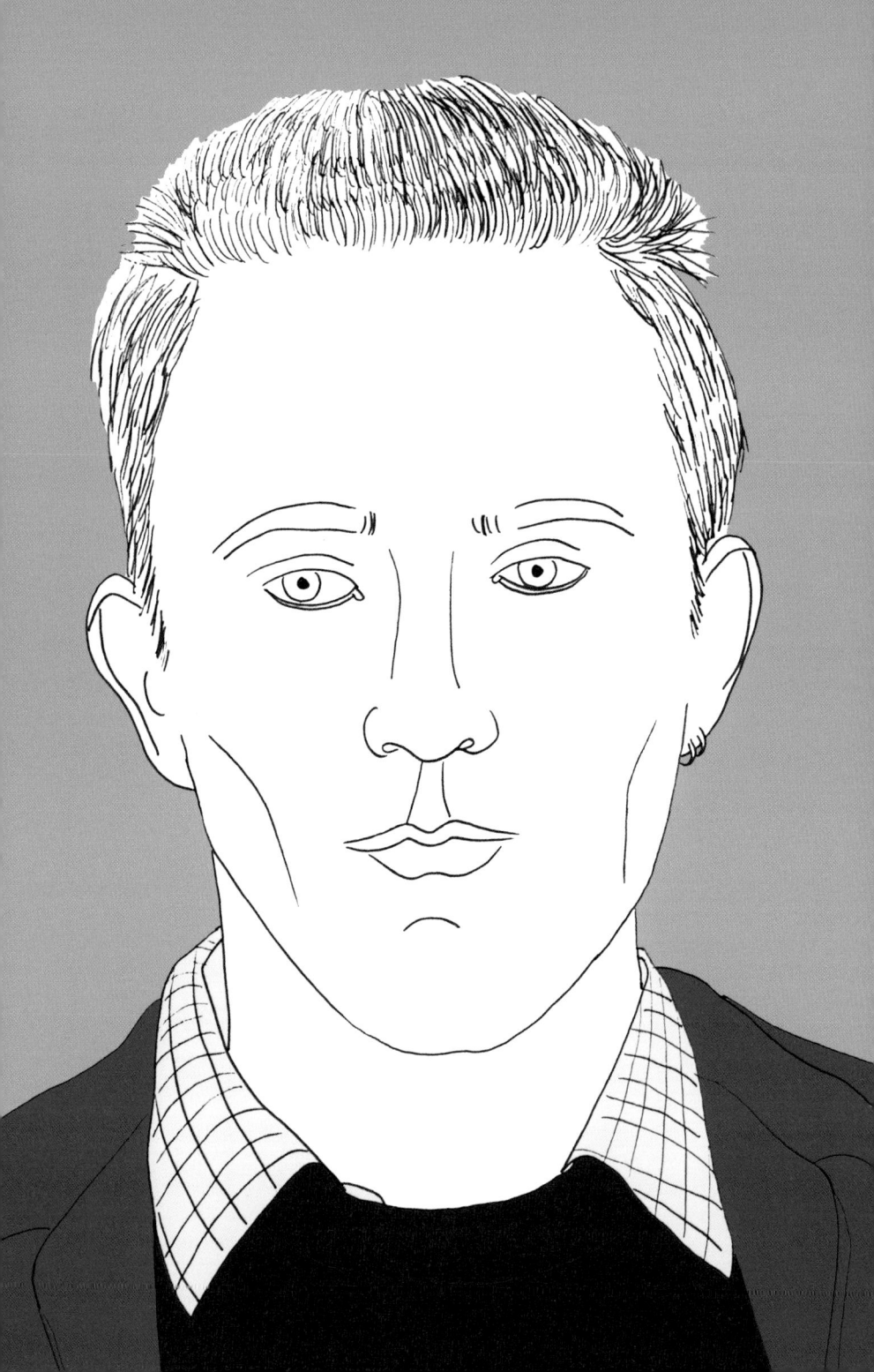

MARK ASHTON'S FIGHT FOR SOCIAL JUSTICE PROVES THAT THE IDEA OF DIFFERENT PROTEST STRUGGLES WORKING TOGETHER TO SUPPORT EACH OTHER IS NOT JUST A MILITANT CONCEPT BUT CAN BECOME A REALITY.

Integrating gay rights activism and left-wing politics, this British activist fought tirelessly for social justice during his short life. After a trip to Bangladesh, where he was shocked by inequalities and the system that created them, he became involved with various communist and gay rights groups in England.

In order to support the striking British miners, while Thatcherite conservative policies raged, he raised funds on the day of the Lesbian and Gay Pride March in London in 1984, and created the group Lesbians and Gays Support the Miners (LGSM) with his friend Mike Jackson.

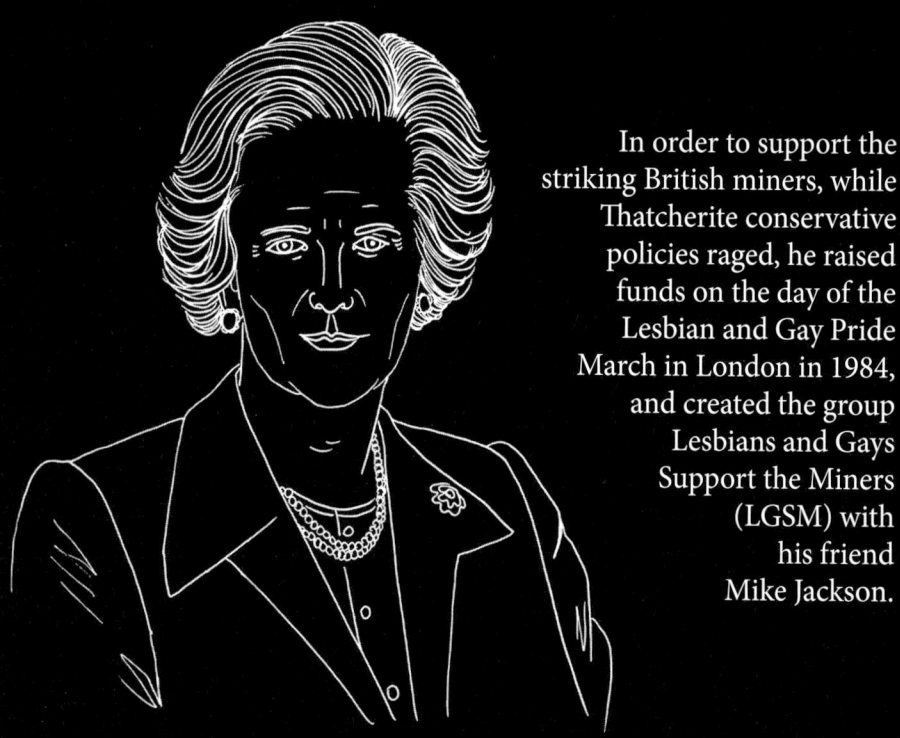

Margaret Thatcher

Mark Ashton

In 1985, miners joined the London Pride parade and that same year, thanks to the support of the National Union of Mineworkers, the Labour Party included in its manifesto a motion to protect LGBT+ rights. LGSM allowed people from two seemingly opposing worlds to come together, as portrayed in Matthew Warchus' 2014 film *Pride*, which tells the story beautifully.

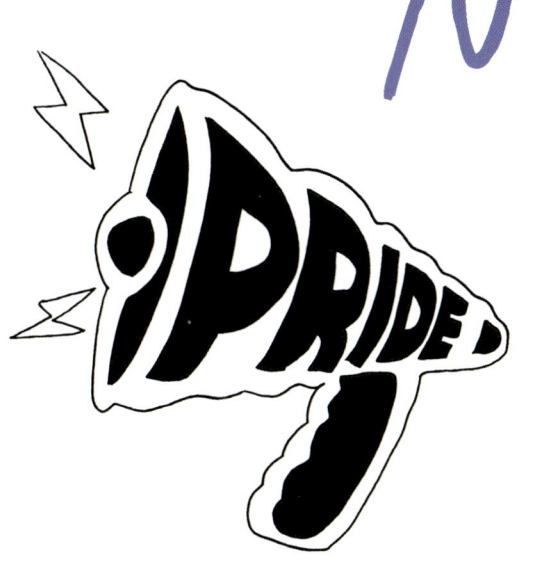

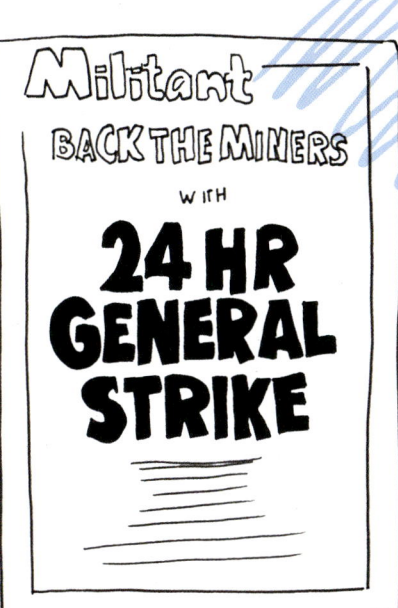

At a time when gay and lesbian struggles were beginning to be recognized in London, and when social and political conflict was erupting in the industrial regions of the North of England, Mark Ashton made the link between these two worlds: between social and institutional violence and the discrimination suffered by these two groups.

"MINING COMMUNITIES ARE BEING BULLIED LIKE WE ARE, BEING HARASSED BY THE POLICE, JUST AS WE ARE. ONE COMMUNITY SHOULD GIVE SOLIDARITY TO ANOTHER. IT IS REALLY ILLOGICAL TO SAY, 'I'M GAY AND I'M INTO DEFENDING THE GAY COMMUNITY BUT I DON'T CARE ABOUT ANYTHING ELSE.'"

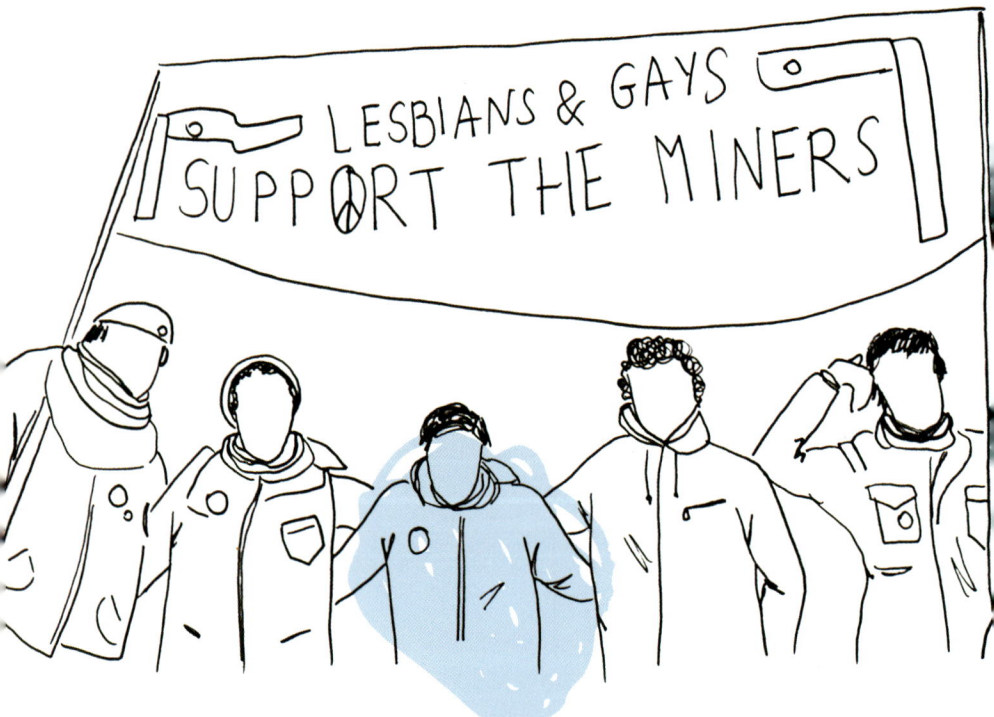

After LGSM, he became involved in the Red Wedge collective, alongside musicians/singers Jimmy Sommerville, Billy Bragg and Paul Weller. He also became the General Secretary of the Young Communist League from 1985 to 1986.

In the 1980s, HIV/AIDS was wreaking havoc within the gay community, but was being treated with total indifference by the general public and politicians. Mark Ashton was appalled by this lack of humanity. The disease took his life a few days after his diagnosis in 1987. He was just twenty-seven years old.

An often-forgotten hero of LGBTQI+ struggles, Mark Ashton nevertheless remains an example of an activist whose work expanded beyond queer struggles. The City of Paris paid tribute to him in 2018 by adding his name to the garden of the Hotel Lamoignon.

Two blue plaques have been installed to commemorate him, one in his home town of Portrush and the other above Gay's the Word bookshop in Marchmont Street, London, where Ashton's LGSM group used to meet.

RuPaul
1960

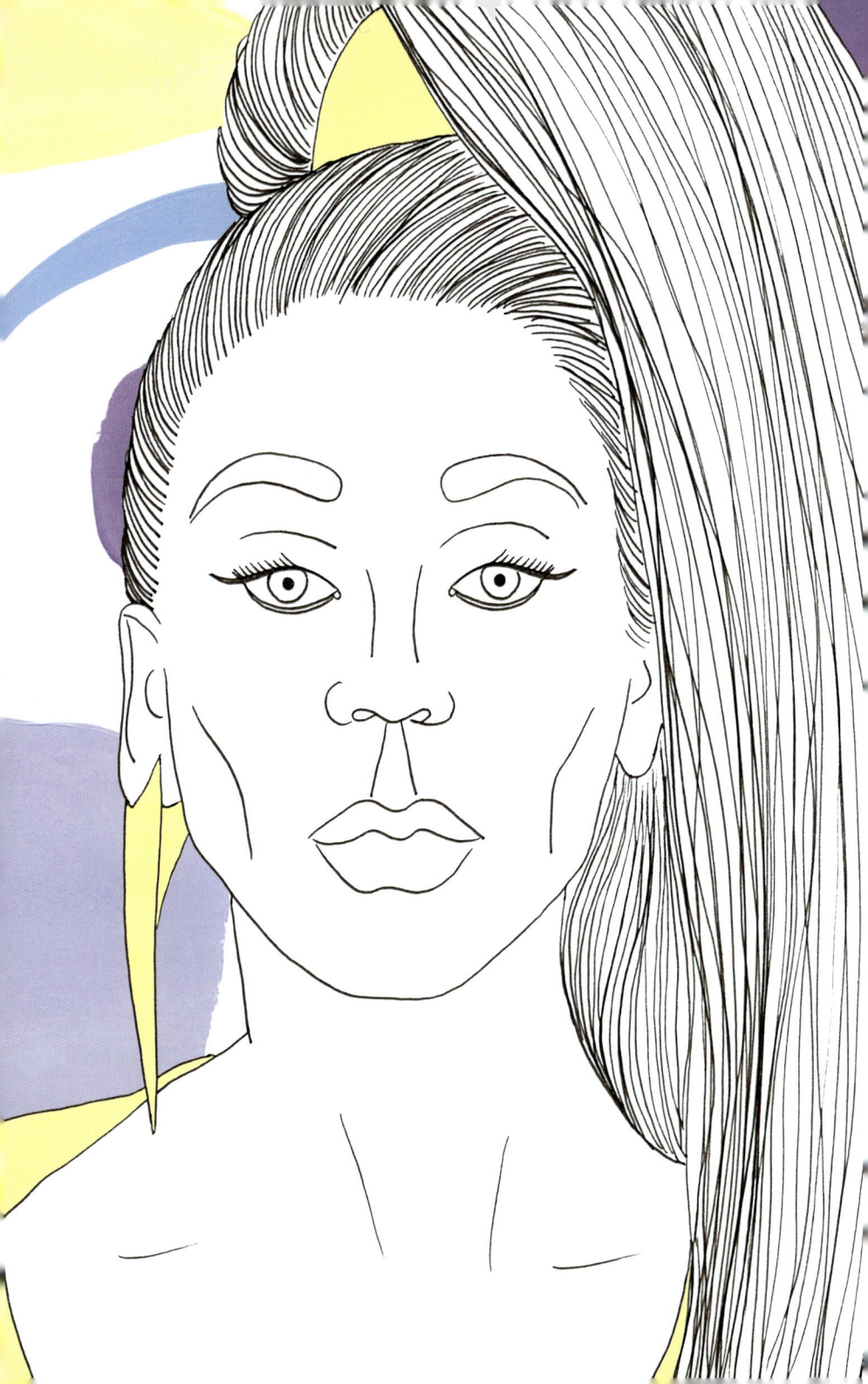

BORN IN SAN DIEGO, CALIFORNIA, AS THE ONLY BOY IN THE FAMILY, SURROUNDED BY THREE SISTERS, RUPAUL CHARLES MOVED TO NEW YORK IN THE LATE 1980S.

He quickly became a local celebrity thanks to his flamboyant drag shows – RuPaul was born. He was crowned "Queen of Manhattan" at a time when, thanks to his local notoriety, he began to rub shoulders with people of the New York underground and artistic scene.

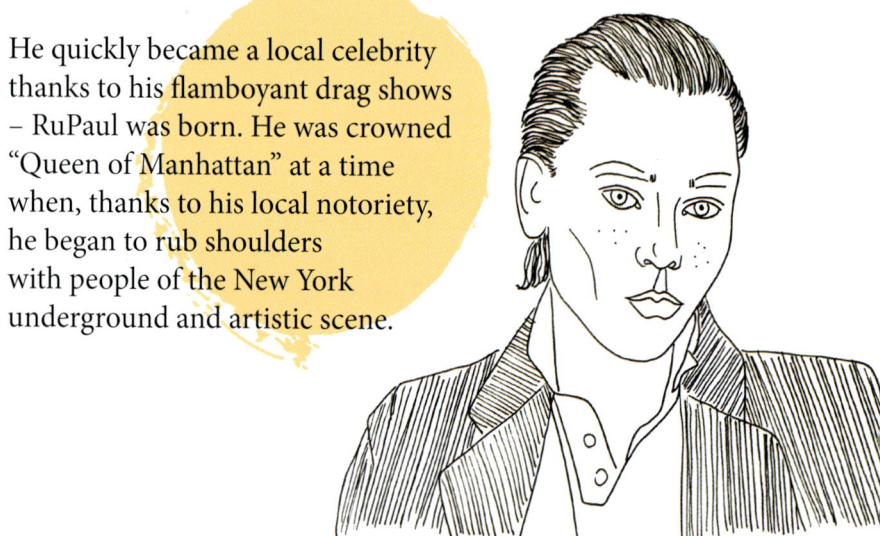

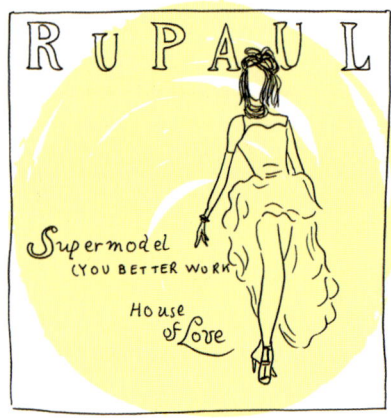

Spotted by a music label, he released his first album in 1993, *Supermodel of the World*, containing the single "Supermodel (You Better Work)". This success gave RuPaul unparalleled visibility and a platform for a Black, gay, drag-wearing man to talk about LGBTQI+ issues, feminism, and racism.

RuPaul

The 1990s were fruitful and rich in projects for RuPaul who recorded a duet with Elton John, released his autobiography, acted in several films, and hosted his own television show… never before had a drag queen been so popular.

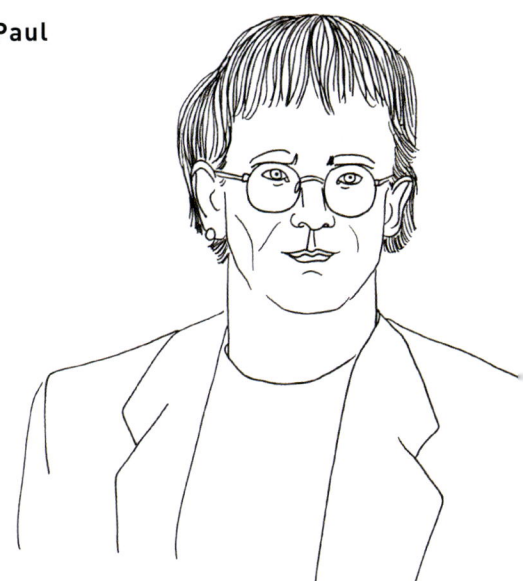

Elton John

In the mid-1990s, he became spokesperson for M.A.C. Cosmetics and the first face of Viva Glam, a lipstick brand whose sales help finance the fight against HIV/AIDS, and which still exists today. Committed to bringing LGBTQI+ issues to the fore and making the community visible, RuPaul received the Vito Russo Award for Artist of the Year at GLAAD (Gay & Lesbian Alliance Against Defamation) in 1999.

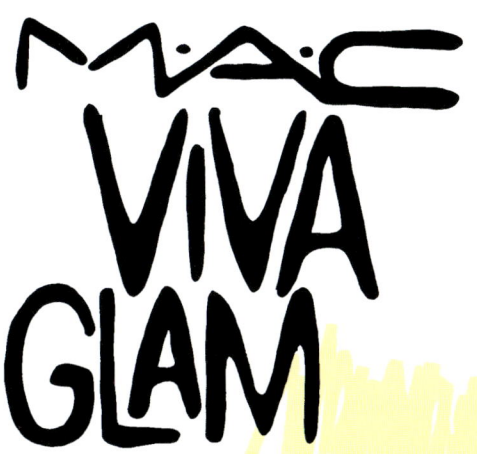

A versatile artist, RuPaul has released several albums (*Glamazon, Born Naked*) and appeared in around fifty films and television shows. For younger generations, RuPaul is above all the host and producer of the super-hit show *RuPaul's Drag Race*, a drag queen competition broadcast on American television for the first time in 2009, which has been running for fifteen seasons and has led to several spin off adaptations around the world.

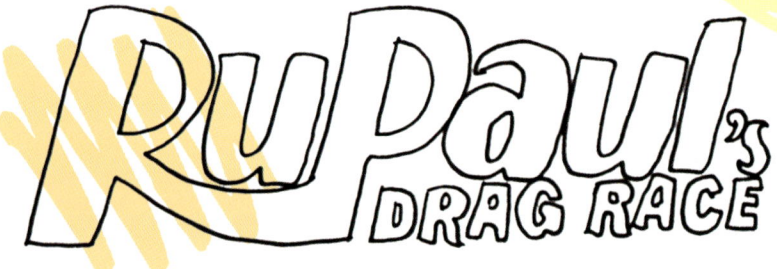

The art of drag and cross-dressing, which has taken time to become accepted by the public, has now firmly established itself in pop culture. The comeback of drag queens since the mid-2010s, thanks in particular to the success of *RuPaul's Drag Race*, and the visibility of drag across social media, has encouraged the birth of new drag queens ready to reinvent this art.

By playing with gendered codes and caricaturing them, sometimes making them ridiculous, funny, or seductive, and by creating larger than life characters beyond the norms, drag is above all a political art. It makes it possible to overturn and question gender constructs but also increases visibility for queer identities.

"THAT IS THE KEY TO NAVIGATING THIS LIFE – DON'T TAKE IT TOO SERIOUSLY. THAT'S WHEN THE PARTY BEGINS."

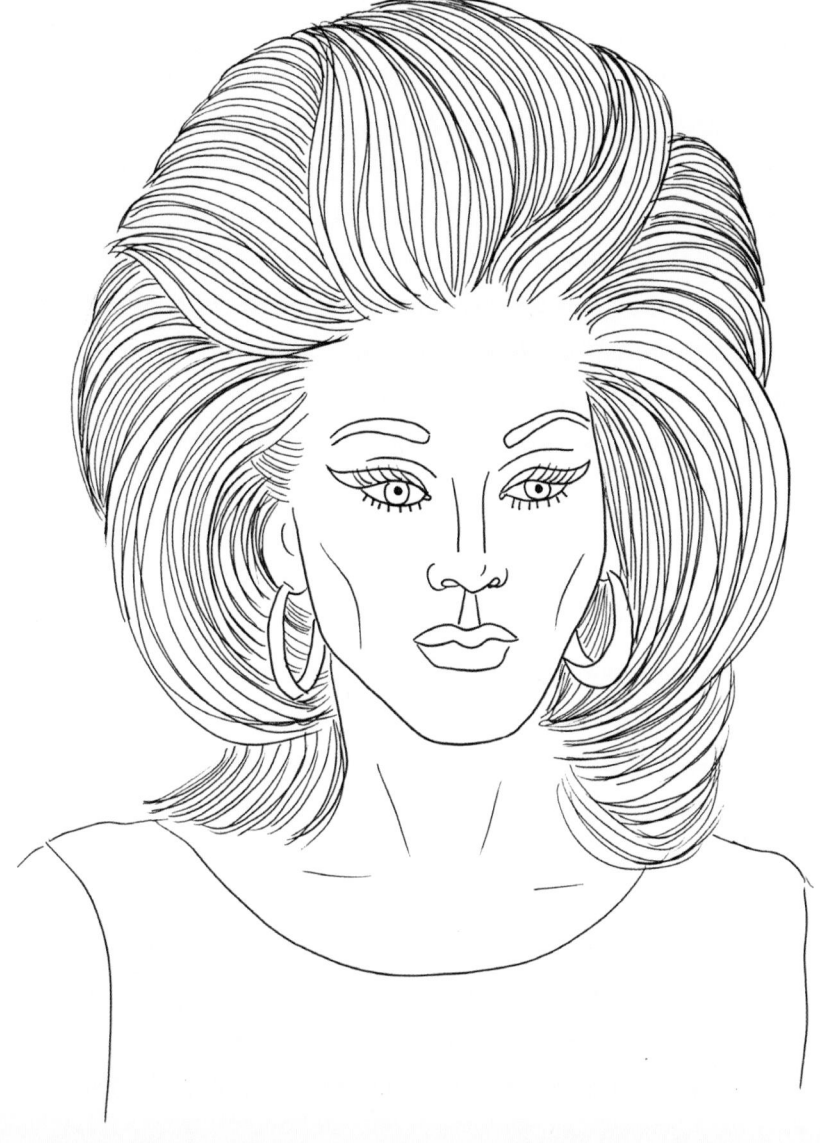

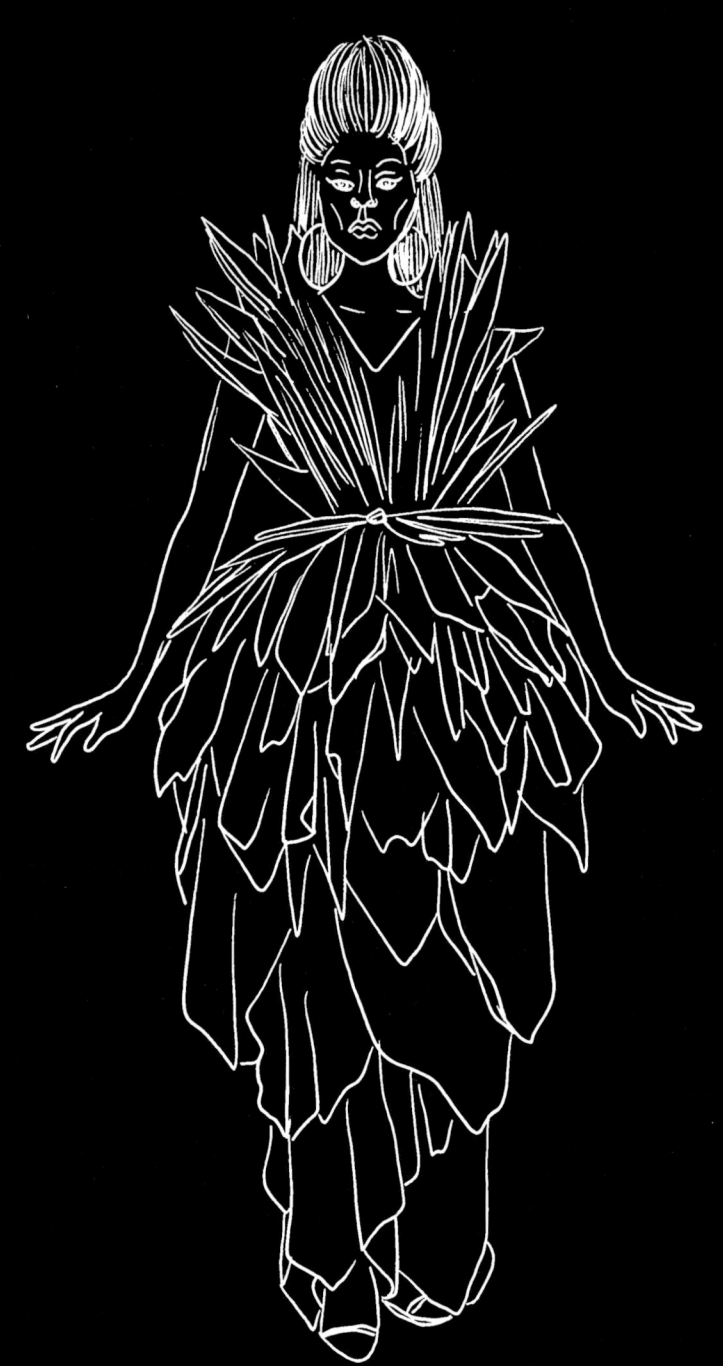

RuPaul

Once considered subversive, transgressive, and highly satirical, the art of drag, born of an underground culture, is now enjoying a renaissance and finding millions of fans on television and within mainstream popular culture. For those who want to challenge the norms and our attitudes to gender identity, this has raised fears amongst some drag queens, about its depoliticization and its loss of the power to shock.

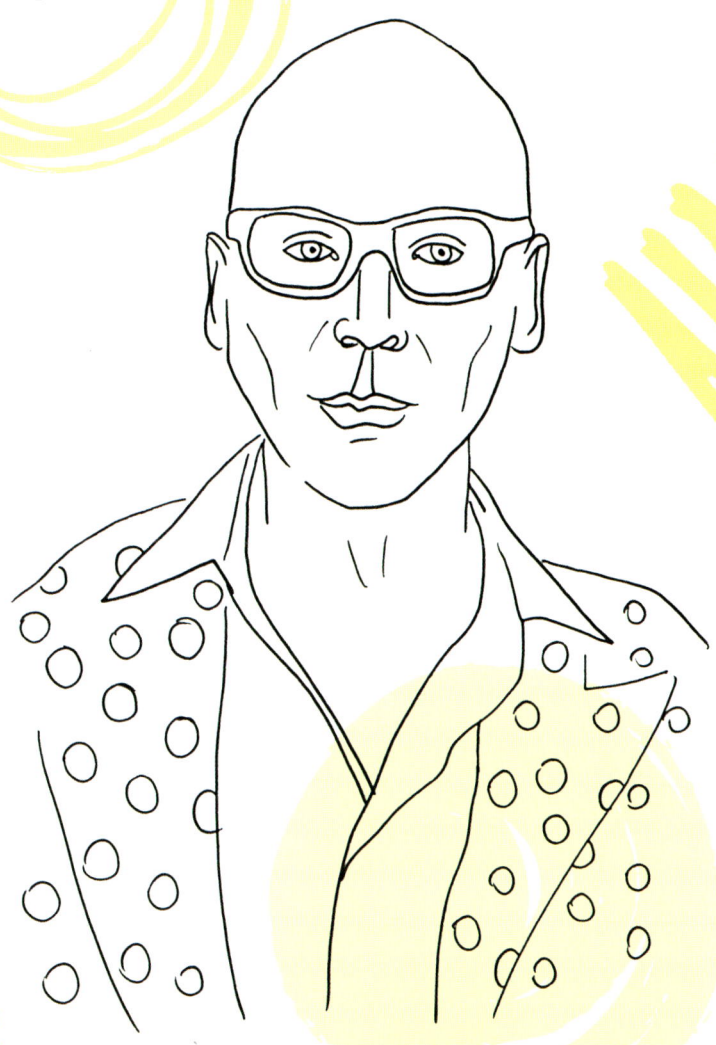

Mary Bonauto
1961

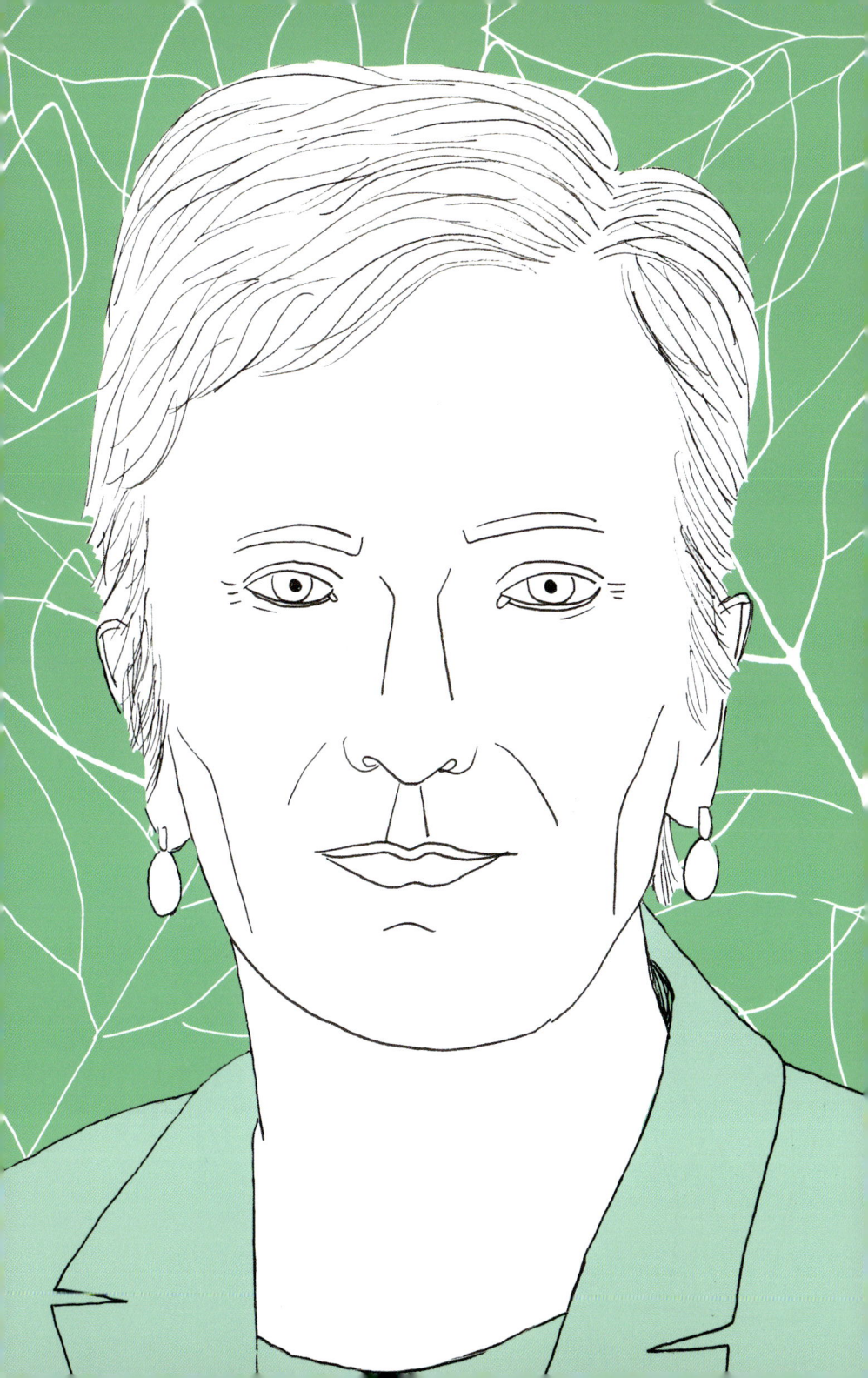

AN AMERICAN LAWYER AND CIVIL RIGHTS ADVOCATE, MARY BONAUTO HAS WORKED AT GLAD (GLBTQ LEGAL ADVOCATES & DEFENDERS) SINCE 1990.

She is one of the leaders of various legal battles that led to the passing of the marriage equality act in the United States. In 1999, she helped establish the first law authorizing same-sex civil unions in the state of Vermont. A first victory that would allow her to become the lead counsel in the case of Goodridge v. Department of Public Health, four years later, in 2003. She won again, leading to Massachusetts becoming the first state in the United States to legally recognize same-sex marriage.

In the years that followed, Mary Bonauto continued her legal battle against the state with a great deal of patience and without losing sight of her wider goal: to have same-sex marriage legalized throughout the country. In 2013, a media and legal spotlight was placed on Section 3 of DOMA (Defense of Marriage Act), which limited the definition of marriage to the union of a man and a woman.

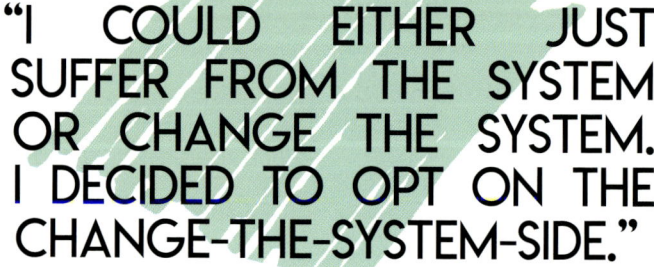

"I COULD EITHER JUST SUFFER FROM THE SYSTEM OR CHANGE THE SYSTEM. I DECIDED TO OPT ON THE CHANGE-THE-SYSTEM-SIDE."

Mary Bonauto

In June 2013, Section 3 of DOMA was declared unconstitutional by the Supreme Court of the United States, forcing all courts in the country to review their marriage legislation.

In 2015, before federal law allowed it, fourteen out of fifty U.S. states still prohibited same-sex marriage. Mary Bonauto once again pleaded before the Supreme Court in Obergefell v. Hodges. Jim Obergefell had married his partner in 2013 in Maryland, but at the time of his death in October 2013, Jim was living in Ohio, a state that did not recognize his union. His status as a "surviving spouse" was therefore denied to him. By five votes to four, on June 26, 2015, the Court ruled in favour of same-sex marriage, allowing all couples to marry in the United States.

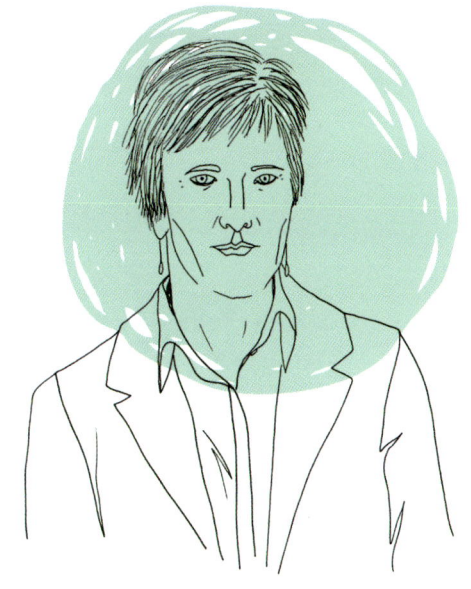

"It's not about me, it's about the people in the lawsuits, the plaintiffs and their stories," she explained. Determined to eradicate discrimination based on sexual orientation, Mary Bonauto continues to use the law to establish the human rights of LGBTQI+ people in the United States, including recently challenging the transgender military ban. On January 25, 2021, President Biden signed an executive order to reverse the ban, allowing most transgender individuals to serve in the United States military.

Mary Bonauto has received several awards including the MacArthur Fellowship in 2014 for her work breaking down legal barriers.

Manvendra Singh Gohil 1965

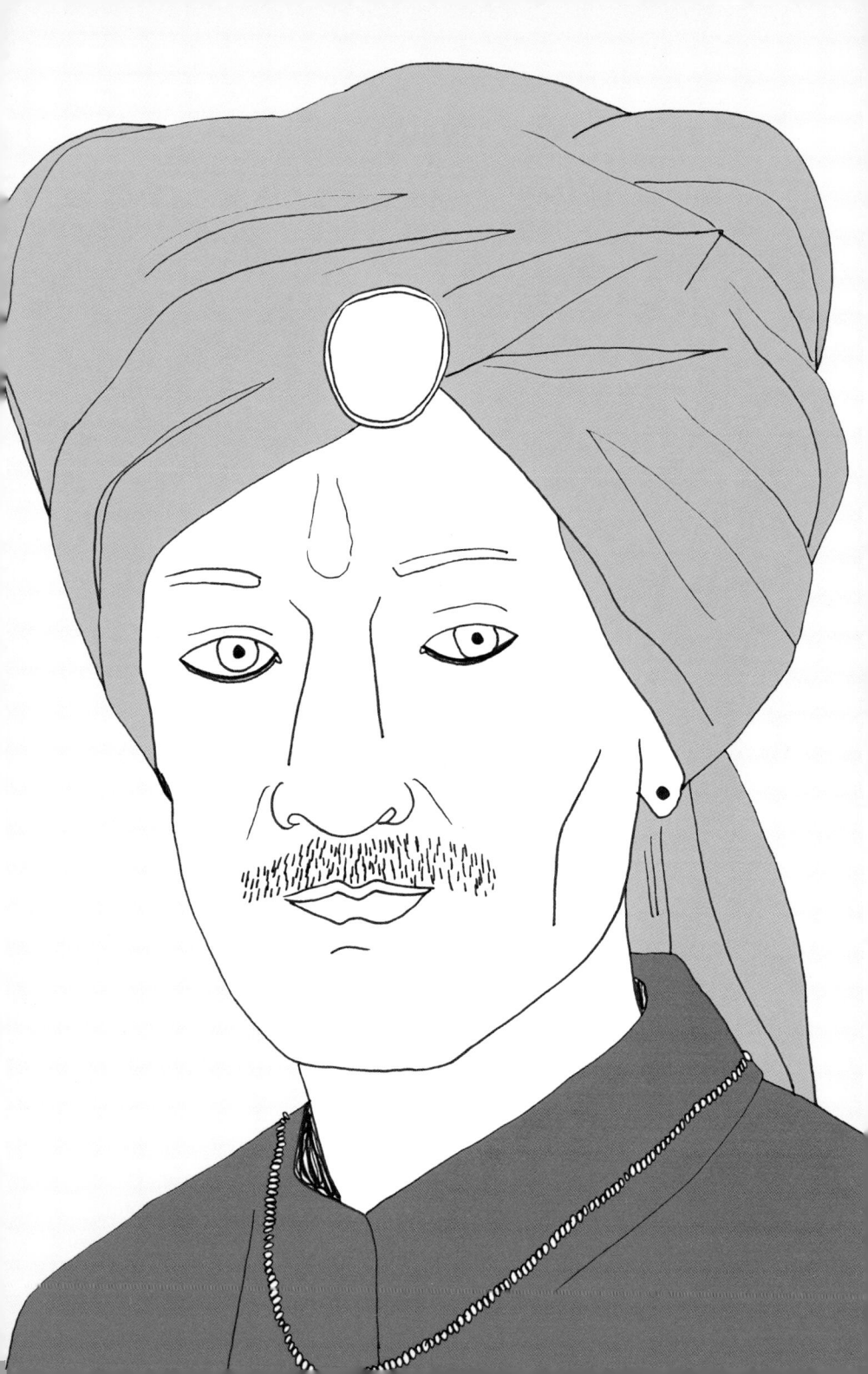

MANVENDRA SINGH GOHIL COMES FROM A LARGE INDIAN ROYAL FAMILY IN THE STATE OF GUJARAT. AFTER BEING MARRIED FOR LESS THAN A YEAR TO A PRINCESS, AND SPENDING SEVERAL YEARS "IN THE CLOSET", HE CAME OUT PUBLICLY AS GAY IN 2006 (AGAINST THE ADVICE OF HIS PARENTS).

In a country where homosexuality is still taboo, and gay sex was illegal up until September 2018, the position of this openly gay prince, who now lives in Mumbai, has made him a leading spokesperson for LGBTQI+ rights in India. He is regularly interviewed by the press and has even been invited on the set of Oprah Winfrey.

For several years, he called for the abolition of Section 377 of the Indian Penal Code, which criminalized "carnal intercourse against the order of nature with any man, woman or animal" and could lead to life imprisonment. The New Delhi High Court of Justice challenged the Article in 2009, but this ruling was later reviewed and quashed, in 2013, by the Supreme Court. However, on September 6, 2018, the Supreme Court ruled to decriminalize gay sex: a historic victory for thousands of Indian people.

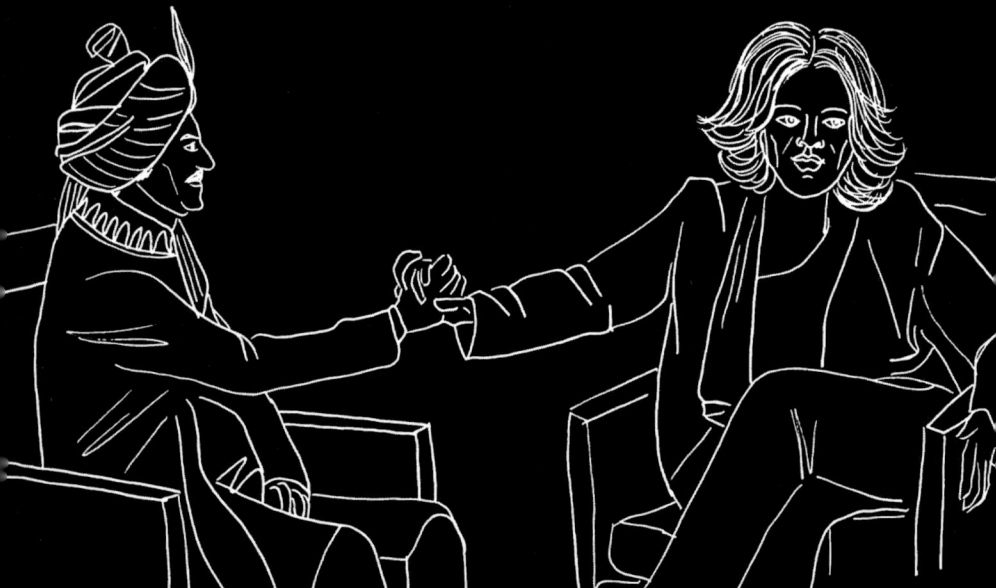

Manvendra Singh Gohil

Sharing his experiences, Manvendra explained, "We are all human beings. We are all equal… All we want is love. Gay rights cannot just be won in the courtroom but in the hearts and the minds of the people we live with."

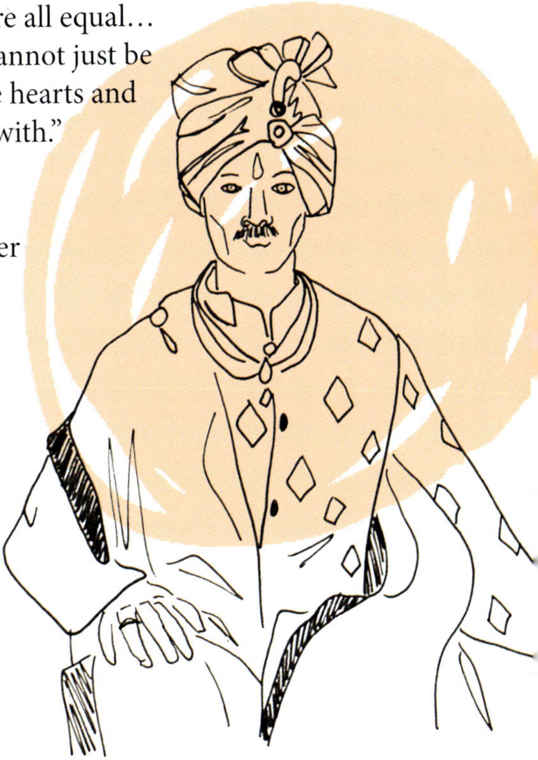

He wants to transform the former family palace of 60,000 m² into a refuge for LGBTQI+ people rejected by their families. "In India we have a family system and we are mentally conditioned to be with our parents. The moment you try to come out, you are told you will be thrown out and society will boycott you," he told the *International Business Times*.

The former family palace

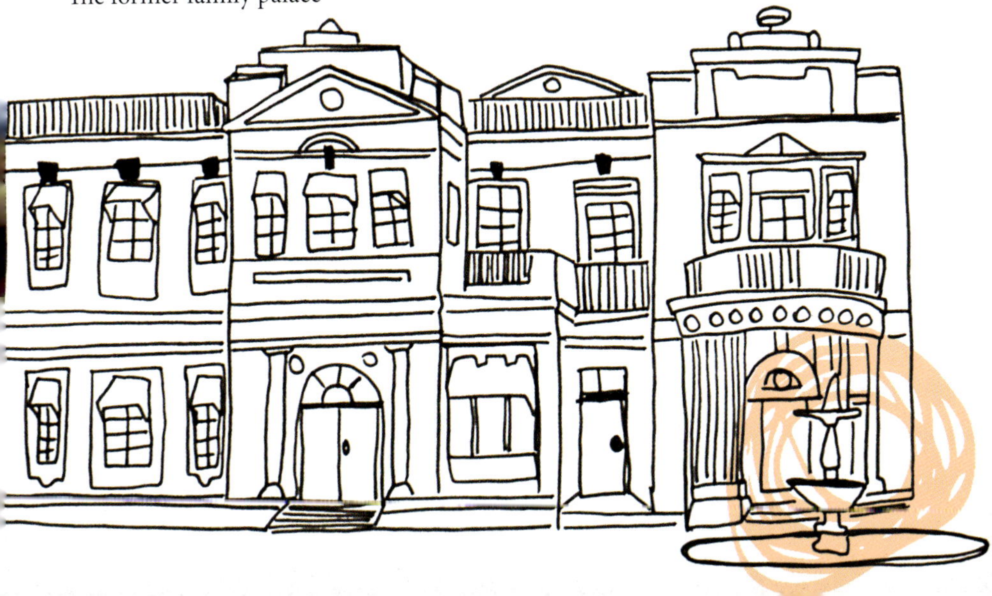

He launched a gay magazine, *Fun*, and founded the Lakshya Trust, which advocates for HIV/AIDS awareness and provides psychological, legal, economic, spiritual, health and social support to LGBTQI+ people in the Gujarat region.
Recently, he launched the very first university course on LGBTQI+ rights at a university in western India.

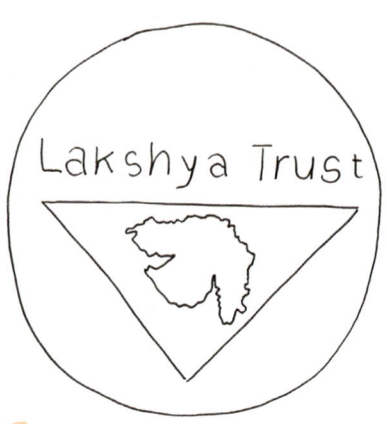

In recent years, Indian society has become more accepting of LGBTQI+ people, and there have been various landmark victories, including the legal recognition of non-binary and transgender people as a third gender in 2014, which Manvendra campaigned for.

However, the country is yet to legalize same-sex marriage, and 2023 saw same-sex couples filing petitions to the Supreme Court, seeking to legalize their union.

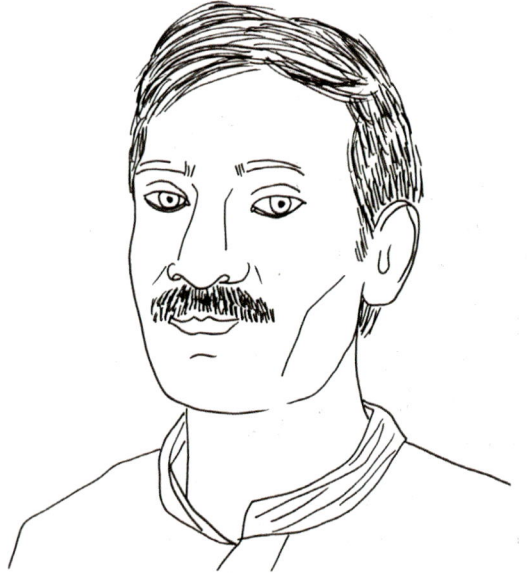

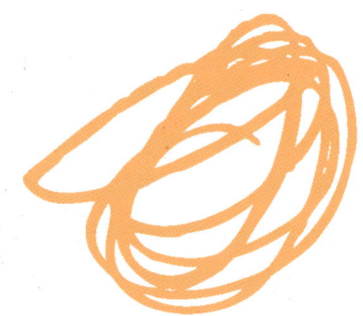

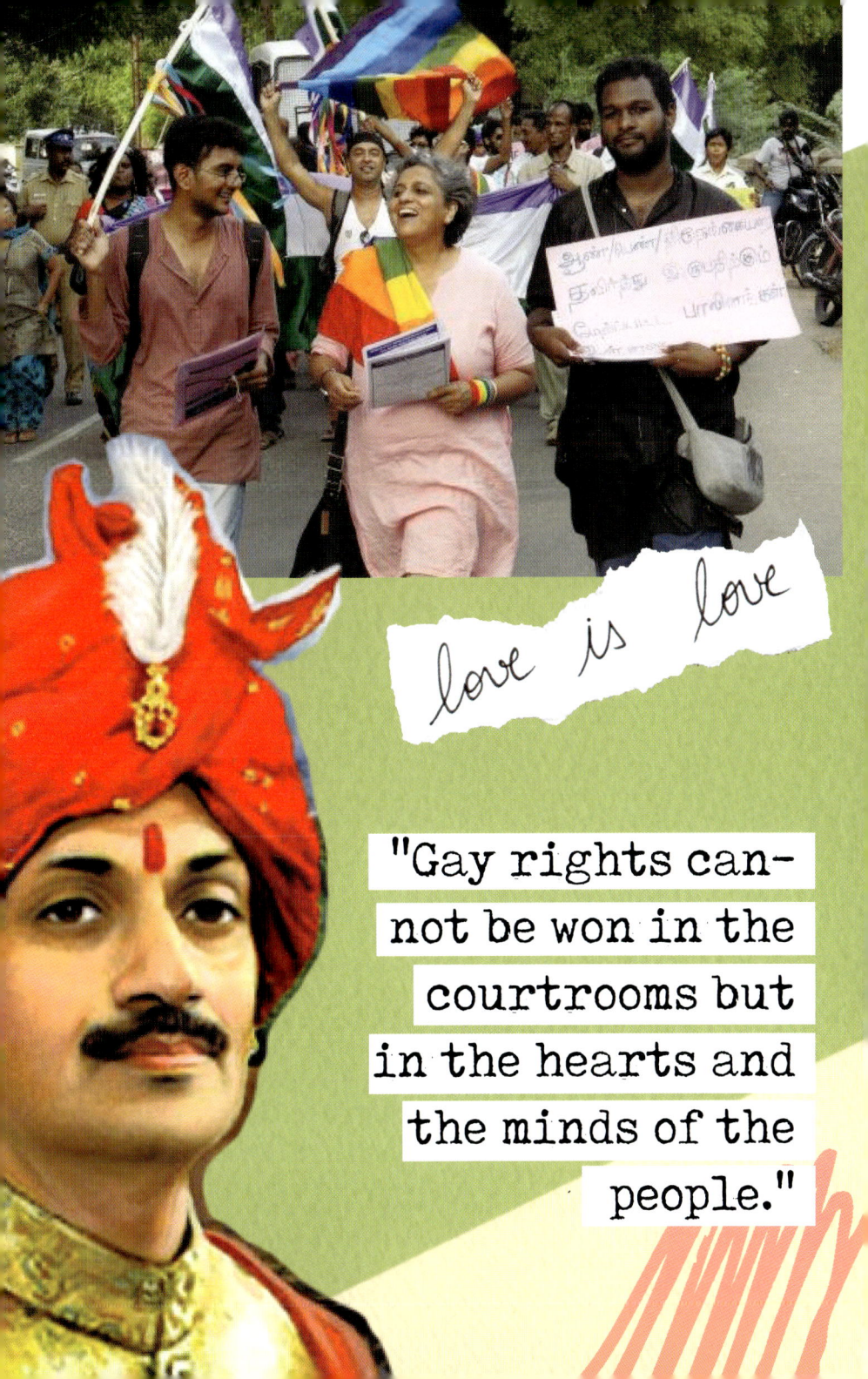

Hida Viloria
1968

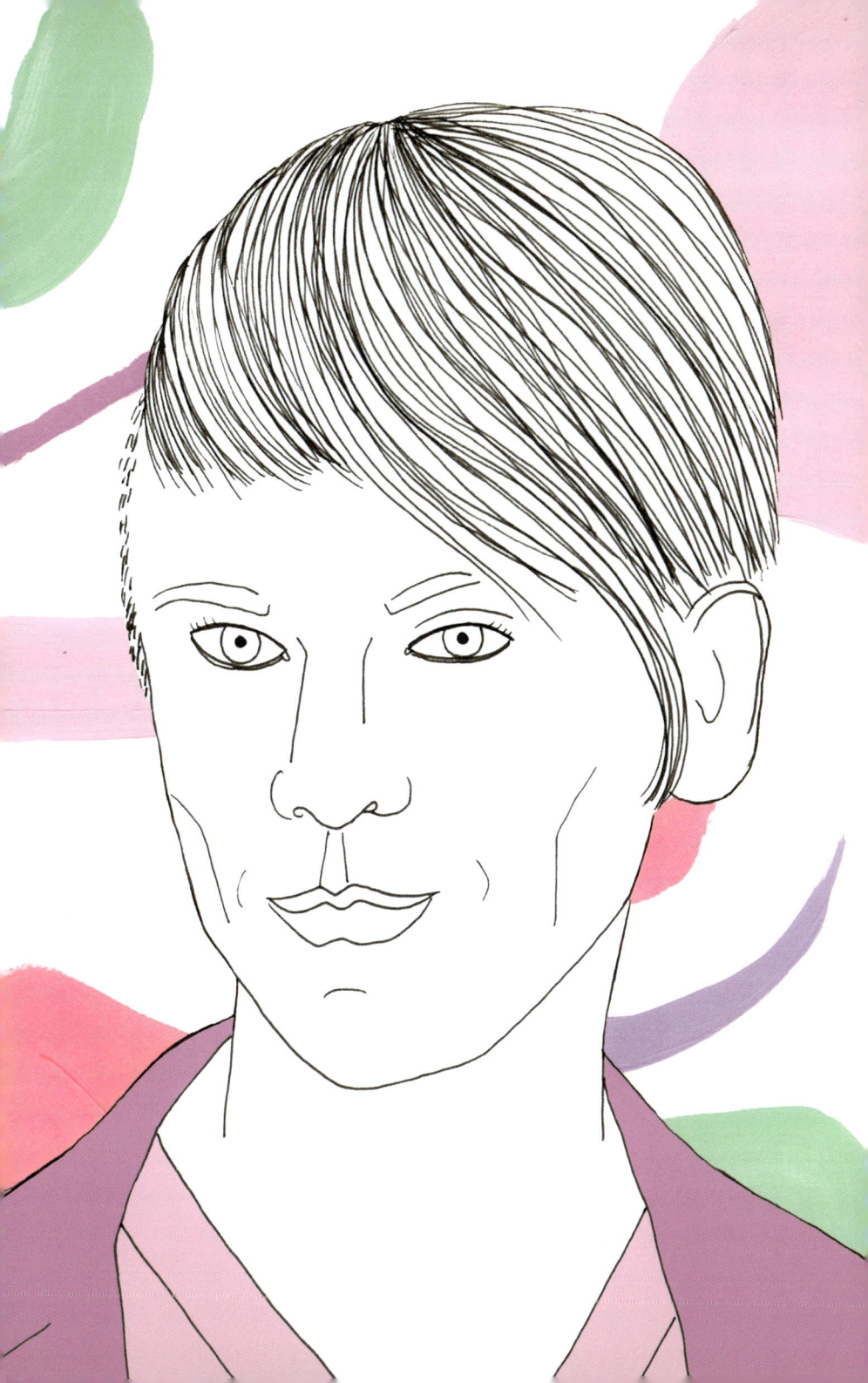

HIDA VILORIA IS A LATINX AMERICAN, INTERSEX, NON-BINARY AND GENDER NON-CONFORMING ACTIVIST RESOLUTELY COMMITTED TO TAKING ACTION FOR THEIR COMMUNITY.

While there are more than thirty different definitions of intersex, the United Nations Human Rights Council defines it as those people: "born with sex characteristics (including genitals, gonads and chromosome patterns) that do not fit typical binary notions of male or female bodies."

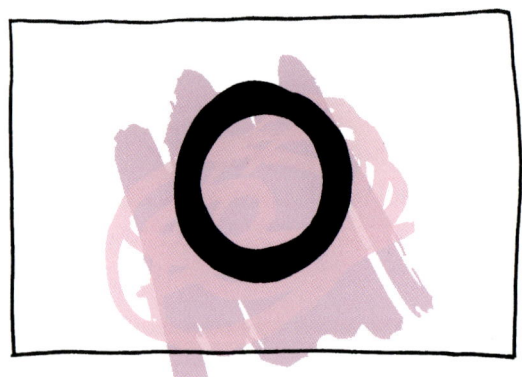

The intersex community flag

When they received their degree from the University of Berkeley in Gender and Sexuality, Hida Viloria quickly utilized their skills to help the intersex cause. They fought against the medical profession's need to "normalize" intersex bodies through surgical interventions, and fought for these bodies to be seen as healthy as they are. The surgical interventions and hormone treatments forced on intersex people are, the vast majority of the time, useless, or even harmful to their health.

Hida Viloria

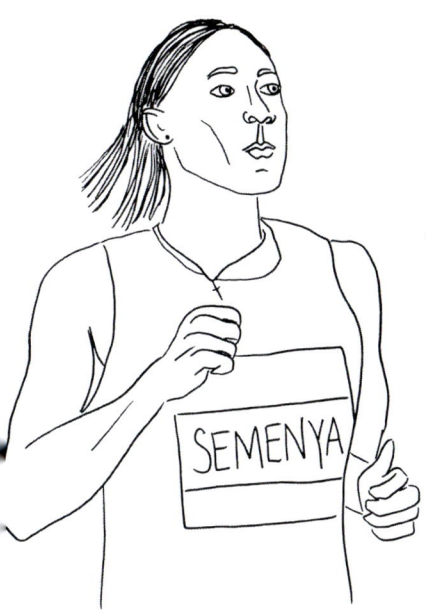

Caster Semenya

In 2010, after supporting the South African intersex athlete Caster Semenya, who was banned from sports competitions because she was hyperandrogenic (having a level considered high of male hormones in the blood), Hida Viloria attended the international Olympic Committee's panel of experts meeting in Switzerland, during which they successfully fought against the pathologization of intersex people. In 2013, they also created an educational resource on this topic for parents of intersex children: *Your Beautiful Child: Information for Parents*.

It was during encounters and interviews with other intersex people that they realized most intersex people have been psychologically and physically scarred by hormonal treatments and childhood medical operations.

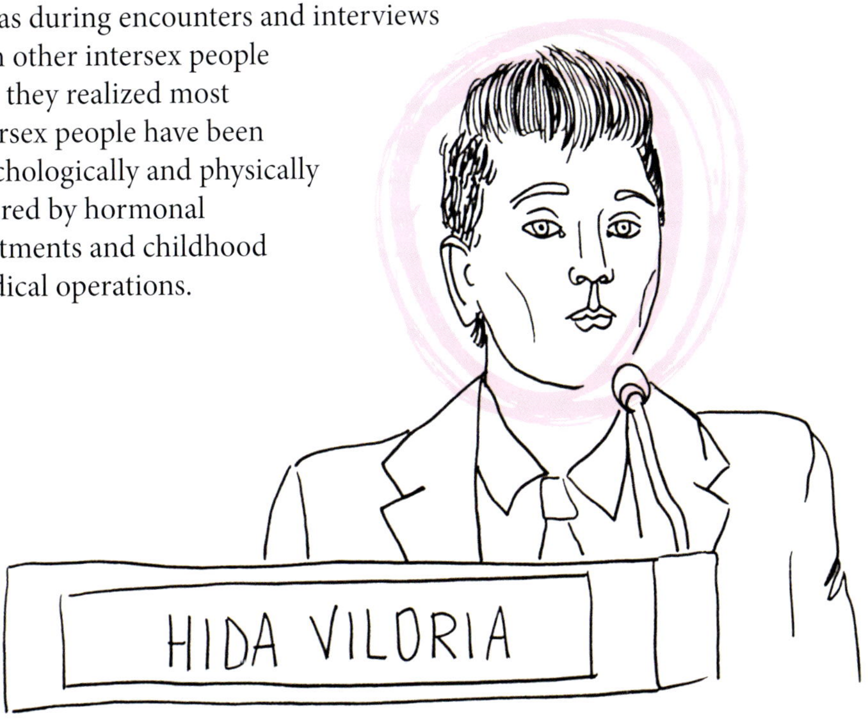

HIDA VILORIA

"I WISH MORE PEOPLE KNEW THAT BEING INTERSEX CAN BE AN EXTRAORDINARILY POSITIVE, PHYSICAL, SPIRITUAL, AND INTELLECTUAL EXPERIENCE."

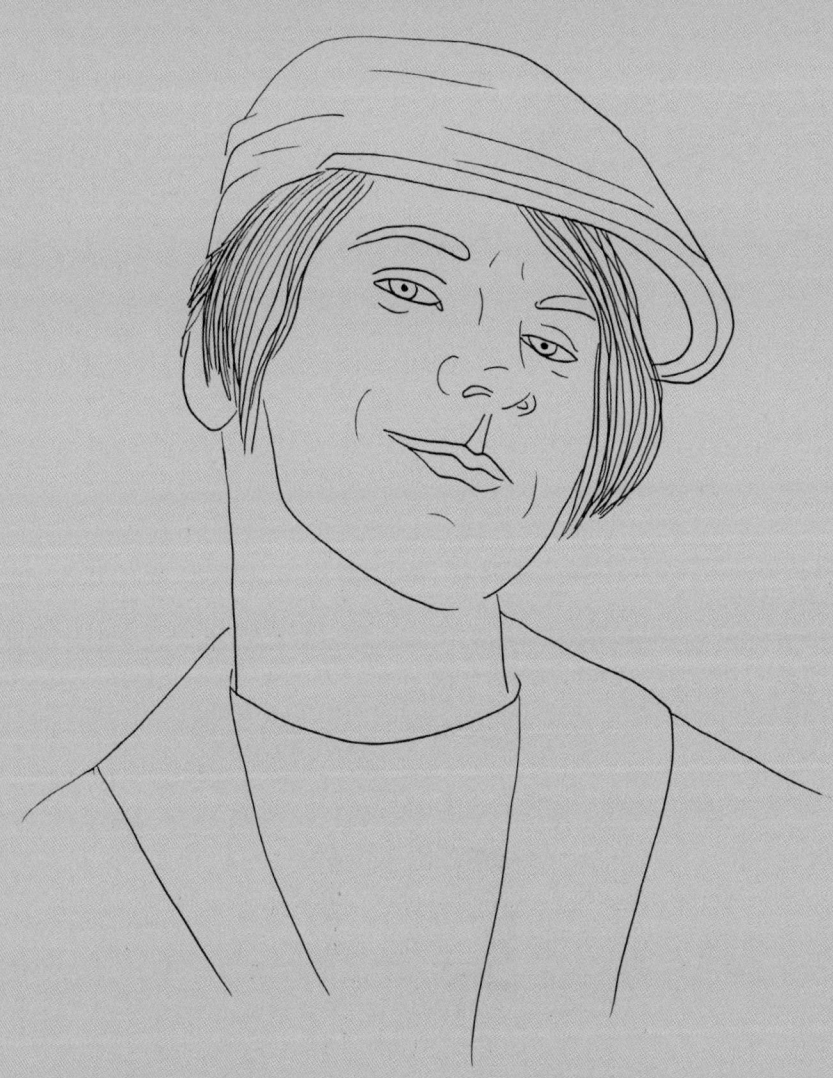

Hida Viloria

They regularly participate in various conferences to raise awareness on these topics and published the book *Born Both: An Intersex Life* in 2017. They recount their life, questions about their gender, activism, and the pressure of gender binaries in society.

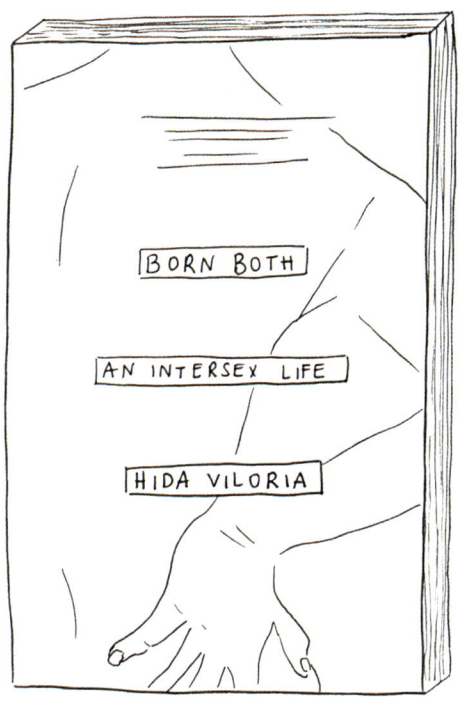

In the preface to the book, they write: "My name is Hida Viloria. I was raised as a girl but discovered at a young age that my body looked different… It wasn't until I was twenty-six and encountered the term 'intersex' in a San Francisco newspaper that I finally had a name for my difference."

Hida Viloria chairs the Organization Intersex International (OII) and founded The Intersex Campaign for Equality (IC4E) which, according to its website, promotes human rights and equality for all intersex people through the arts, education, and actions.

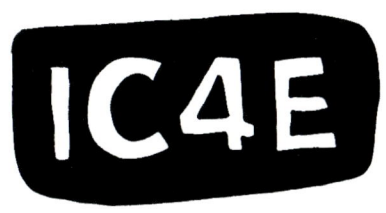

Bamby Salcedo
1969

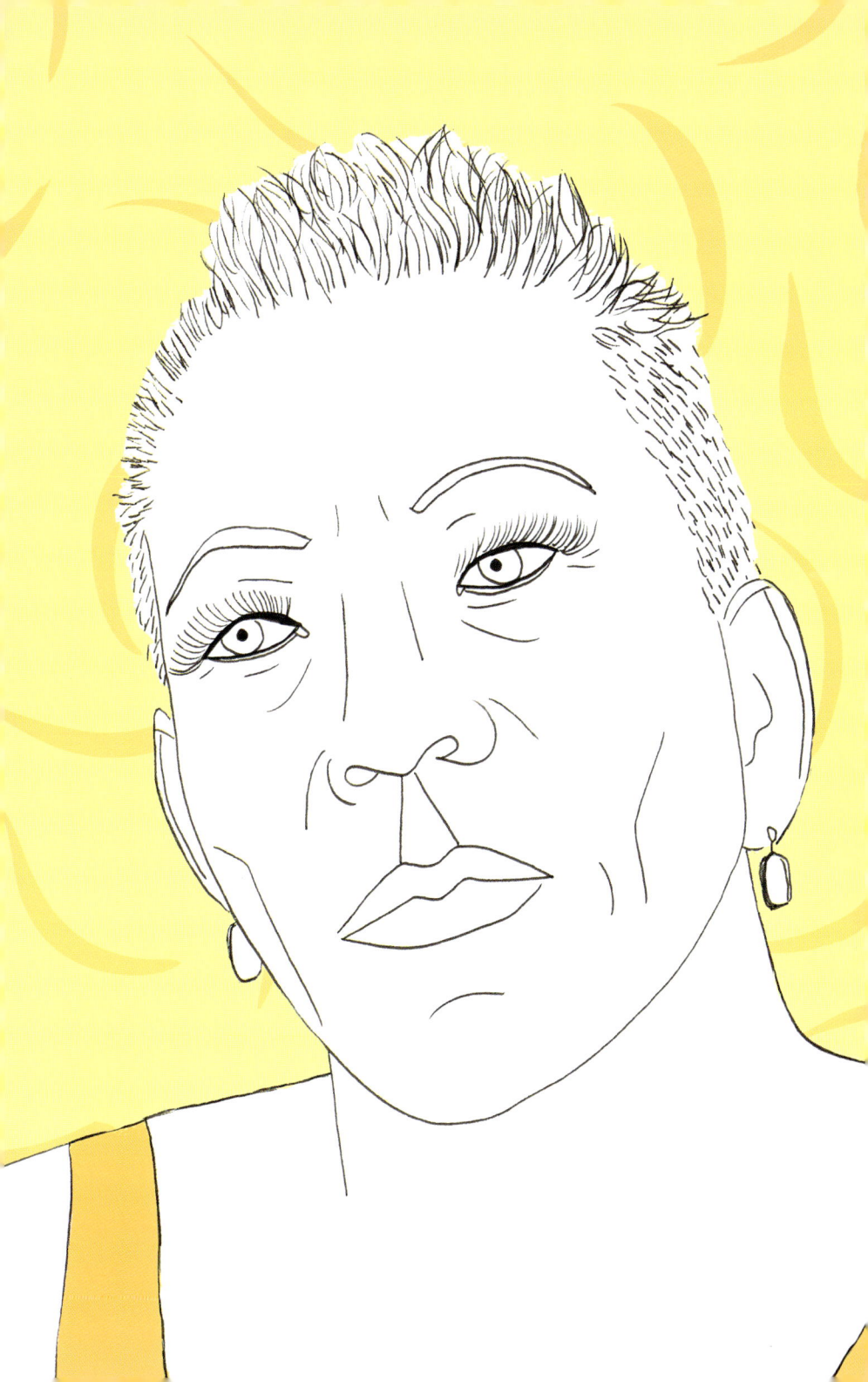

"I AM A MIRACLE. YO SOY A MILAGRO. I AM NOT SUPPOSED TO BE HERE... I'M REALLY NOT SUPPOSED TO BE HERE." THIS INTRODUCTION TO BAMBY SALCEDO'S BIO ON HER WEBSITE SAYS A LOT ABOUT THE LIFE OF THIS TRANS ACTIVIST FROM THE POOR NEIGHBOURHOODS OF GUADALAJARA.

Bamby Salcedo is a prominent and celebrated transgender Latina activist, who advocates for and addresses the issues of transgender Latinas throughout the United States.

After many years spent on the streets of Guadalajara, a Mexican city where crime, drugs, juvenile detention centres and gangs rocked her daily life, Bamby Salcedo emigrated to the United States, at the age of seventeen. She was homeless, became a sex worker, took drugs, and got arrested and sent to prison. After the murder of transgender teenager Gwen Araujo in 2002, she decided to dedicate her life to the defence of trans people.

In 2009, Bamby Salcedo created the TransLatin@Coalition. Based in Los Angeles, this organization aims to improve the quality of life of trans Latina women in the United States, defend their rights, protect them, and work towards their integration into society. It also develops various programs in partnership with other organizations around HIV, trans youth, trans visibility, and LGBTQI+ discrimination. She has advised on how to provide competent health care services for transgender people as well as health care for LGBTQI+ people and human rights in Latin America and The Caribbean.

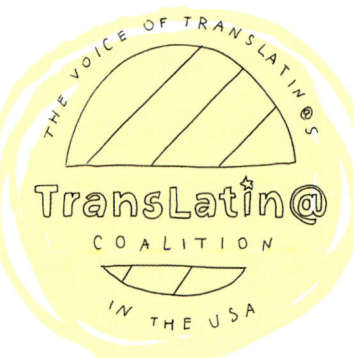

Bamby Salcedo

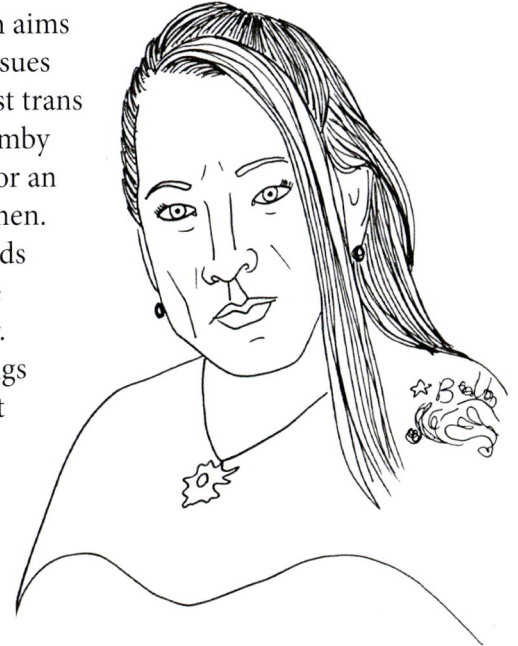

Initiator of the Trans Lives Matter National Day of Action, which aims to "affirmatively address the issues of institutional violence against trans people within our society", Bamby Salcedo is an inspiring voice for an entire generation of trans women. A woman whose various awards have not diminished her drive to change things for the better. "There are two important things I've learned in my life, the first is knowing my history… but even more important is that we don't forget where we come from," she explains.

Always ready to step up and take action, she cut her hair on stage during a speech in Seattle to symbolize physical freedom and self-determination. She chose the name Bamby because she managed to evade the police at the age of twelve, by running as fast as a deer. She created the "Angels of Change" program which involves the production of a trans photo calendar and a runway show for young transgender people each year, to boost self-esteem and confidence.

Her life story has been the subject of two documentary films, *TransVisible: Bamby Salcedo's Story* and *LA QueenCiañera*.

Phyllis Akua Opoku-Gyimah
1974

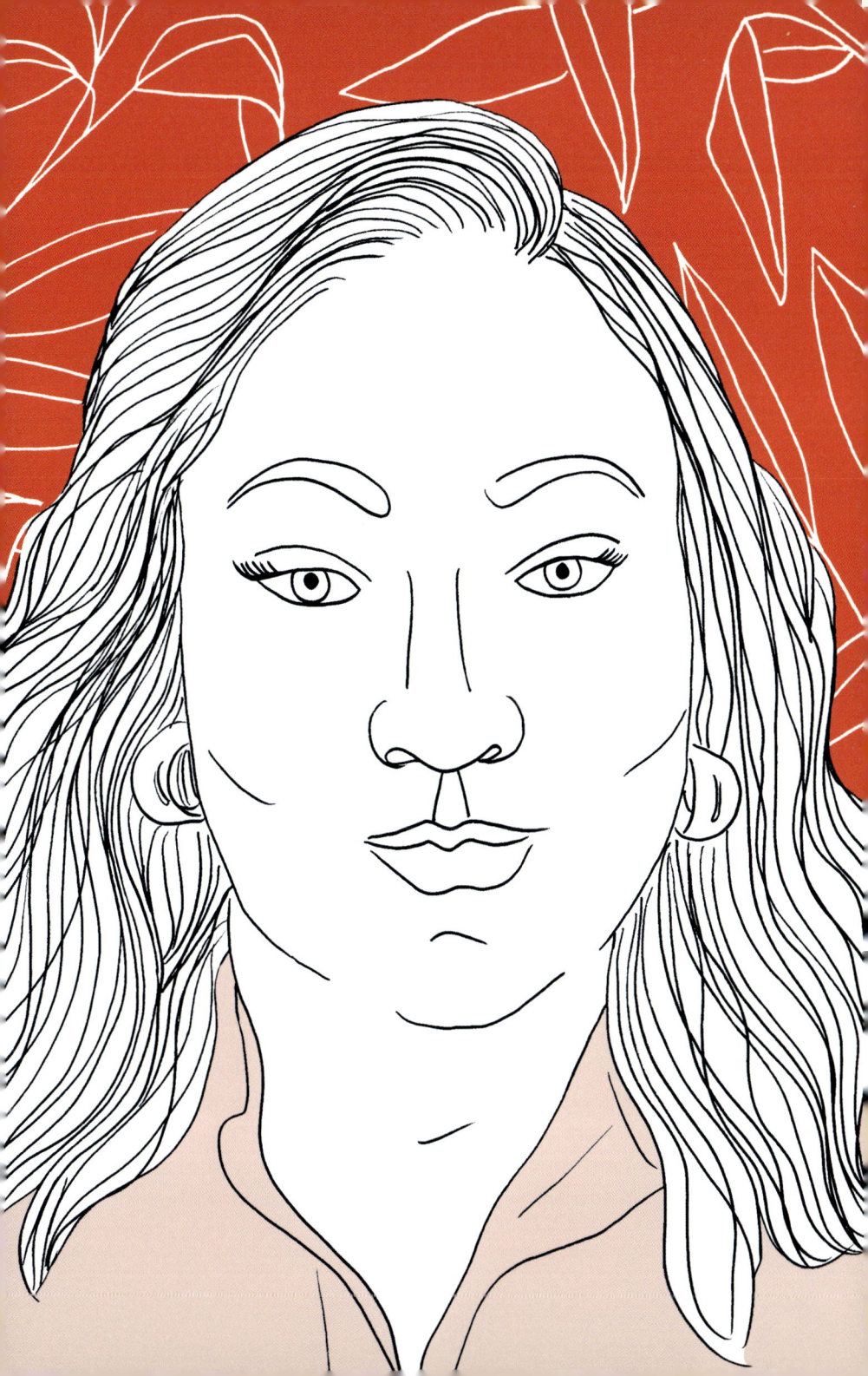

PHYLLIS AKUA OPOKU-GYIMAH, BETTER KNOWN AS LADY PHYLL, IS A POWERHOUSE WITHIN BRITISH ACTIVISM. ONE OF BRITAIN'S MOST PROMINENT LESBIAN ACTIVISTS, SHE HAS INCREASED VISIBILITY AND ADVOCACY FOR LGBTQI+ PEOPLE OF COLOUR IN THE UK AND BEYOND.

Lady Phyll first became politically active whilst she was still in school, as she started questioning the white, Euro-centric version of history taught to British students:

"Why were we only being taught about the Battle of Hastings and Henry VIII's wives? I wanted to know about slavery, the history of Africans and Asians. My requests were declined. Instead, I sat in the library and taught myself, reading books about Marcus Garvey, Martin Luther King and Malcolm X."

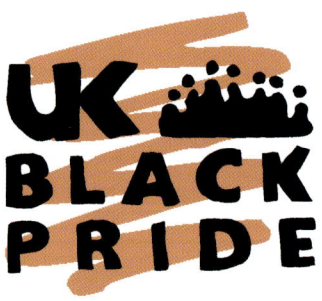

This questioning and desire to challenge the status quo has carried into her adult life. She is co-founder and director of UK Black Pride, which was set up partially in criticism of the lack of diversity celebrated at Pride in London. UK Black Pride is the largest celebration for LGBTQI+ people of colour, and aims to "promote and advocate for the spiritual, emotional, and intellectual health and wellbeing of the communities [they] represent."

Phyllis Akua Opoku-Gyimah

Being queer and a person of colour results in specific challenges not faced by white queer people, and Lady Phyll hopes that by discussing, advocating for change, and supporting one another, UK Black Pride will mean that nobody feels alone.

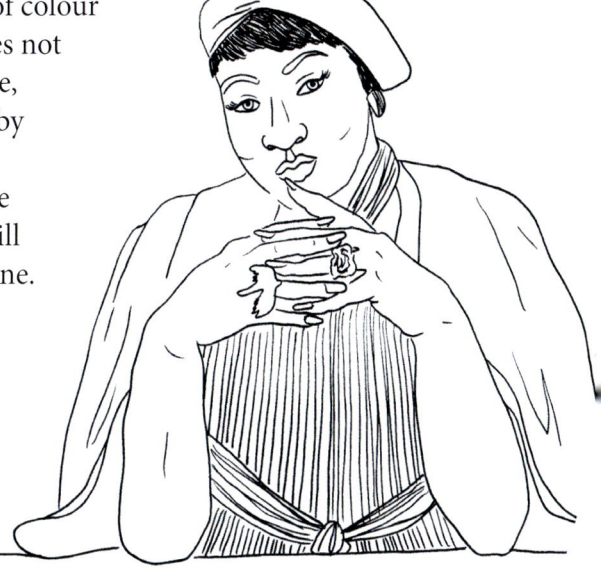

In 2016, she was awarded an MBE in the New Year Honours in recognition of her advocacy work. However, she publicly refused it in protest against the continued persecution of LGBTQI+ people around the world as a consequence of British colonial rule.

She was a trustee of Stonewall for three years, only standing down when the charity partnered with Black Pride. She has also been heavily involved with the Trades Union Congress, serving on their Race Relations Committee.

She co-edited *Sista!: An anthology of writings by Same Gender Loving Women of African/Caribbean descent with a UK connection* in 2018, and was named in the 100 Great Black Britons list in 2020.

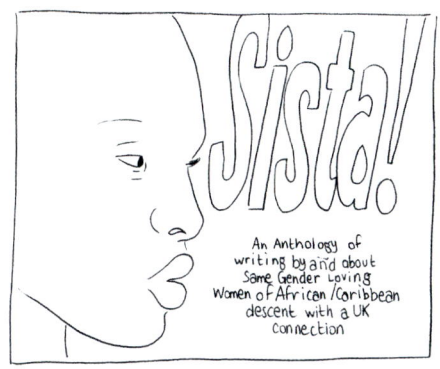

Xulhaz Mannan
1976 – 2016

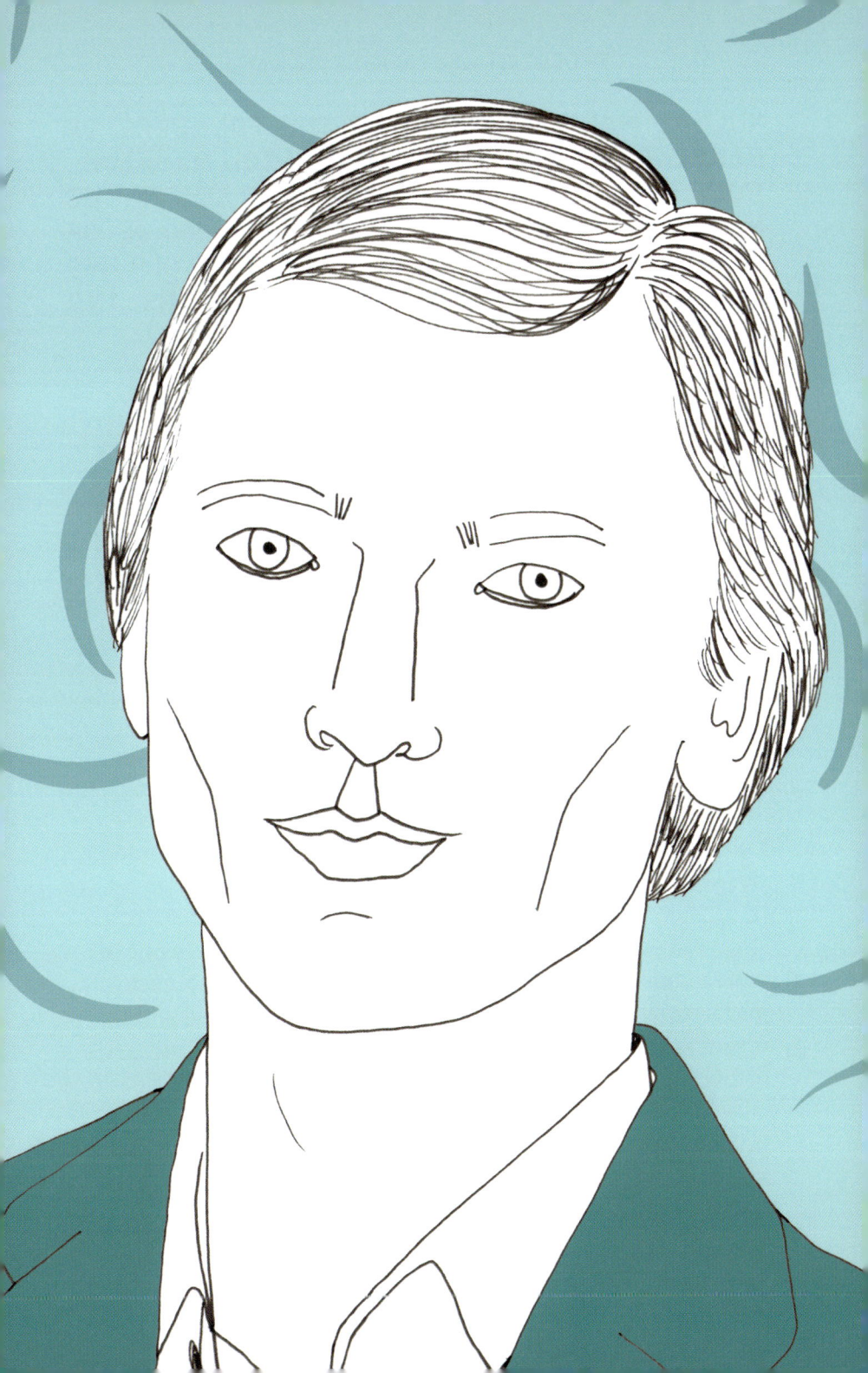

XULHAZ MANNAN IS ONE OF THE FOUNDERS OF BANGLADESH'S FIRST AND ONLY LGBTQI+ MAGAZINE, *ROOPBAAN*, LAUNCHED IN 2014. THE AIM OF THE MAGAZINE WAS TO GIVE A DIFFERENT IMAGE OF LGBTQI+ PEOPLE, TO CHALLENGE THE CLICHÉS AND STIGMAS PROPAGATED BY POLITICIANS AND INFLUENTIAL RELIGIOUS FIGURES.

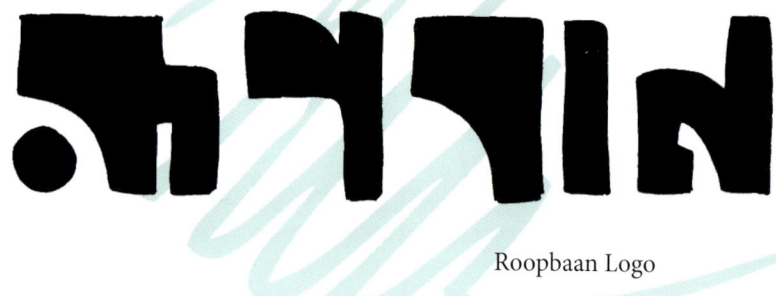

Roopbaan Logo

In April 2016, the bodies of Xulhaz Mannan and his partner, Tanay Mojumdar, were found dead in their homes, violently stabbed by men posing as couriers. Responsibility for the murder was later claimed by Ansar al-Islam, a branch of Al-Qaeda.

"I have only one life and I refuse to split it in two in the name of good morals. I'm the way I am and that's it," he said in French gay magazine *Têtu* in 2015. Openly gay, he also participated in the organization of a "rainbow rally" on 14th April in 2014 and 2015, before it was cancelled by the police in 2016.

In May 2019, eight extremists were charged by Bangladesh police for the murders. Four of the eight are in custody and police are still searching for the others.

Xulhaz Mannan

As a result of his murder, many LGBTQI+ people left Bangladesh, whilst others erased all traces of their activism online. The murder of Xulhaz Mannan and his partner was part of a series of killings of activists, bloggers, and intellectuals in the months leading up to his death. The situation for LGBTQI+ people in Bangladesh is still precarious according to reports from several NGOs.

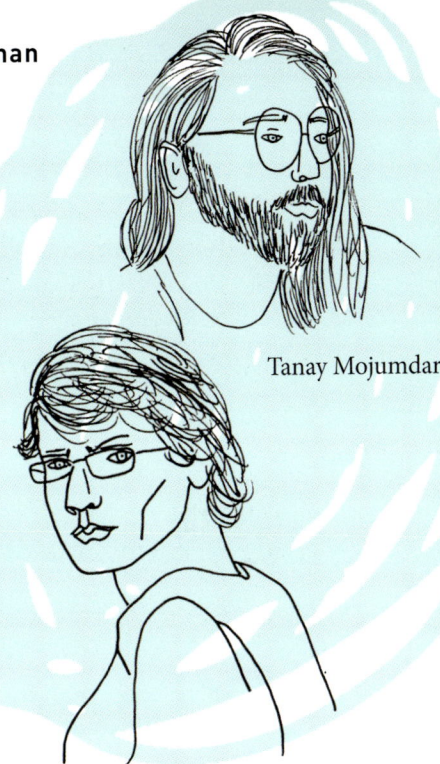

Tanay Mojumdar

Xulhaz Mannan

Twenty-seven men were arrested on suspicion of homosexuality at a community centre in Dhaka, the country's capital, in 2017.

In a country of 163 million people, where homosexuality is criminalized under Article 377 of the Penal Code, LGBTQI+ people fear for their lives. However, Bangladesh is one of the countries that has legally recognized a third gender, and there are estimated to be around 100,000 people who identify as 'hijra'. In 2000, hijra sex work was declared legal by the Bangladeshi High Court.

Xiaogang Wei
1976

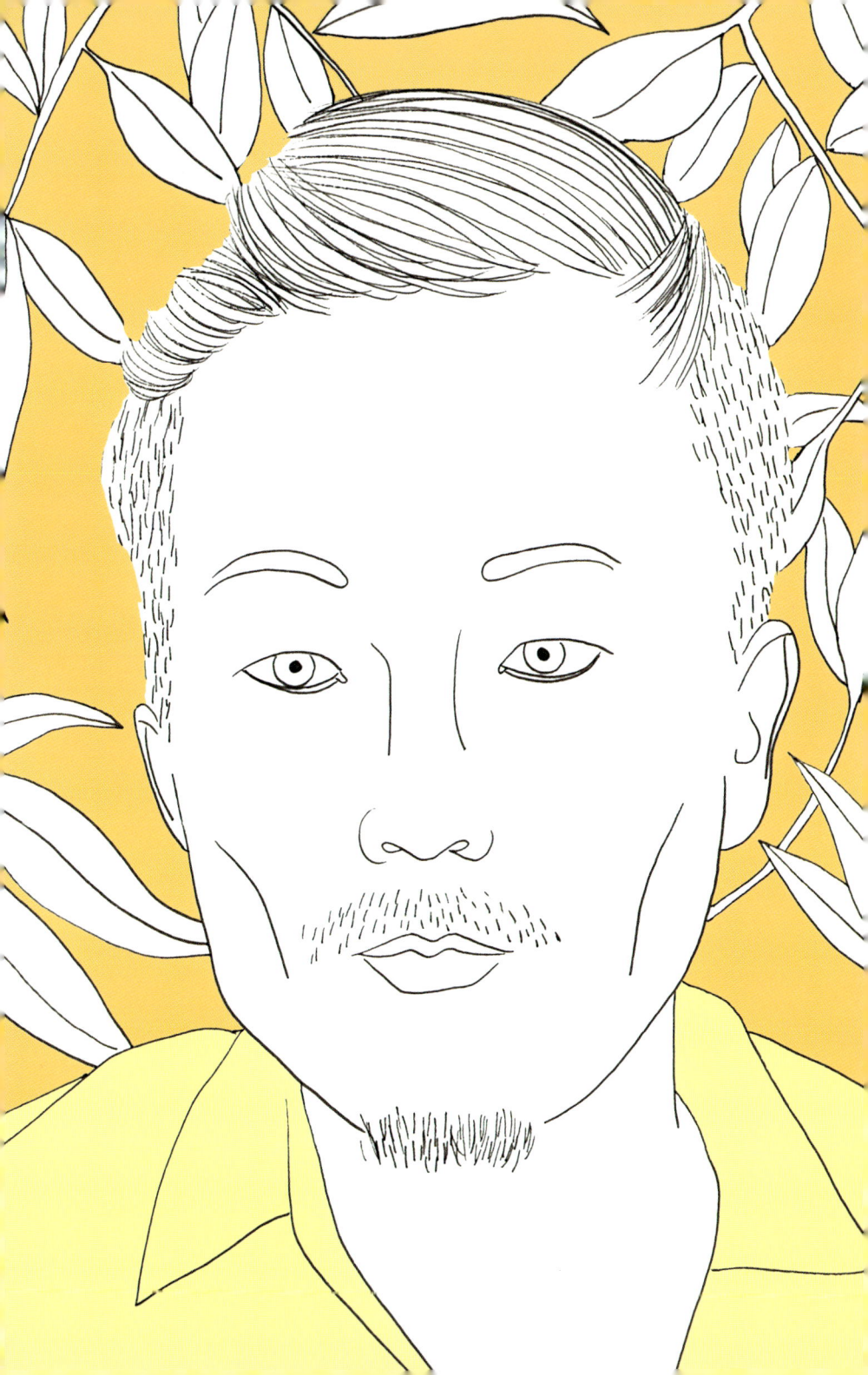

XIAOGANG WEI IS THE CO-PRODUCER, ACTOR AND DIRECTOR OF SEVERAL DOCUMENTARIES AND FILMS ON HIV/ AIDS AND LGBTQI+ ISSUES IN CHINA, AMONG OTHERS: *MEN AND WOMEN* (1999), *OLD TESTAMENT* (2001), *LIVING POSITIVE* (2005), *THE CREAM OF THE QUEER CROP* (2010), *CHINA PK QUEEN* (2020).

Xiaogang Wei is also an organizing member of the Beijing Queer Film Festival. He used to be a member of the board of directors of the Beijing LGBT Center and a consultant for UNICEF.

In addition, he is the founder of Queer Comrades, a website that offers content for LGBTQI+ people. Since 2007, Xiaogang Wei has hosted a talk show under Queer Comrades, in which he invites Chinese queer people to come and discuss their lives in China. The website is monitored by the government, but continues to offer information, documentation, and entertainment, giving visibility to a community still widely discriminated against.

Queer Comrades also aims to create LGBTQI+ archives in China while promoting major community events.

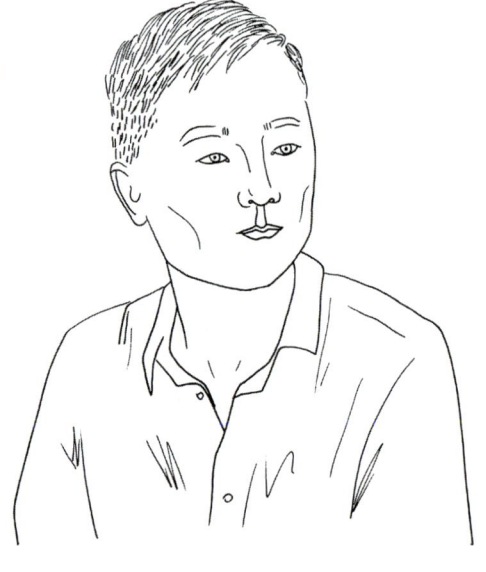

In China, the issue of homosexuality, and LGBTQI+ issues, is relatively ambiguous. While homosexuality has not been considered a mental illness since 2001, President Xi Jinping banned the broadcast of "abnormal sexual relationships and behaviour" in film and television in 2015, removing all LGBTQI+

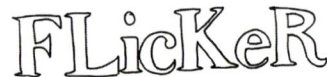

characters from the country's media, TV series and films. Gay and lesbian dating apps are regularly suspended without explanation, and censorship on the social network Weibo (the equivalent of Twitter in China) is strict.

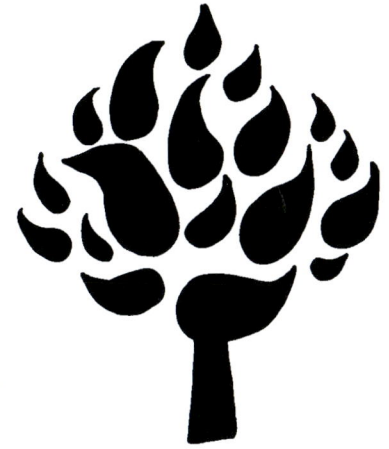

LGBTQI+ events are often banned, including Shanghai Pride, which was the longest running LGBTQI+ event but was shut down in 2020. "It's very hard to understand what you have the right to do," says the director of the Beijing LGBT Center. Some hospitals in the country offer conversion therapies using electroshock (ECT) and hypnotherapy to "cure homosexuality". For Chinese LGBTQI+ people, coming out is almost always faced with difficulty. According to a study by the Beijing LGBT Center, only 5% of Chinese gay people fully embrace their sexuality.

"WHEN GAY CHINESE TALK ABOUT THE CONDITIONS IN CHINA, THEY OFTEN MENTION THAT THERE ARE GAY BARS AND GAY SITES, BOTH SYMBOLS THAT A CHANGE HAS OCCURRED, BUT THESE BARS AND WEBSITES ARE INSUFFICIENT; THEY DON'T MEAN WE HAVE A SOCIETY WITH EQUAL RIGHTS FOR ALL."

Ludovic-Mohamed
Zahed
1977

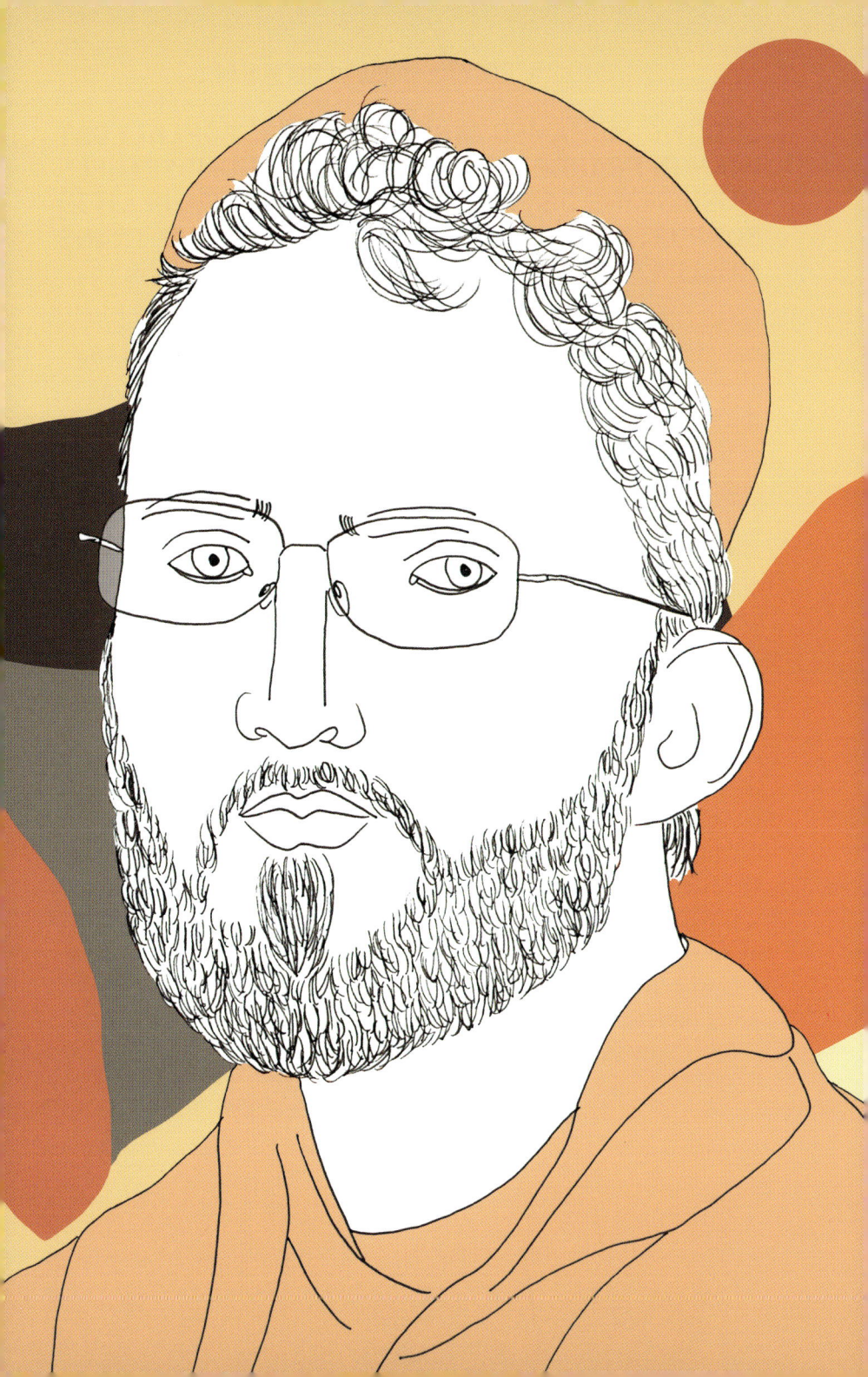

LUDOVIC-MOHAMED ZAHED IS THE FIRST OPENLY GAY IMAM IN FRANCE. HE ALSO FOUNDED HOMOSEXUELS MUSULMANS DE FRANCE (HM2F), AN ORGANIZATION SUPPORTING GAY, LESBIAN, BISEXUAL AND TRANS MUSLIM PEOPLE.

He has lived in Marseilles since 1995, where he took refuge during the Algerian Civil War, but grew up in Algiers, where he was born, and entered a Quranic school at the age of twelve. It was around the age of seventeen that he became aware of his sexuality. Two years later, he learned that he was HIV positive, before coming out at the age of twenty-one. He then cut his ties with his religion, feeling forced to choose between his faith and his sexuality. During this time, he became involved with HIV/AIDS activism and then turned to Buddhism.

At the age of thirty, he immersed himself in studying the Quran and carried out research for two doctoral theses on minorities within religious communities. He discovered that there was never any mention of homosexuality in the Quran and from that point on refused to choose between his religion and his sexual orientation.

Ludovic-Mohamed Zahed

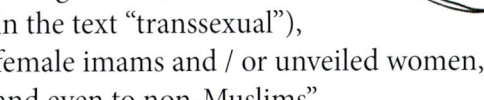

In 2010, he created the Association Homosexuels Musulmans de France (HM2F). He inaugurated two mosques open to all, the first in Paris in 2012 and another in Marseilles in 2015, which aim to be "an 'inclusive' place of worship, open to homosexuals, bisexuals, transgenders (modified in the text "transsexual"), female imams and / or unveiled women, and even to non-Muslims".

He got married in South Africa in 2011, and now wants to see a progressive Islam adopted in France, one that rejects the use of conversion therapy. He published *The Qur'an and the Flesh* in 2012, which tells the story of his life. He now runs CALEM, a spiritual institute that trains new generations of imams including women and LGBTQI+ people.

For religious people, having to choose between faith and gender identity and/or sexual orientation can be a traumatic experience. If religious LGBTQI+ people rarely speak out on this subject, it is because it is often difficult to find one's place when religious institutions deny your existence, reject you, or try to "convert" you through conversion therapies which are still allowed in many countries. France banned conversion therapy in 2022. The climate towards LGBTQI+ people in Algeria is still hostile with only around a third of people in Algeria said to be in favour of homosexuality; fines and imprisonment are still in force.

Nikolai Alekseev
1977

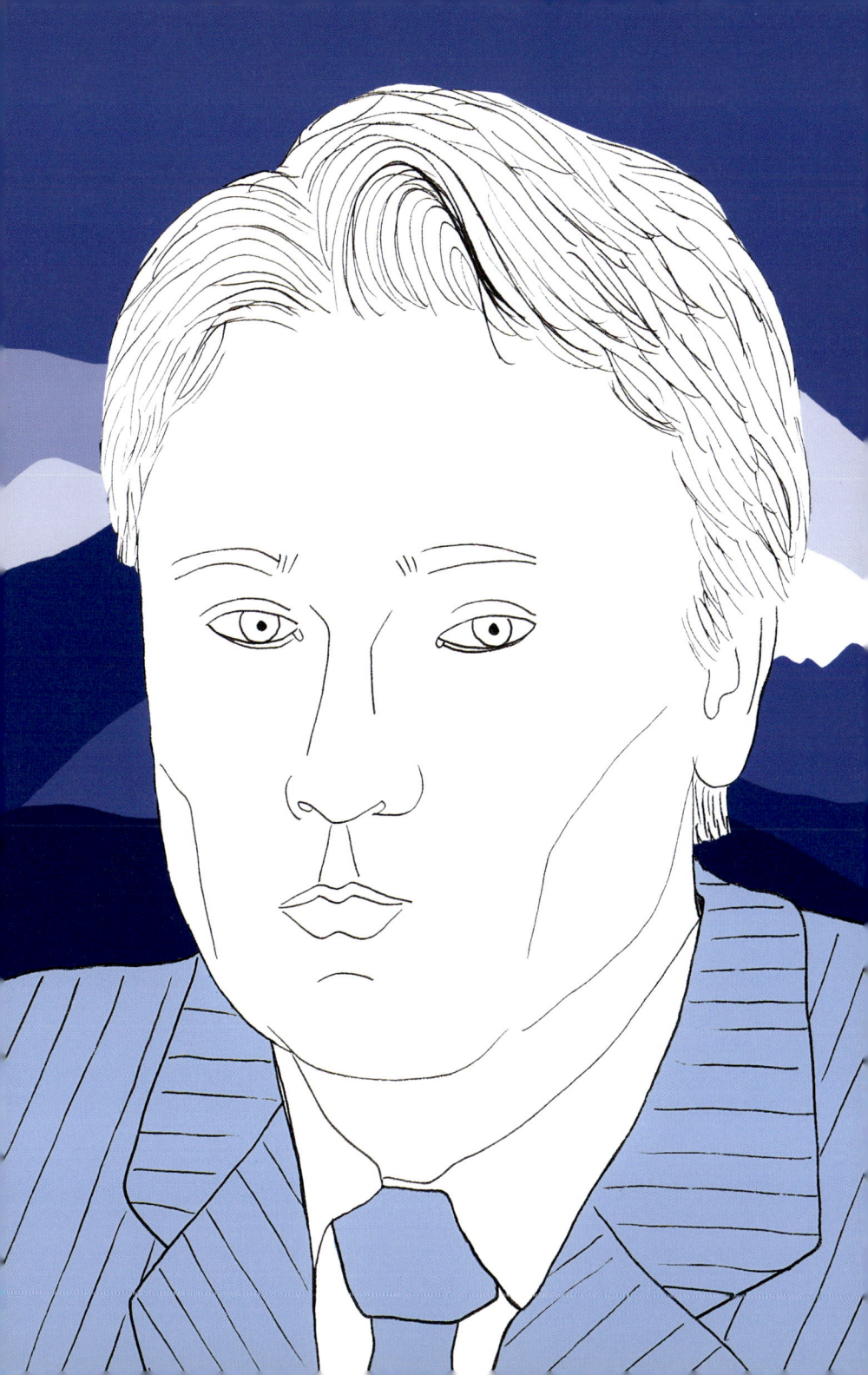

NIKOLAI ALEKSEEV IS A RUSSIAN GAY ACTIVIST, AND THE HEAD OF GAYRUSSIA.RU, AN LGBT ORGANIZATION IN RUSSIA THAT LEADS VARIOUS DEMONSTRATIONS AND PUBLIC PROTESTS. HE IS ALSO A MEMBER OF THE ORGANIZING COMMITTEE OF THE MOSCOW PRIDE MARCH.

In 2006, he launched the very first Pride March in the Russian capital, despite a ban introduced by the mayor at the time, Yuri Luzhkov. The march is banned every year and is violently repressed by the police, even if the demonstration is peaceful. In 2012, a Moscow court banned the Pride March until 2112, for a period of 100 years. Despite various arrests and intimidation by the Russian authorities, Nikolai Alekseev has repeatedly filed complaints with the European Court of Human Rights (ECHR) denouncing the actions of Russia and its President towards LGBT people. The ECHR ruled in his favour in 2010 and condemned Russia for "violating freedom of assembly" (Article 11).

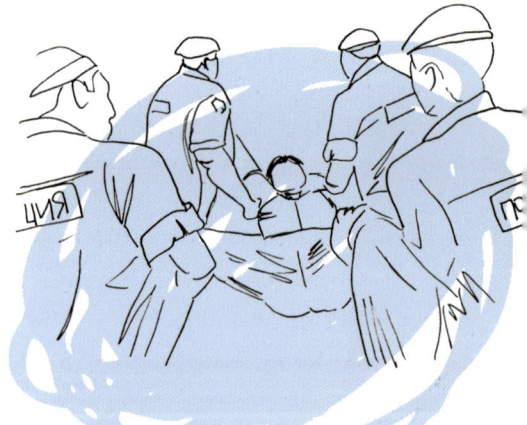

In a country where a federal law introduced in 2013 prohibits distribution of "propaganda of non-traditional sexual relations among minors", punishable by a fine and imprisonment, the plight of LGBTQI+ people is a cause for concern.

Nikolai Alekseev

Beyond enforcing censorship, this law has legitimized LGBTQI+phobic acts and reinforced the conflation between paedophilia and homosexuality in the minds of many Russians. In short, homosexuality is not illegal in the country, but it must not be visible or made public. In 2022, a new "LGBT propaganda" law was passed, banning any mention of gay, lesbian, bisexual and transgender people in film, books, and online.

According to surveys carried out in 2020, one in five Russian people want to "eliminate" gay and lesbian people from society, which is proof of the effectiveness of the government's efforts in influencing public sentiment. Despite the threats against him, Nikolai Alekseev continues to speak in the media, and at conferences, to alert the international community to the situation in Russia.

Beyond Gay: The Politics of Pride, a Canadian documentary by Bob Christie features the organization of the third Moscow Pride March in 2008. In 2009, France 4 aired *Global Resistance* featuring Nikolai Alekseev and his fellow activists from Russia and Belarus. Australian Logan Mucha filmed the attempts to organize Slavic Gay Pride in Minsk, Belarus, in May 2010, and the role played by Nikolai Alekseev, in his documentary film *East Bloc Love.* (2011)

Yelena Grigorieva
1978 – 2019

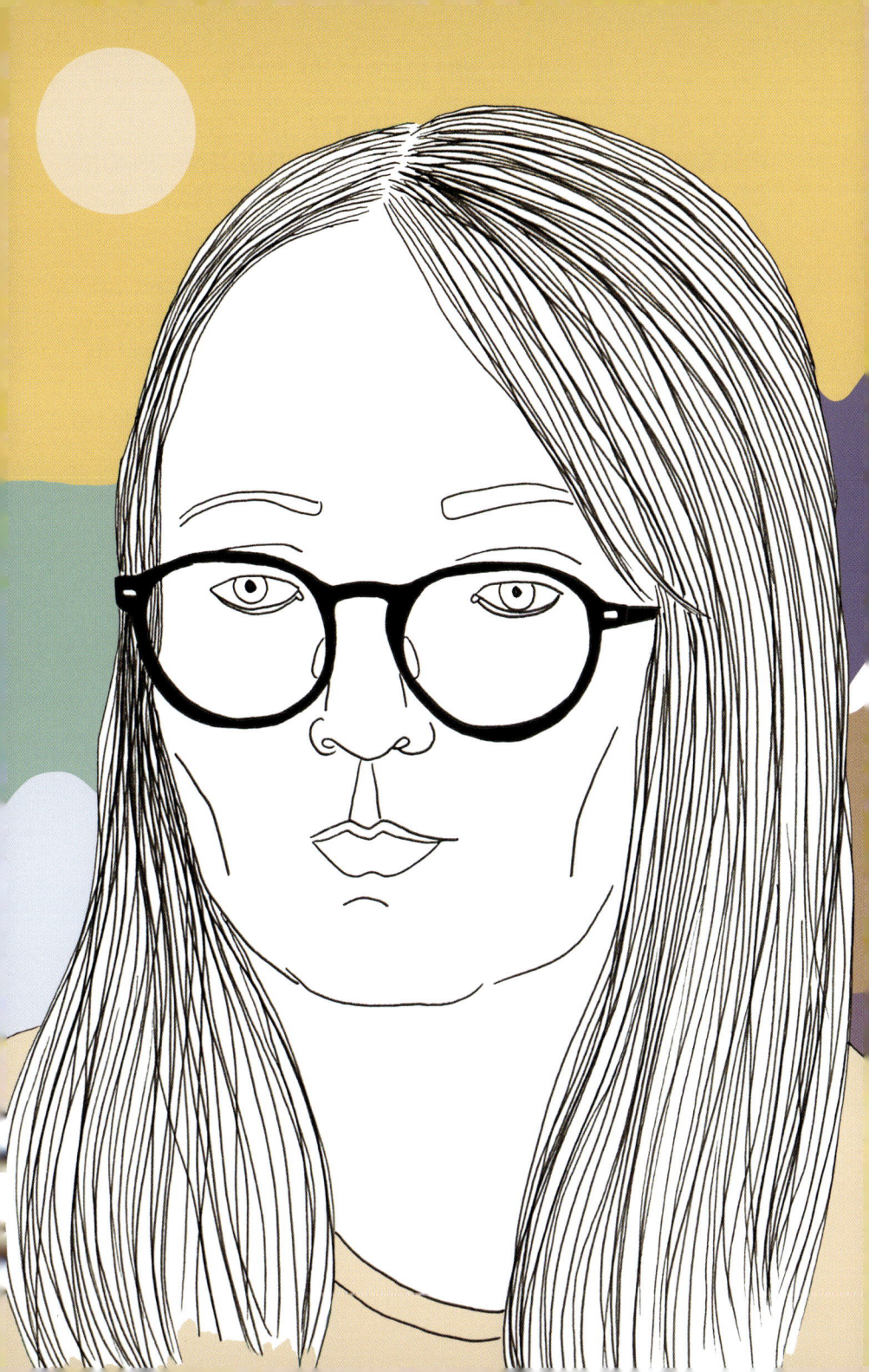

BRUTALLY STABBED TO DEATH IN 2019 IN ST. PETERSBURG, RUSSIA, YELENA GRIGORIEVA IS ONE OF TOO MANY LGBTQ+ ACTIVISTS WHO HAVE DIED FIGHTING FOR THEIR RIGHTS.

Before her body was found in a bush near her home, the activist had received several threats and filed a complaint with the police who failed to take any action. In April 2018, a website called Pila [Saw] was launched, on which they not only published a list of gay men and lesbians, but called for them to be shot. The list included the name of Yelena Grigorieva. She had publicly protested in support of the Khachaturyan sisters, who were arrested for murdering their abusive father in 2018.

The bisexual activist openly posted her opinions on her Facebook profile and participated in various demonstrations and rallies on sensitive topics in Russia, such as the issue of political prisoners and her opposition to Russia's annexation of Crimea. She was killed because she refused to remain silent. However, the assassination of Yelena Grigorieva provoked protests in St. Petersburg. The Pila website disappeared soon after the activist's death as other prominent activists took the case to the media.

This gruesome attack was part of a wave of violence and threats against LGBTQI+ people in Russia where, since 2013, it has been prohibited by law to "promote homosexuality" among minors.

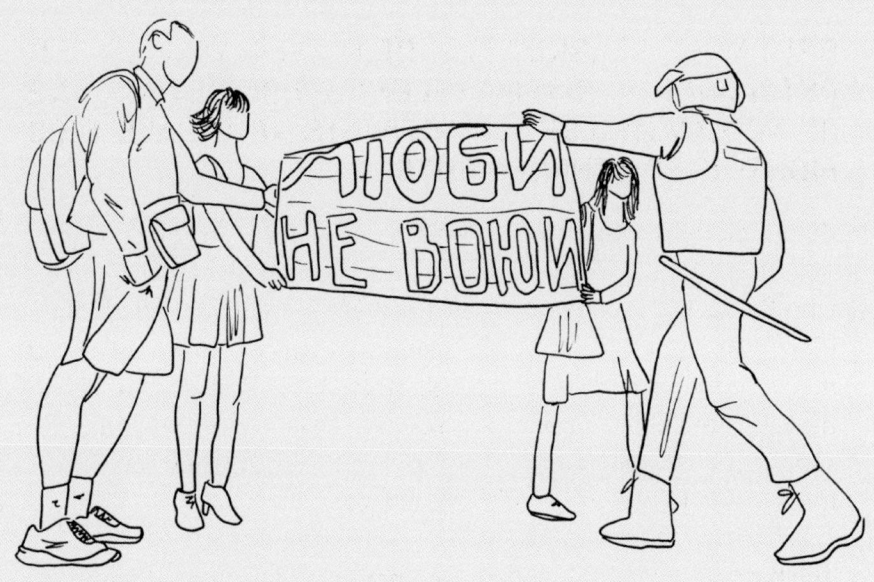

"Many people would like to do in reality what Pila is threatening us with. The idea has emerged that killing people over their sexual orientation is not just normal, but noble," says Mikhail Tumasov, an activist whose name was also featured on the Pila website. The state authorities have failed to take the threat of Saw seriously, even accusing LGBTQI+ activists of creating it to gain asylum in the West. Similar websites continue to operate and threats have continued to be made to LGBTQI+ supporters and activists including to Vitaly Bespalov, the editor of an LGBTQI+ website called Parni PLUS and a friend of Yelena Grigorieva.

In recent years, the former Soviet bloc has hardened its attitudes on LGBTQI+ issues, fuelled by nationalist policies, whether in Chechnya where queer people continue to be hunted, locked up and tortured, in Poland where there are "LGBT-free zones", or in Hungary where anti-LGBT laws were introduced in 2021. Similar sentiment can be seen across Bulgaria and Romania, raising fears about a wider regression of LGBTQI+ rights in Eastern Europe.

Georges Azzi
1979

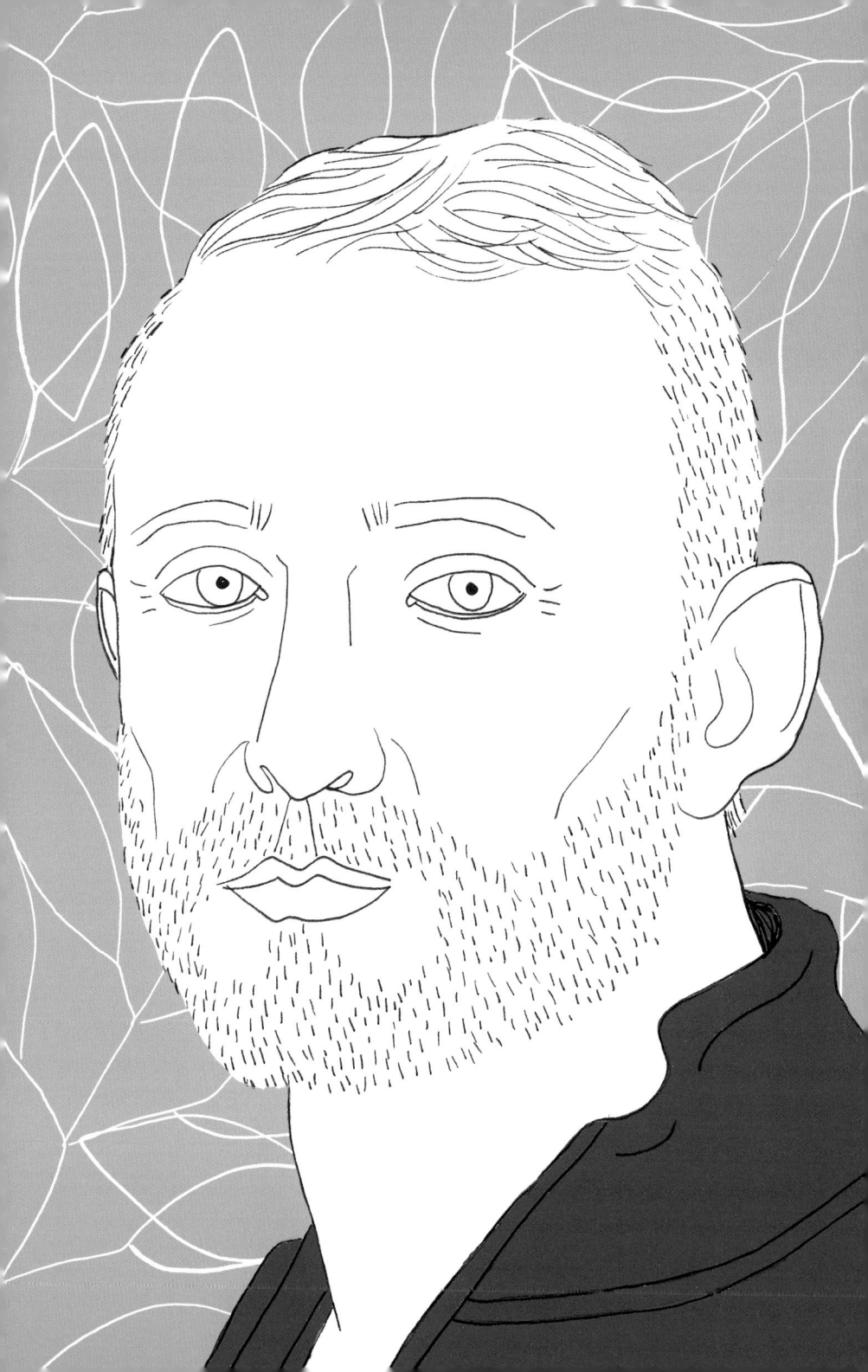

GEORGES AZZI IS THE FOUNDER OF HELEM, WHICH MEANS "DREAM" IN ARABIC. CREATED IN 2004, IT IS THE FIRST ORGANIZATION SET UP TO DEFEND LGBTQI+ PEOPLE IN THE ARAB WORLD, AND OFFERS FREE SCREENINGS, SUPPORT GROUPS AND LEGAL ASSISTANCE, AMONGST OTHER THINGS. HE IS ALSO THE EXECUTIVE DIRECTOR OF THE ARAB FOUNDATION FOR FREEDOM & EQUALITY (AFE), WHICH AIMS TO "ENCOURAGE, PROTECT AND SUPPORT SEXUAL HEALTH, SEXUALITY, GENDER, AND HUMAN RIGHTS MOVEMENTS IN THE MIDDLE EAST AND NORTH AFRICA."

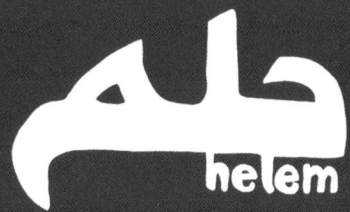

Georges Azzi moved to Paris in 2000, where he earned a degree in engineering, multimedia, and communications and became involved in LGBTQI+ activism. Back in Beirut, and living as an openly gay man, he was the first activist to speak publicly about gay rights on Lebanese television. "I think broadcasting the conversation about LGBT rights is the reason we've made so many advances," he told *Hornet* in March 2018.

In a country where no less than eighteen different religious communities coexist, it is often difficult for LGBTQI+ people to make their voices heard. The Pride March is regularly cancelled, but according to Georges Azzi, Lebanon has made a lot of progress and the LGBTQI+ community has benefited from greater visibility since 2004.

Georges Azzi

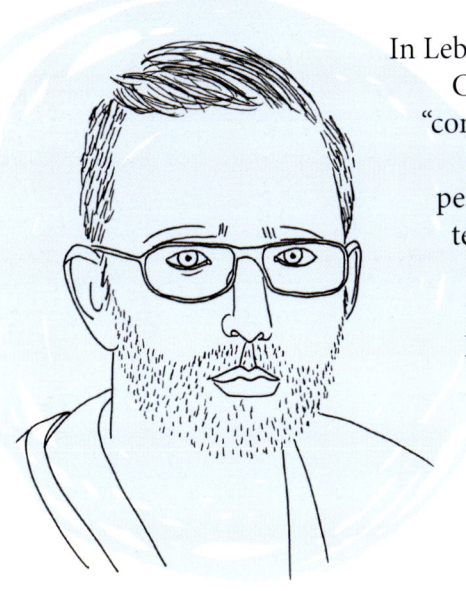

In Lebanon, Article 534 of the Penal Code prohibits sexual relations "contradicting the laws of nature", which allows gay and lesbian people to be sentenced to prison terms ranging from one month to one year. But in July 2018, the Court of Appeal in Mount Lebanon came to a judgement which acquitted nine people accused of homosexuality.

Under his leadership, the first International Day Against Homophobia and Transphobia was celebrated in Lebanon in 2005, bringing visibility to the LGBTQI+ community. He also helped create the first LGBTQI+ publication, *Barra* [Out] Magazine, and a brochure to advise on safe-sex practices for those with HIV, in association with the Ministry of Health.

The treatment of LGBTQI+ people is varied in Lebanon. It is considered one of the most liberal countries in the Middle East, and Beirut is fairly open, with gay bars common in the streets of the capital. However, in June 2022, Lebanese authorities decided to ban LGBTQI+ gatherings, violating LGBTQI+ people's constitutional rights.

Helem has also helped support the human rights of Syrian refugees to Lebanon. Following the Beirut explosion in August, 2020, which damaged the building in which Helem was based, the organization has nevertheless continued to offer support to LGBTQI+ people in the city.

Marielle Franco
1979 – 2018

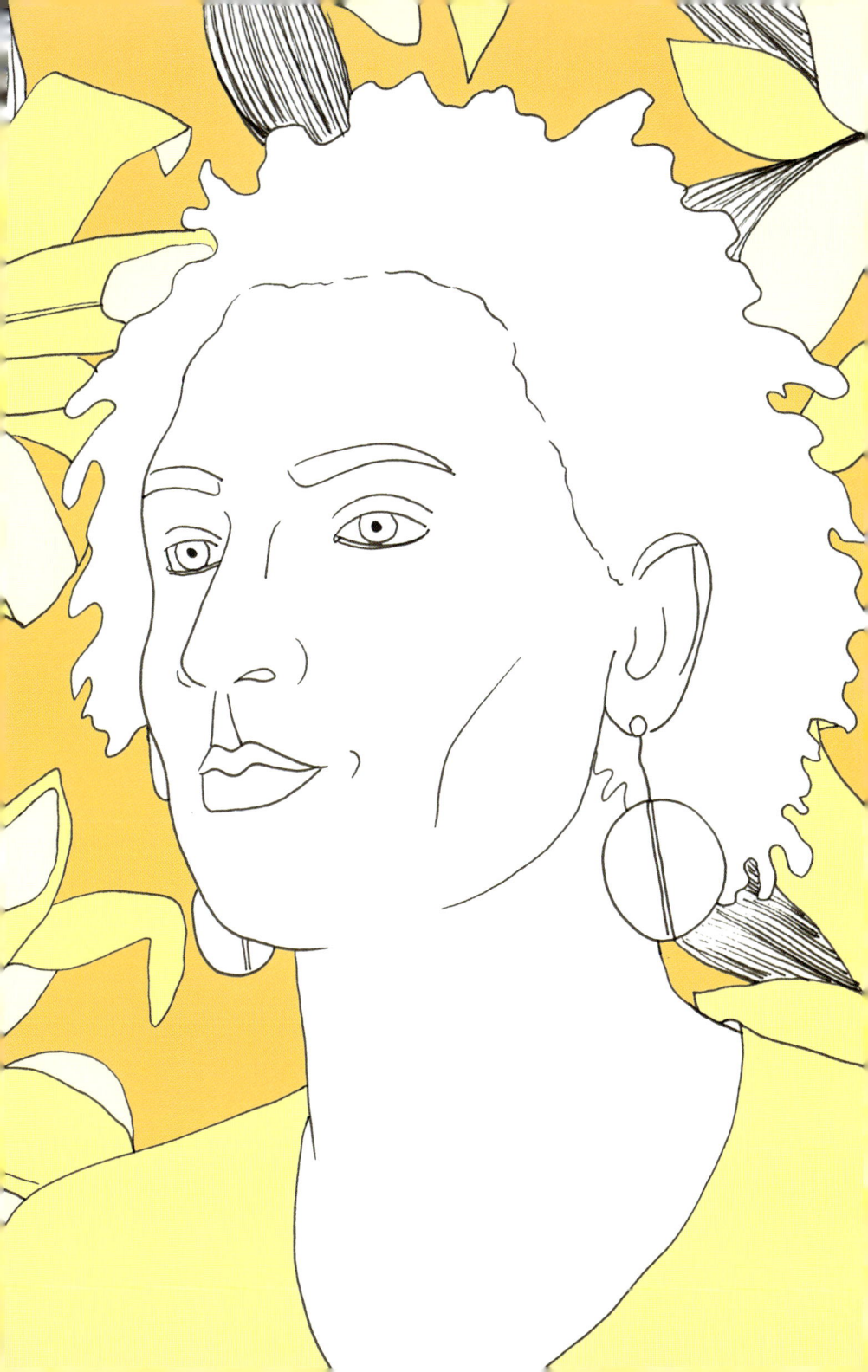

A BLACK, LESBIAN WOMAN FROM THE COMPLEXO DA MARÉ FAVELA IN RIO, MARIELLE FRANCO FOUGHT ALL HER LIFE FOR THE MARGINALIZED: WOMEN, BLACK PEOPLE, LGBTQI+, AND UNDERPRIVILEGED PEOPLE. SHE WAS ASSASSINATED IN 2018.

Her commitment to human rights began after a friend, still a student, was killed by a stray bullet in a shooting. Openly lesbian, she did not hesitate to appear in public with her spouse at a time when she held a position as a municipal councillor of the city of Rio de Janeiro, and was a member of the PSOL (the Socialism and Freedom party). She was convinced that the political face of the country must be diversified.

Even though more and more LGBTQI+ people are voted into political office around the world, the first openly LGBTQI+ person to lead a country was only elected in 2009, in Iceland. Since 2011, elections of LGBTQI+ leaders have been successful in Ireland, Luxembourg, Belgium, and Serbia which shows that attitudes to LGBTQI+ people seem to be changing in Western countries.

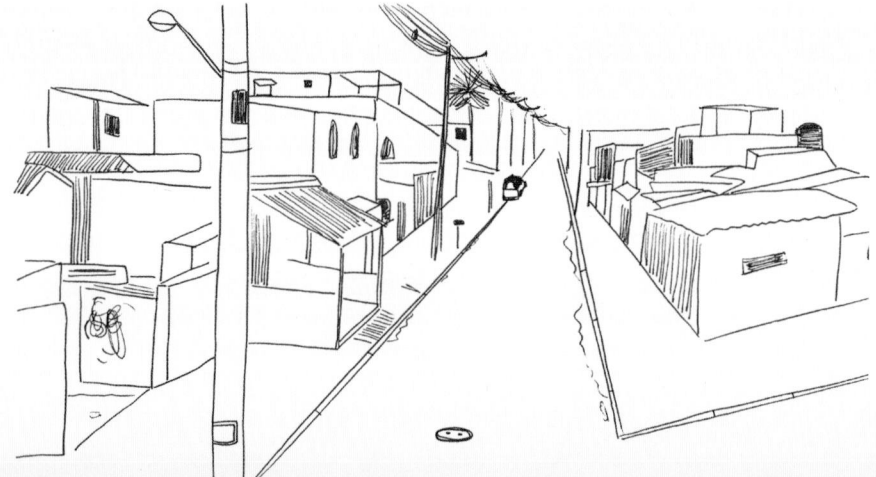

Marielle Franco

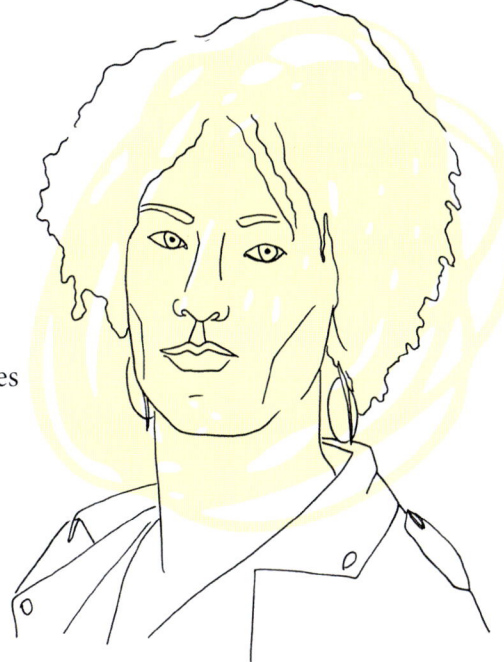

Marielle Franco represented Brazil's political revival, and was assassinated for her activism. She was shot in the head on 1st March 2018, while sitting in her car with her driver and assistant. Marielle Franco is now one of the long list of people who died for the causes they defended.
"They thought they were burying us but we were seeds," she repeated during her meetings and reunions. Her death was seen as a way to silence her on issues considered "embarrassing" for her opponents.

Marielle Franco had spoken passionately, a few days before her death, against police violence and President Michel Temer's decision to give the military full security control of Rio. The investigation into her death progressed slowly despite dozens of marches and several rallies held in her memory, and it wasn't until 2019 that two officers were arrested for her murder. Her partner, Monica Benicio, continues the fight for LGBTQI+ rights.

In Brazil, a country of more than 200 million inhabitants, LGBTQI+ people are extremely vulnerable, particularly when Jair Bolsonaro, the openly LGBTQI+phobic president, came to power. According to research by Statista, an average of 300 LGBTQI+ people are killed in Brazil because of their gender or sexuality every year. The end of Bolsonaro's leadership in 2022 gives some LGBTQI+ campaigners hope of future reforms and a change of public sentiment.

Kasha Jacqueline Nabagesera
1980

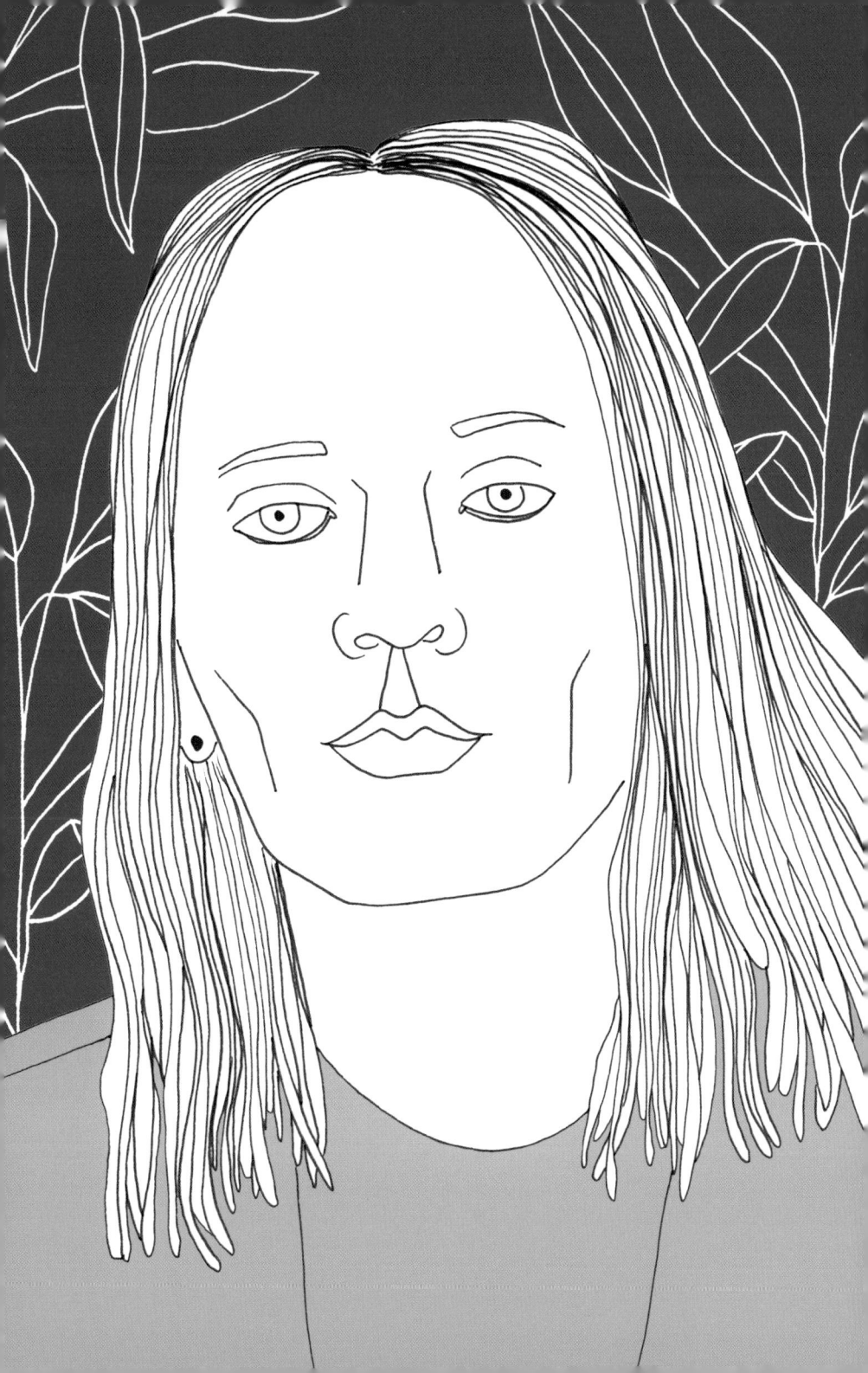

KASHA JACQUELINE NABAGESERA IS A UGANDAN LESBIAN ACTIVIST AND FEMINIST, BORN IN 1980 IN KAMPALA. IN 2003, SHE CREATED FREEDOM AND ROAM UGANDA (FARUG), THE FIRST UGANDAN LGBTQI+ ASSOCIATION.

In 2011, one of her close friends, activist David Kato, was murdered. This only strengthened her determination to advance LGBTQI+ rights in her country. Although she is regularly threatened and assaulted, she knows that many LGBTQI+ people in Uganda need her voice to be heard.

In 2012, she organized the country's first Pride March and, two years later, launched *Bombastic* magazine in Uganda, the country's first LGBTQI+ magazine.

"...history shows us that seemingly insurmountable challenges to equality – the institution of slavery, the denial of women's suffrage, colonial rule and apartheid – have been contested, challenged and repudiated. I believe that through court judgments, through advocacy and through sensitizing our people on the full meaning of fundamental human rights, we shall overcome. And that the day is not far when discrimination against people based on who they love will also be left behind in the wastebasket of history," she said in a speech, accepting an award in 2015.

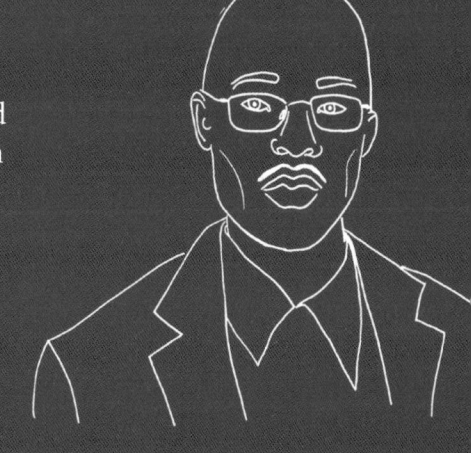

David Kato

Kasha Jacqueline Nabagesera

In Uganda, a gay or lesbian person can be sentenced to life in prison because of their sexuality. New bills raise concerns about the future of LGBTQI+ rights in Uganda, such as in 2019 when a law, which was promulgated and then abolished a few months later, proposed to criminalize any "promotion" of homosexuality and force the population to denounce gay people and lesbians. Activists are already subjected to insults, discrimination, imprisonment, violence and murder; many have left the country.

With each new law aimed at suppressing their rights, the LGBTQI+ community becomes more fearful. The press fuels this homophobic climate by regularly publishing lists of suspected gay people and lesbians, stirring up hatred in a country where religion and the Church have a strong influence.

Kasha Jacqueline Nabagesera received the Martin Ennals Award in 2011 and, in 2015, the Right Livelihood Prize (sometimes known as the alternative Nobel Prize) for her commitment to LGBTQI+ people in Uganda. She also made the cover of the European, African and Middle East version of *Time* magazine in 2015, giving international recognition for this activist with exemplary courage.

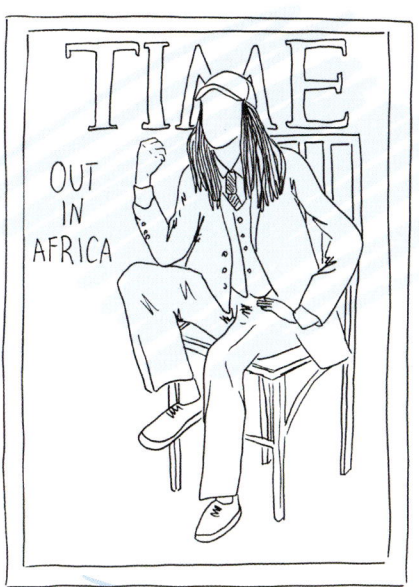

She said: "I may not live to see the freedom I am fighting for but I am just happy to be part of the foundation for change."

David Jay
1982

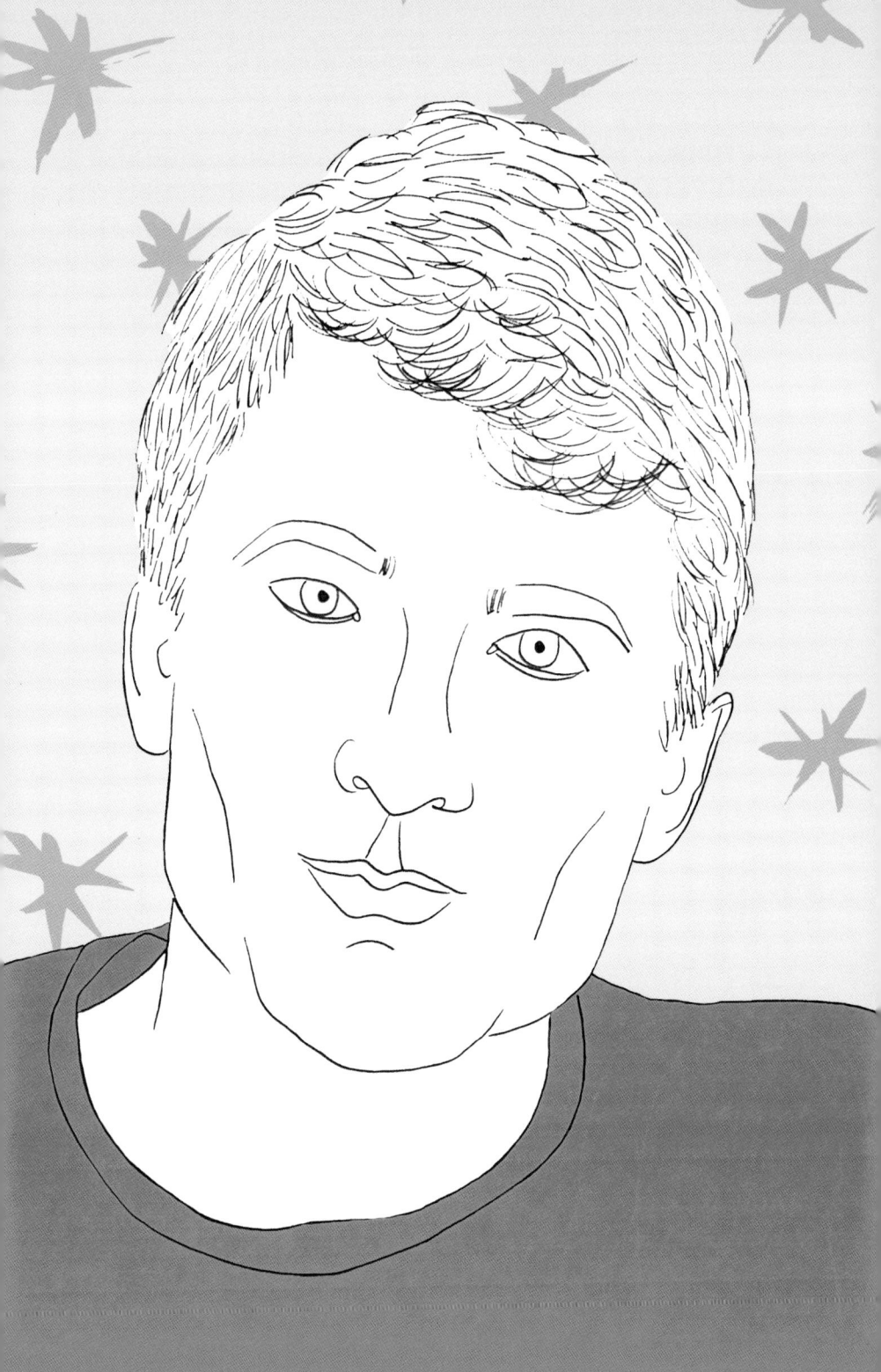

DAVID JAY IS A NORTH AMERICAN ASEXUAL ACTIVIST. HE FOUNDED THE ASEXUAL VISIBILITY AND EDUCATION NETWORK (AVEN), WHICH AIMS TO SHARE INFORMATION, PROMOTE ADVOCACY, AND WIDEN VISIBILITY OF ASEXUALITY.

Asexuality is a sexual orientation like homosexuality, heterosexuality, bisexuality or pansexuality. An asexual person is a person who does not feel sexual attraction but may experience feelings of love for a person. About 1% of the world's population is believed to be asexual, according to the only study on the subject conducted in 2004 by psychologist Anthony Bogaert.

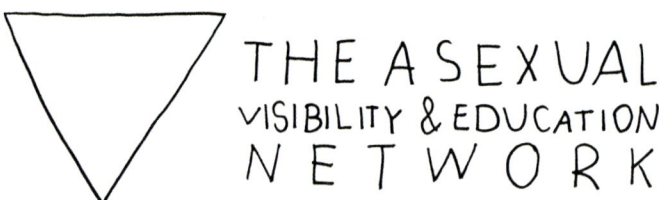

In a hypersexualized world, David Jay is often confronted with questions and sometimes even contempt. "People are very intrigued, they find it strange. They find it hard to imagine that sex can play no role in a life. What is the hardest thing for them to grasp is the link between sexuality and love," he explains.

In 2001, frustrated to find so few resources on the subject, David Jay created a website where asexual people could exchange information. This was the beginning of AVEN.

David Jay

"When I realized I was asexual, I spent a lot of time discovering what it meant to me," says the activist. In 2006, he launched a major campaign with the American media to amplify the voices of asexual people, who are often misunderstood and perceived as outcasts with medical or mental disorders. The lack of representation in the media has impacted how asexuality is perceived by the general public.

In 2011, the documentary *(A)sexual* was released and featured David Jay.

AVEN now has about 70,000 members and serves as a resource and information centre for asexual people, those who have questions, academic researchers, and the press. AVEN members make their cause visible, distribute information brochures, lead workshops, and organize meetings. Even if the road to full recognition is still long, this fight is paying off and since 2013, asexuality is no longer recognized as a pathology by the American Psychiatric Association, but as a sexual orientation.

The first International Asexuality Day was celebrated on 6 April, 2021 with over 25 different national asexuality organizations participating. Asexuals have faced discrimination from other queer groups and some LGBTQI+ organizations are unwilling or unsure whether to include them within the LGBTQI+ community.

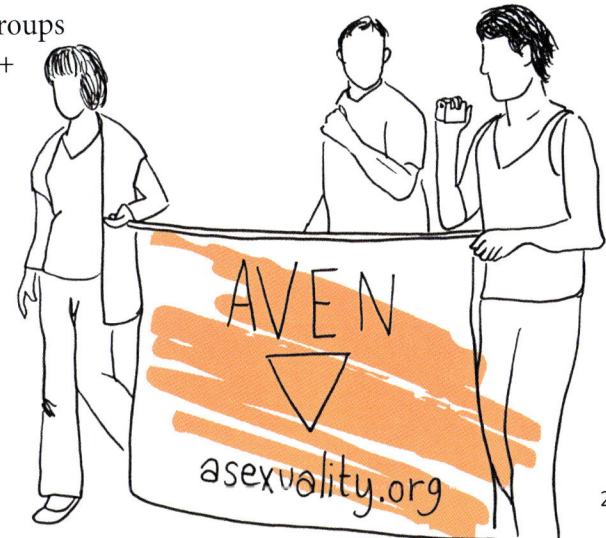

Linda Baumann
1982

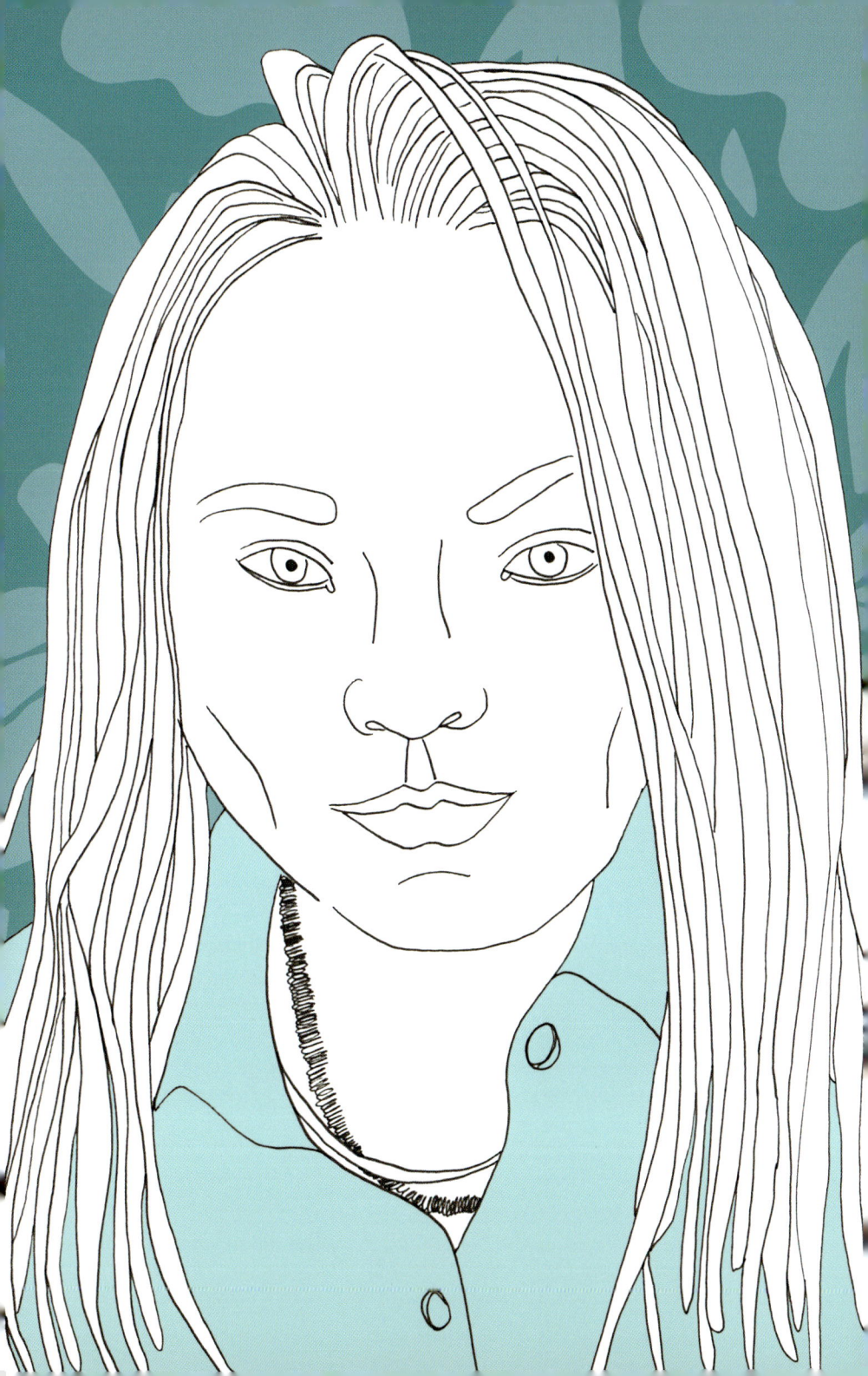

A TIRELESS AND DETERMINED ACTIVIST, LINDA BAUMANN FIGHTS FOR THE EMANCIPATION OF LGBTQI+ PEOPLE IN NAMIBIA AND RESPECT FOR THEIR EXISTENCE.

After volunteering for the Red Cross while still a teenager, Linda Baumann began campaigning for community rights at a meeting of a local LGBTQI+ organization in 2001. "I saw so many people who looked like me," she said, after she had spent years rejecting her sexuality. Linda also worked at the Namibia Planned Parenthood Association (NAPPA) where she was an advocate for sexual and reproductive health and the rights of young people in particular.

In 2003, she co-founded the Coalition of African Lesbians (CAL), "a feminist, activist and Pan-Africanist network of fourteen organizations in ten countries in sub-Saharan Africa committed to advancing freedom, justice and bodily autonomy for all women on the African continent and beyond," according to its website.

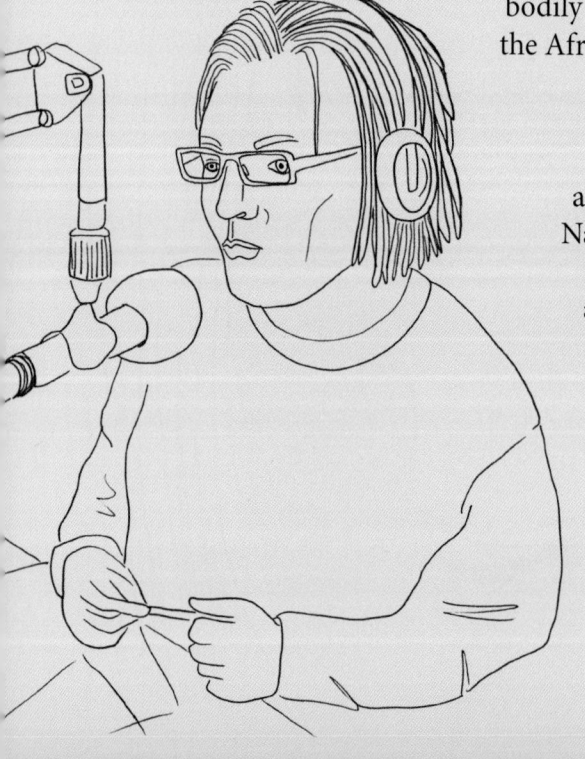

For two years, she hosted and produced *Talking Pink*, a Namibian radio show focused specifically on queer issues, and also frequently spoke to the Namibian media about LGBTQI+ rights. Gaining a public media profile in Namibia has unfortunately not been without consequences, and Linda Baumann is regularly the target of threats and intimidation.

Linda Baumann

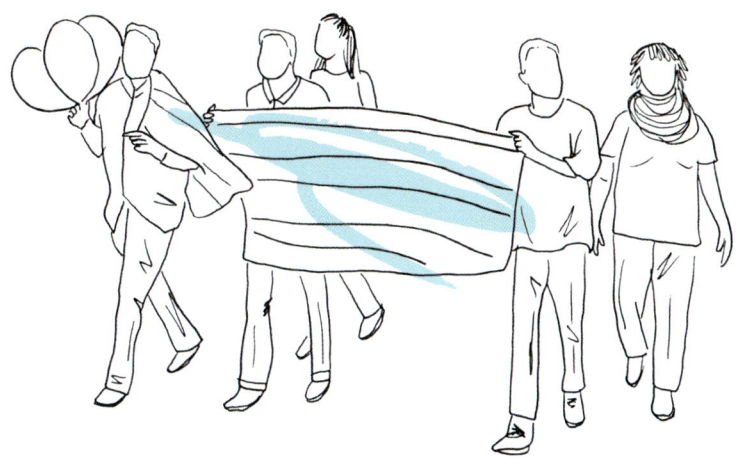

In Namibia, relations between men, considered "against nature", are prohibited by a law passed in 1927, when the country was under colonial rule. Although no convictions have taken place since Namibia's independence in 1990, the law's existence helps to justify LGBTQI+-phobic acts and hate crimes. Nevertheless, the first Pride March in the country's capital, Windhoek, in 2017, and the organization of a lesbian festival in 2018, suggest that attitudes are changing. Organized by OutRight Namibia, led by Linda Baumann, the march brought together 200 people, and took place without incident, while allowing LGBTQI+ people to celebrate and become publicly visible for a few hours.

The activist now works for the Namibia Diverse Women's Association, an intersectional feminist organization, and remains very active in various forums, national and international NGOs.

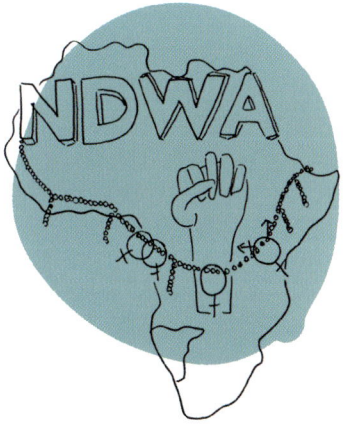

Her work has earned her recognition in her country and in the rest of the world. She was awarded the African Feather of the Year Award in 2019 for her LGBTQI+ activism.

Megan Rapinoe
1985

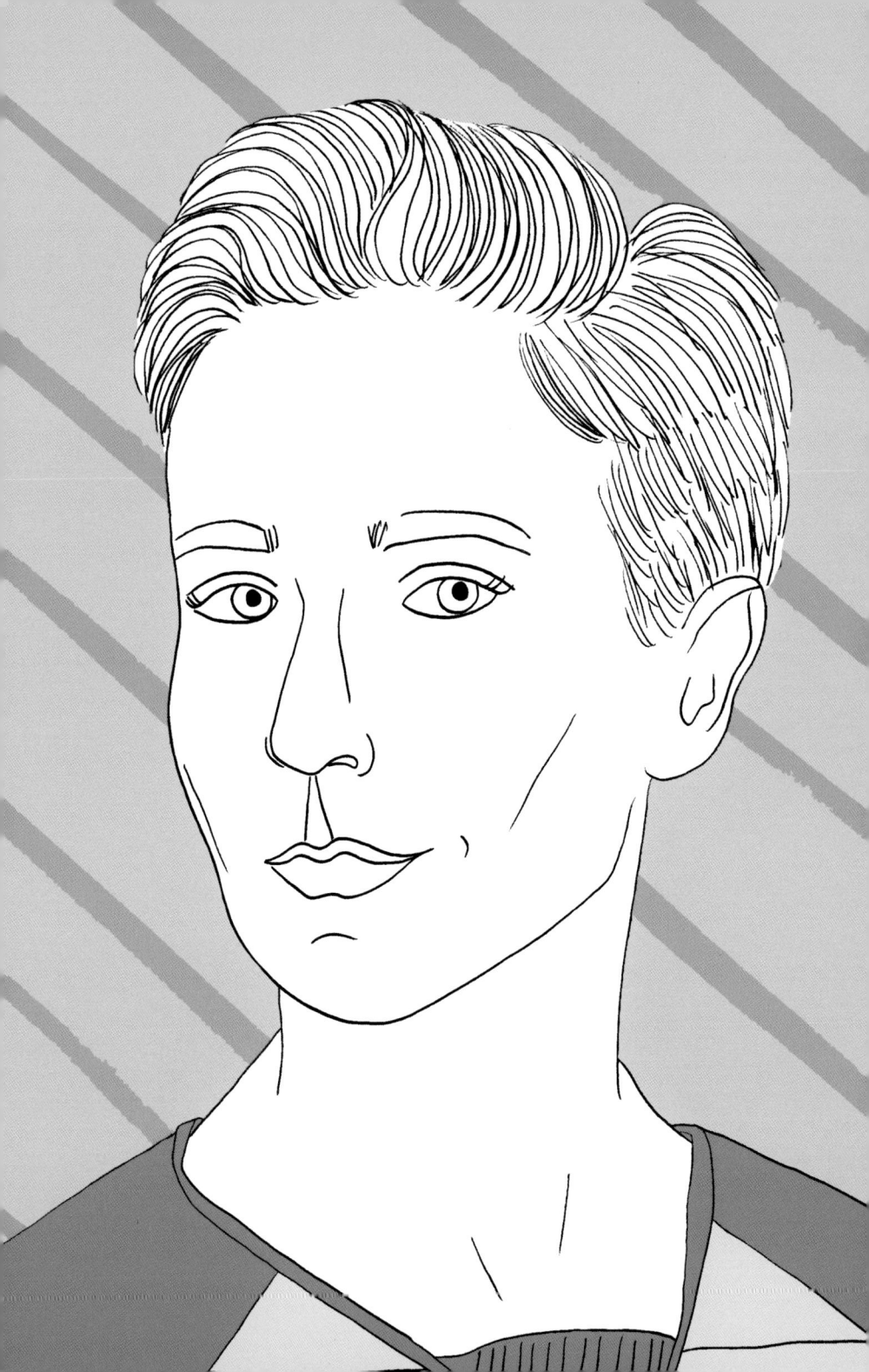

MEGAN RAPINOE IS AN ICONIC AMERICAN FOOTBALL PLAYER AND AMBASSADOR FOR ATHLETE ALLY, A NON-PROFIT FOCUSED ON ENDING HOMOPHOBIA AND TRANSPHOBIA WITHIN SPORTS.

Megan has used her international popularity to further various social causes. She was the first white athlete to kneel during the American national anthem, a movement started by Colin Kaepernick to protest police brutality against African Americans.

Megan began playing football at an early age, and was the star of the University of Portland's women's soccer team as a student there. She graduated in 2008, and almost immediately started playing professionally. After a few years playing for various club teams in the U.S., she started playing for international teams in Australia and France. Meanwhile, she was still playing for the U.S. on an international level, and helped the U.S. Women's National Team win a gold medal at the 2012 Olympics, and win the 2015 and 2019 Women's World Cups.

She publicly came out in *Out* magazine in 2012, stating that she felt there was a need for people to see queer representation within sport. "I feel like sports in general are still homophobic, in the sense that not a lot of people are out. I feel everyone is really craving [for] people to come out. People want – they need – to see that there are people like me playing soccer for the good ol' U.S. of A."

She has been involved in several campaigns relating to women and LGBTQI+ equality. In 2013, she became an ambassador for Athlete Ally. She's also worked with Gay, Lesbian & Straight Education Network (GLSEN) and the United States Olympic & Paralympic Committee.

Megan Rapinoe

In 2019, she was part of a group of women who brought a lawsuit against the United States Soccer Federation, hoping to achieve equal pay.

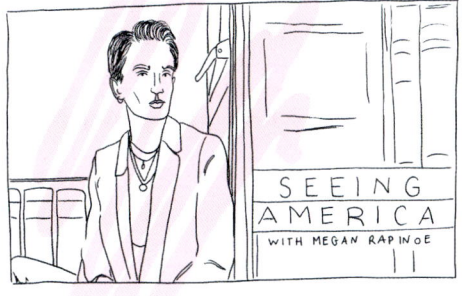

Megan has not been shy in politics either, criticizing Donald Trump and endorsing Elizabeth Warren in the 2020 Democratic Party presidential primaries. Her 2020 television programme *Seeing America with Megan Rapinoe* saw her in conversation with Alexandria Ocasio-Cortez, amongst other progressive thought-leaders.

Megan has been dating her fiancé, fellow athlete Sue Bird, since 2016. In 2018, they became the first same-sex couple to appear on the cover of *The Body Issue*.

Her outspoken nature and distinctive appearance has definitely brought new attention to women's football around the world. To those who are just discovering the game, particularly after the 2022 European Cup, she says "Welcome, everybody, to the party. You're extremely f***ing late, but fine."

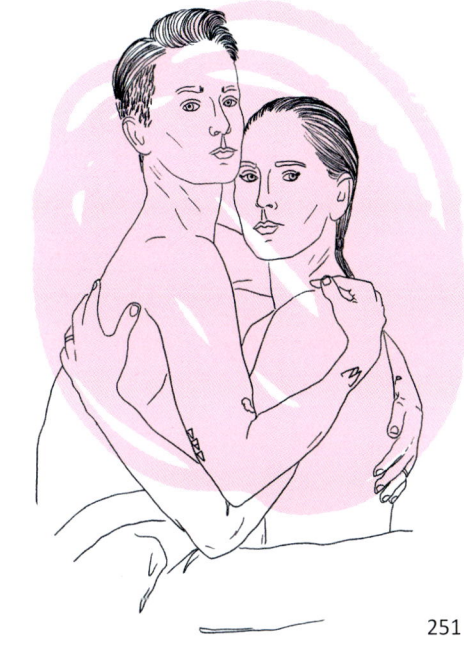

In July, 2022, she was presented with the Presidential Medal of Freedom, the highest honour given to American civilians, by President Joe Biden in a ceremony at the White House.

Elliot Page
1987

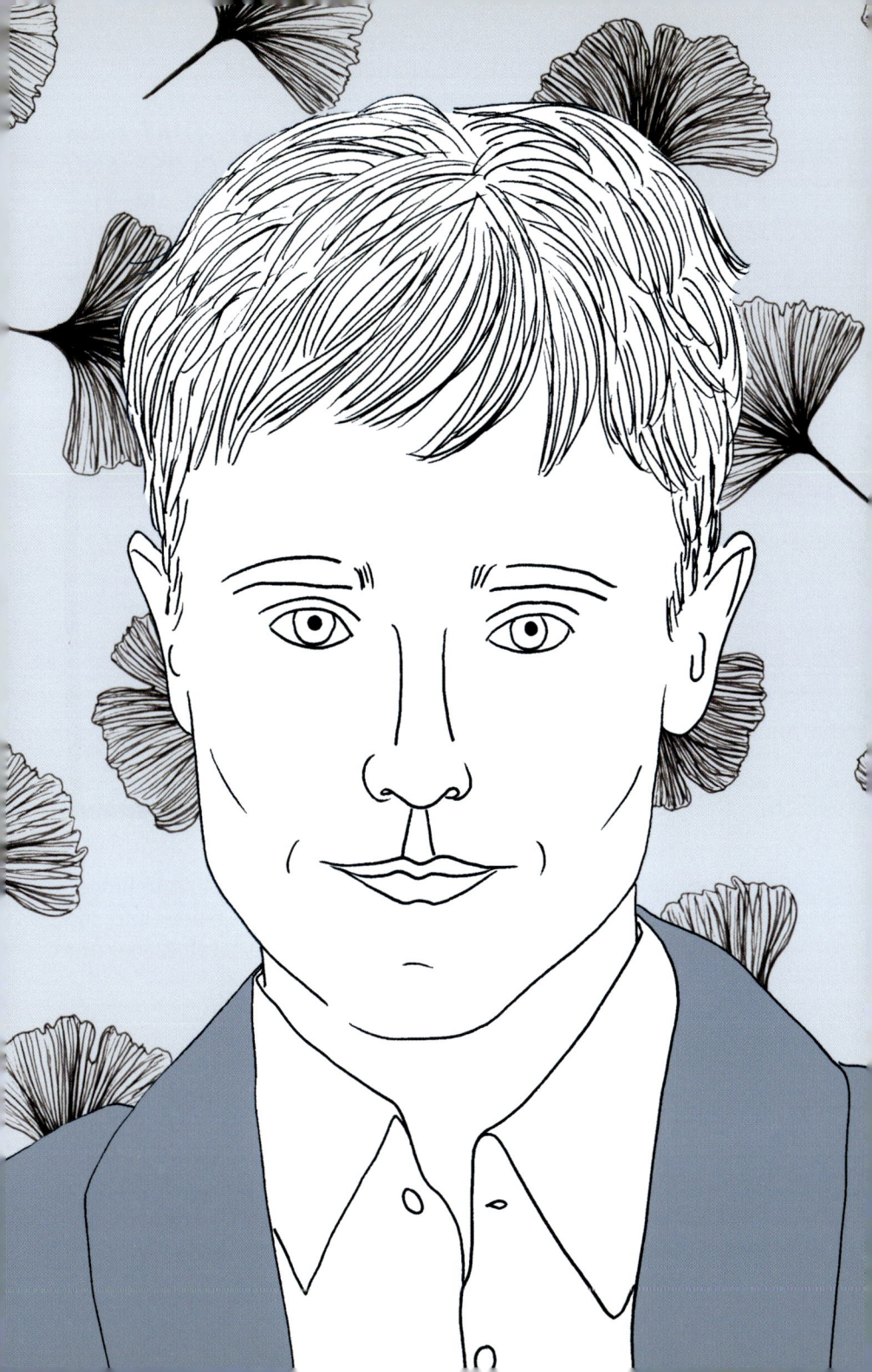

"I LOVE THAT I AM TRANS. AND I LOVE THAT I AM QUEER. AND THE MORE I HOLD MYSELF CLOSE AND FULLY EMBRACE WHO I AM, THE MORE I DREAM, THE MORE MY HEART GROWS AND THE MORE I THRIVE.", ELLIOT PAGE WROTE IN A LETTER TO HIS SOCIAL MEDIA FANS IN 2020.

Growing up in Nova Scotia in Canada, Elliot Page (formerly Ellen Page) began acting in television roles from the age of ten. His break out role was playing Juno, the young woman character in the film of the same name (2007). Other major roles followed in *Inception*, *X-Men* and more recently in the series *Umbrella Academy* streaming on Netflix. However, Elliot Page is now also well-known for his role in transgender and feminist activism.

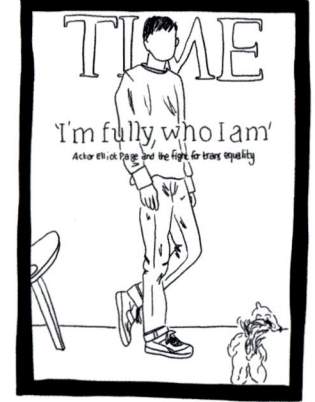

He came out as a lesbian in 2014 in a moving speech at the "Time to Thrive" event, organized by the HRC (Human Rights Campaign). Some time later, he spoke in interviews about the pressure he had long suffered, behind the scenes of the film industry, to hide his sexuality. In 2020, he publicly came out as transgender and, in 2021, became the first transgender man to appear on the cover of *Time* magazine.

He co-starred with Julianne Moore in the 2015 film *Freeheld*. Inspired by a true story, it tells the fight of Inspector Laurel Hester who falls in love with a young woman, Stacie. Things go fine until Laurel discovers she has lung cancer and wants to donate her pension to Stacie. The County Freeholders refuse. Not being married, and marriage for all not being legal, they must fight to win their case. They win their case just before Laurel's death,

Elliot Page

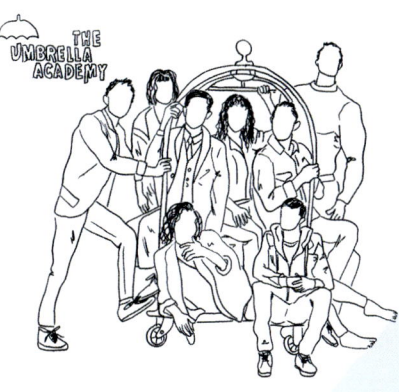

laying the foundations of marriage equality in the United States.

Bringing underrepresented stories and experiences to the screen is what Elliot Page wants to do. By reminding us that every right is hard-won and how inequality can destroy lives, this activist is aware of the platform given to him. He said in a speech: "It has become increasingly clear to me that we all need to use our influence, whatever it may be, to help others." In 2016, along with his friend Ian Daniel, he launched a documentary series, *Gaycation*, and went to meet LGBTQI+ communities around the world to discuss the different rights granted to each community. He does not hesitate to challenge homophobic American personalities, and politicians introducing anti-LGBTQI+ measures.

While American films and TV series continue to underrepresent LGBTQI+ people, progress has been made in recent years. In 2019, according to a study conducted by GLAAD, the number of LGBTQI+ characters regularly seen on U.S. television during prime-time reached more than 10%. A record helped by Elliot Page's character in the television series *Umbrella Academy* who transitions along with him.

Hanne Gaby Odiele
1988

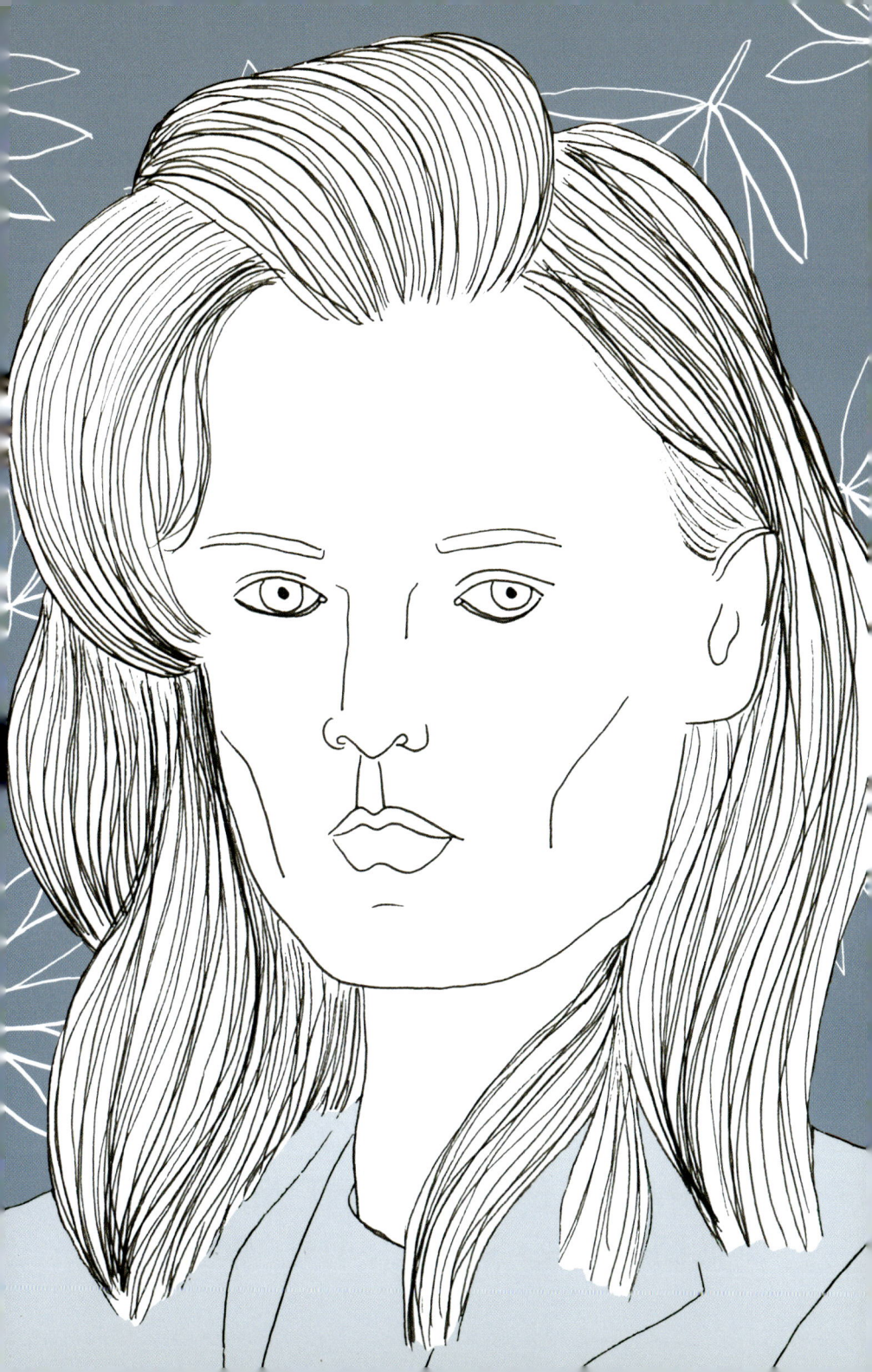

HANNE GABY ODIELE IS A BELGIAN INTERSEX MODEL. CHANEL, LOUIS VUITTON, BALENCIAGA, JEAN-PAUL GAULTIER... SHE HAS MODELLED FOR THE BIGGEST FASHION BRANDS AND APPEARED IN *VOGUE*.

INTERSEX RIGHTS are HUMAN RIGHTS

In many countries, when a child is born intersex, it is doctors and parents who choose the gender of the child. They are then operated on to "correct" their sex or appearance, and sometimes subjected to hormonal treatments. According to the United Nations, 1.7% of the population is born intersex, (the same percentage who are born with red hair).

Beyond the physical suffering associated with this surgery, the psychological and emotional damage is considerable. These operations, which are not necessary in the majority of cases, often lead to complications.

This is what happened to Hanne Gaby Odiele, who underwent an operation at the age of ten to remove their internal testicles, and a vaginal reconstruction operation at the age of eighteen, even though they were born with no uterus or ovaries. Neither they, nor their parents, had heard of the term "intersex" before they came across an article of a young woman recounting the same operations with unfortunate consequences for her physical and mental health.

"I AM VERY PROUD TO WORK WITH INTERACT. I DON'T WANT ANY OTHER CHILDREN TO SUFFER THE WAY I DID."

Hanne Gaby Odiele

"Like most intersex kids, I have been subjected to irreversible, unconsented and unnecessary surgeries… People want to put us in boxes: male or female. But in reality, sex is on a spectrum. Intersex is just proof of that. It's important for me to speak up now: those surgeries have been happening for way too long and I want them to stop now," she stated on her Instagram account.

Since they disclosed their intersex status, they have been an advocate for intersex human rights, working with interACT, a non-profit organization that campaigns for the rights of intersex youth to choose what happens to their bodies.

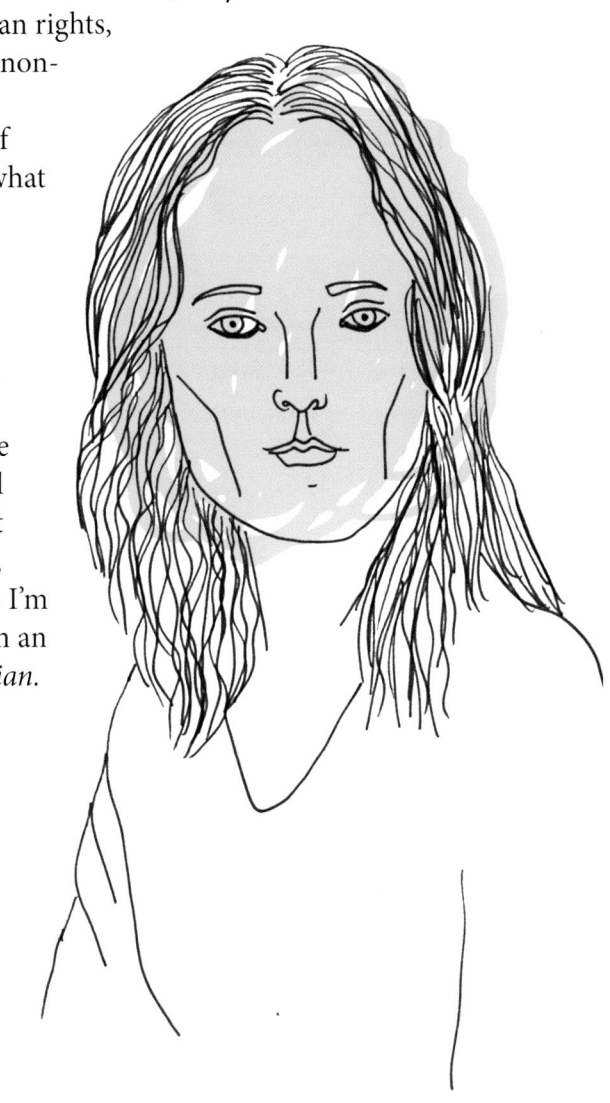

"There's a kind of shame placed on our bodies, like we're not supposed to talk about it," she says. "I will never know what it is to be a cis-gender woman, I will never be able to talk about a period or having a child, but I'm not a man either – I'm proud intersex," she said in an interview with *The Guardian*.

In 2019, they came out as non-binary in Flemish newspaper *De Morgen*. By telling their story they have made visible a subject still rarely discussed in the media.

Olly Alexander
1990

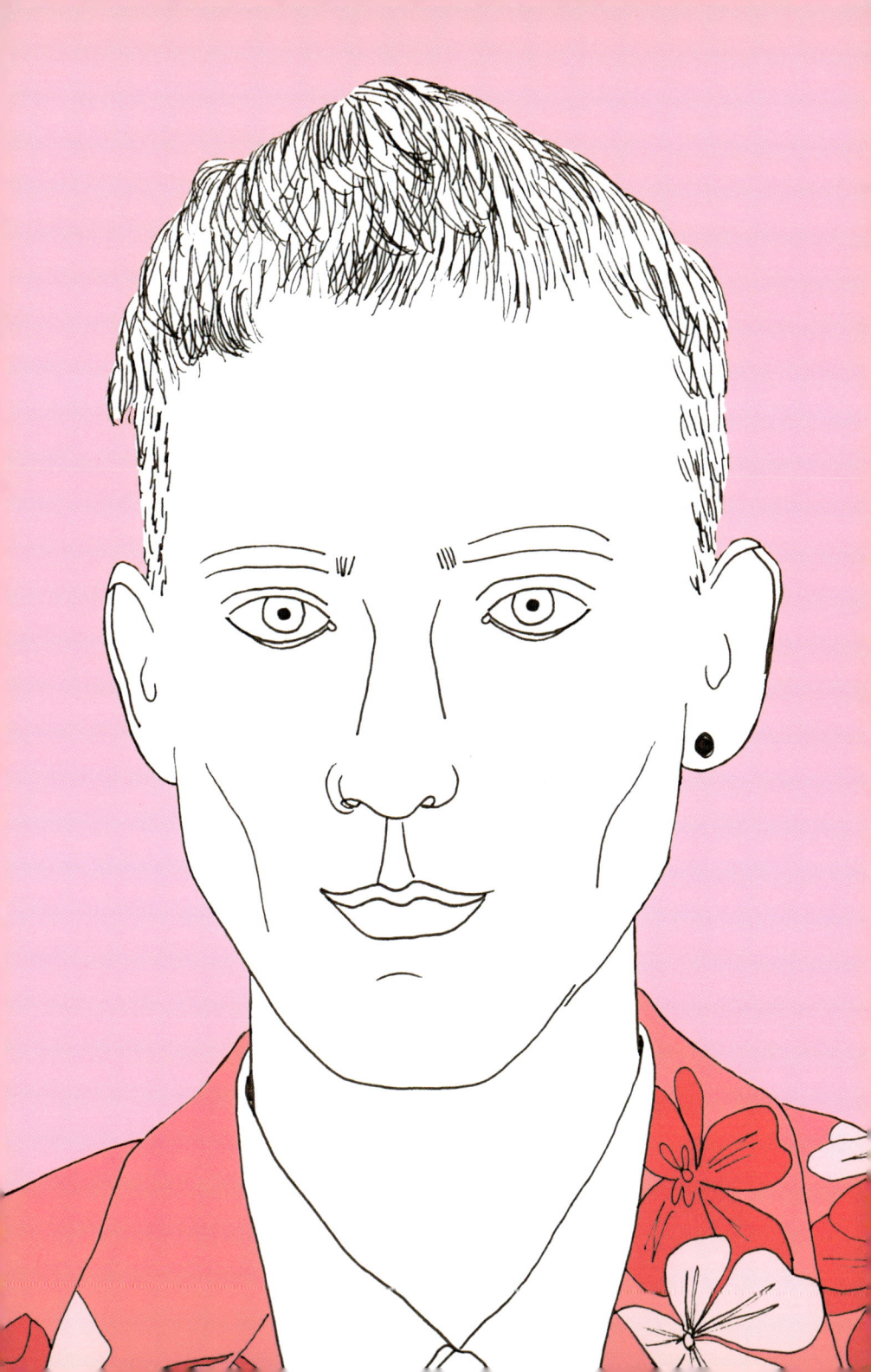

ACTOR AND LEAD SINGER OF THE BRITISH POP GROUP YEARS & YEARS, OLLY ALEXANDER IS PART OF A MODERN GENERATION OF ARTISTS BORN IN THE 1990S, WHOSE DISCOURSE ON GENDER AND SEXUALITY IS MUCH MORE OPEN AND UNINHIBITED THAN THAT OF HIS ELDERS.

Openly gay, the singer of the hits "King" and "Take Shelter" no longer hesitates to shake up the codes and conventions of the pop music genre, which is arguably too heteronormative. The lyrics of some of his songs speak openly about love and sexual relationships between men, such as the single, "Sanctify", which is about heterosexual men who experiment sexually with gay men.

In an interview, Olly Alexander also denounced the homophobia which persists in the music industry: "We wouldn't be where we are today without all the gay artists that have come out before us and broken down so many barriers. But the barriers aren't gone. Particularly for less privileged members of the queer community. There is this very insidious casual homophobia that exists in the fabric of everything including the music industry."

Aware of representing only a part of the LGBTQI+ community, Olly Alexander nevertheless tries to push the envelope through his music and his speeches. On *Palo Santo*, the band's second album with more assertive lyrics, he says: "I don't think I could have written the new songs ten years earlier."

The music industry has seen the emergence of a multitude of queer artists in recent years, such as MNEK, Sophie, Troye Sivan, Kehlani, Hayley Kiyoko, and Perfume Genius, who do not hesitate to speak out, in their songs or publicly, about their sexuality, gender or the stigma experienced by LGBTQI+ people.

Olly Alexander

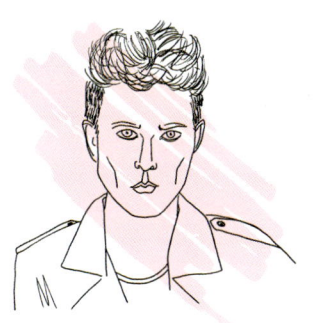
Perfume Genius

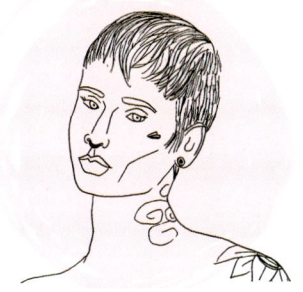
Kehlani

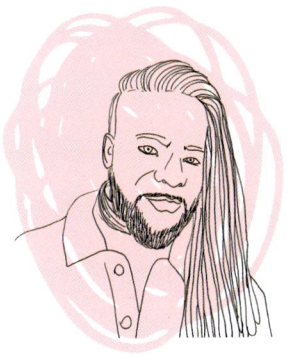
MNEK

In 2017, in the BBC documentary *Growing Up Gay*, Olly Alexander talked about his childhood and looked at why LGBTQI+ people are more likely to suffer from mental illness and suicidal thoughts. The documentary looks back at Olly's journey and childhood; he talks about his depression, his mental health, the harassment he suffered, and also goes to meet other queer people who are victims of LGBTQI+phobia. Depression, anxiety, eating disorders, self-harm, suicide… LGBTQI+ youth are between two and seven times more likely to attempt to end their lives, according to a report by SOS Homophobia published in 2018.

In 2021, Olly Alexander starred in the TV series *It's a Sin*, which depicts the lives of a gay friendship group during the HIV/AIDS crisis in London from 1981 to 1991. Based on the lives of Russell T Davies' friends, the TV show brought the realities of the crisis to a new generation, and led to an increase in HIV testing in the UK.

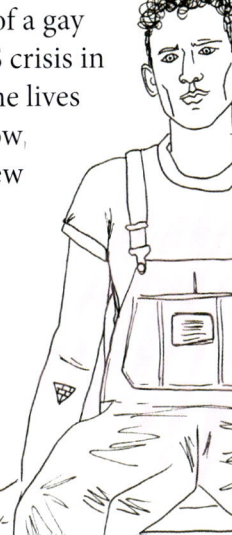

Artist and activist, Olly Alexander continues to speak out for LGBTQI+ people in a society where there is still a great deal of homophobic and transphobic discrimination.

Hande Kader
1993 – 2016

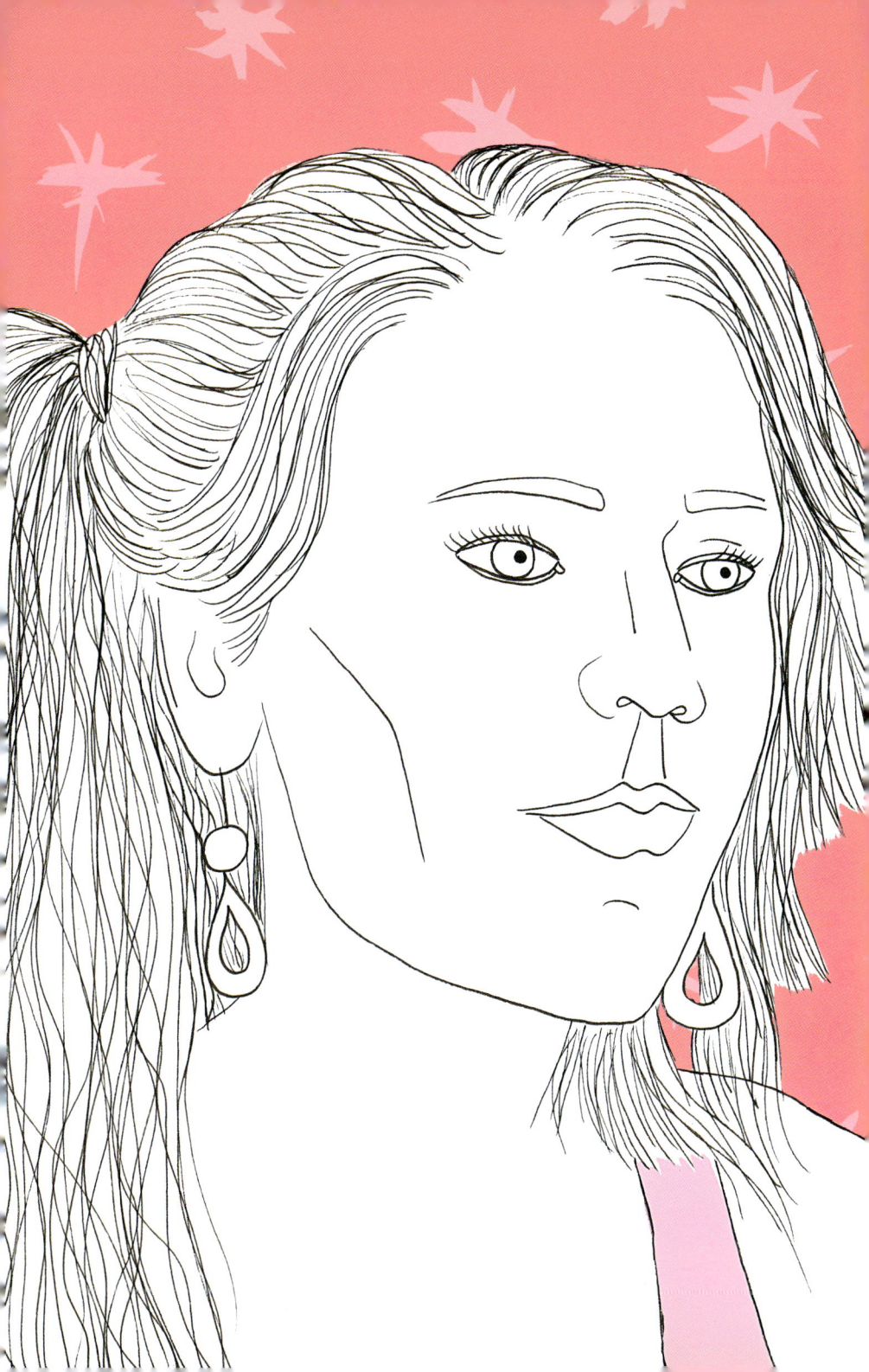

HANDE KADER WAS A TURKISH TRANSGENDER ACTIVIST AND SEX WORKER WHO ROSE TO PROMINENCE AFTER CHALLENGING THE POLICE AT THE ISTANBUL PRIDE MARCH IN JUNE 2015.

Tear gas, rubber bullets, and water cannons were used against a crowd that came to demonstrate peacefully. The march was violently repressed and cancelled just a few hours before its launch following the orders of President Erdogan, under the pretext of "maintaining public order" and because it clashed with Ramadan. Photos and videos of the twenty-two-year-old standing up to the police spread around the world.

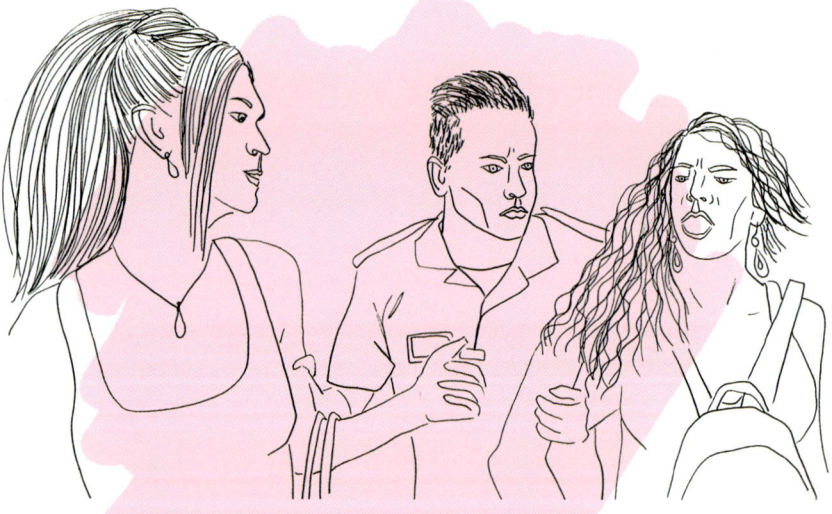

Last seen getting into a customer's car in early August 2016, Hande Kader's body was found burned and mutilated on the side of a road on August 8, 2016. Hundreds of LGBTQI+ people have suffered the same fate in Turkey in recent years, including a gay Syrian refugee in 2016, who was found hanged and maimed. The country's LGBTQI+ associations denounced the media silence on Hande Kader's murder and called for demonstrations a few days after the discovery of her body.

Hande Kader

Although same-sex sexual relations are not illegal in Turkey, there has been an evident decline in LGBTQI+ rights since 2013.

The government, which emerged from the Islamic-conservative AK (Justice and Development Party), has banned Istanbul Pride marches for several years and has also suspended all LGBTQI+ events in the country. "From November 18, 2017, considering public sensitivities, all film events, shows, round tables, conferences, exhibitions, etc. organized by LGBTQI+ communities will be banned until further notice in our province, in order to guarantee peace and security," read the website of the provincial government of the capital, Ankara. These decisions followed various remarks made by President Erdogan and members of the government such as Selma Aliye Kavaf, Minister of Family and Women, who in 2010 described homosexuality as a "disease" to be "treated".

Banning these events and reducing the visibility of LGBTQI+ people means depriving thousands of Turkish LGBTQI+ people of a necessary platform and safe spaces. Beyond the bans, it is also a way to further stigmatize LGBTQI+ people and fuel LGBTQI+phobic discrimination.

In 2021, the International Lesbian,Gay, Bisexual, Trans and Intersex Association in Europe ranked Turkey second to last on the legal equality index, stating that LGBTQI+ people faced "countless hate crimes".

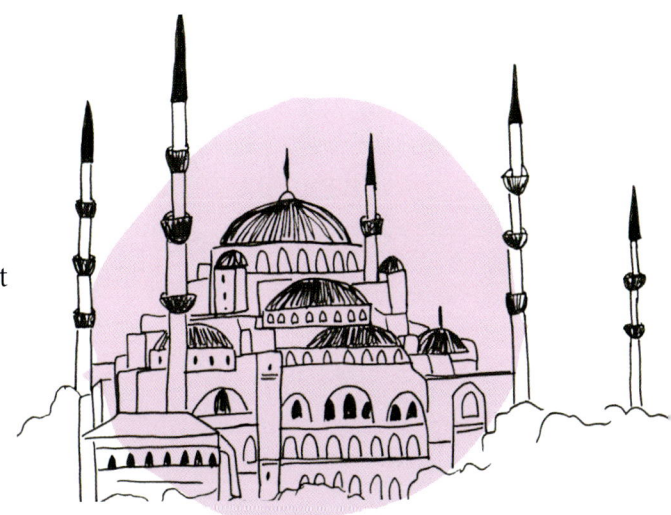

Bouhdid Belhadi
1993

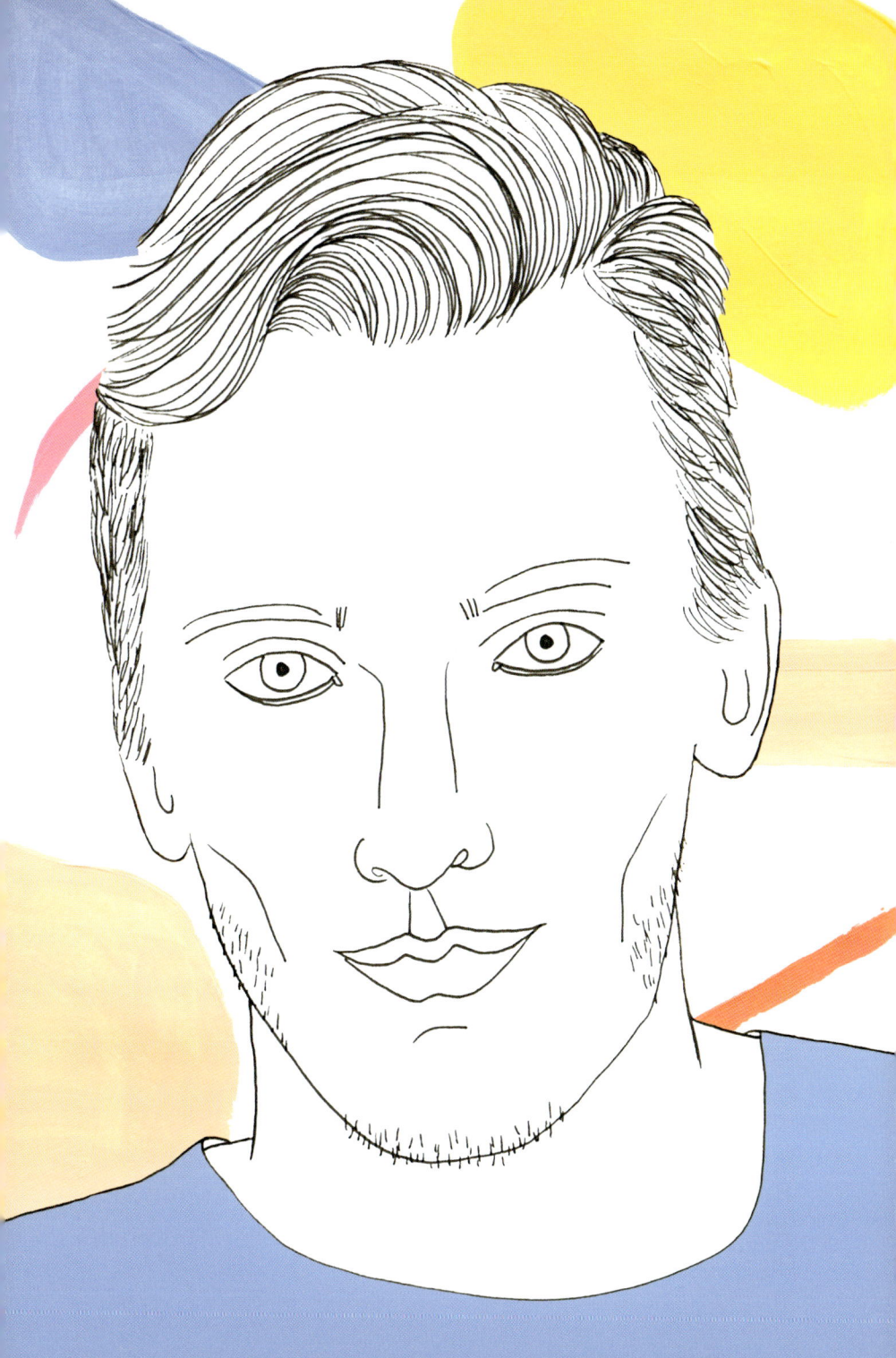

BOUHDID BELHADI IS A LAWYER AND EXECUTIVE DIRECTOR OF THE ASSOCIATION, SHAMS, CREATED IN 2015 AND AIMED AT DEFENDING THE RIGHTS OF LGBTQI+ PEOPLE IN TUNISIA.

He is also the director of the first LGBTQI+ online radio station in the Arab world, *Shams Rad*, which gives a platform to a community too often silenced. Shams (which means sun in Arabic) aims to "raise awareness among the Tunisian population, ordinary citizens and political decision-makers, about homophobia in society and to defend individual liberties," Bouhdid Belhadi told the media. At its launch, the young activist received thousands of threats and insults on social media while religious and political groups called for the closure of the association and its radio station. Determined not to be intimidated and to continue the fight, Shams launched *Shams Mag* in 2017, the first LGBTQI+ magazine in Tunisia.

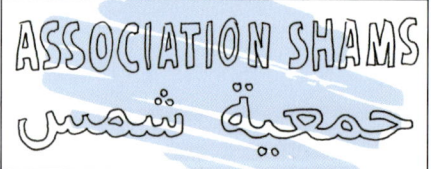

In a country that criminalizes homosexuality with sentences of three years in prison, LGBTQI+ people face an ongoing struggle to be visible and acquire new rights. Some researchers believe that the historical criminalization of homosexuality in Tunisia dates back to the time when the country was still a French protectorate. Bouhdid Belhadi said in an interview: "They should cancel laws that were put in place under French colonial rule – Law 230 of the penal code – which criminalizes homosexuality in Tunisia, and dates from 1913."

It was the Tunisian revolution of 2011 that made Bouhdid Belhadi, then seventeen, want to fight for his rights. In 2018, he was part of the group of LGBTQI+ activists violently repressed by the police at a peaceful demonstration.

Bouhdid Belhadi

While the country saw the first openly gay candidate in its history run for president in 2019, even if he would later be dismissed, for Bouhdid Belhadi things are changing too slowly. The anal test (a forensic act used by the Tunisian justice system that serves as evidence for the practice of sodomy and aims to "prove" a person's "homosexuality"), is considered torture by Amnesty International, but is still practised in Tunisia.

Shams made a documentary, *Au pays de la démocratie naissante* [In the country of emerging democracy], which portrayed the precariousness of life for sexual minorities in Tunisia. The film was shown at film festivals and at an international LGBT Conference in Montréal in 2017. Shams was awarded the Medal of the City of Paris in the same year.

In 2021, the president of Shams, Mounir Baatour, was sentenced to a year in prison for a Facebook post which was considered blasphemous by a judge. Violence is experienced in the daily lives of many LGBTQI+ people, sometimes even from within the family circle.

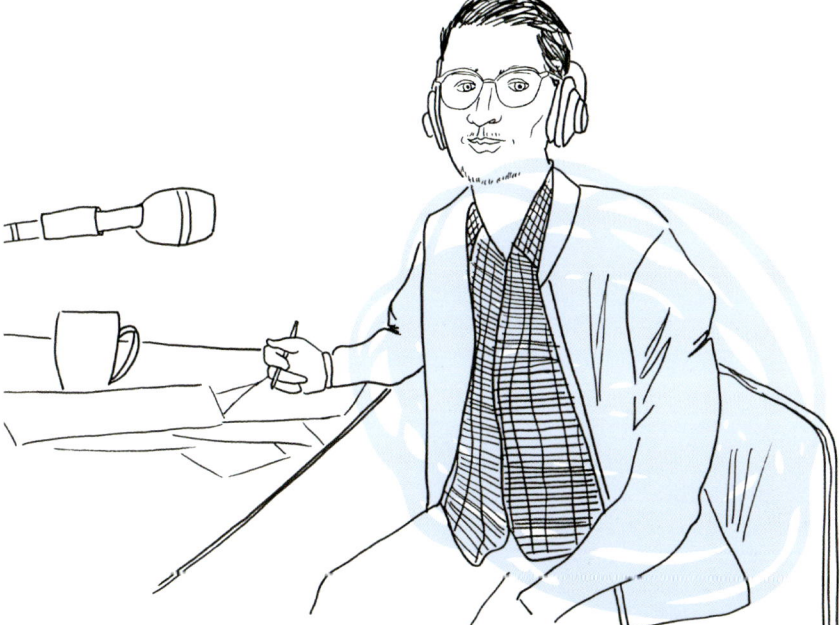

Aaron Rose Philip
2001

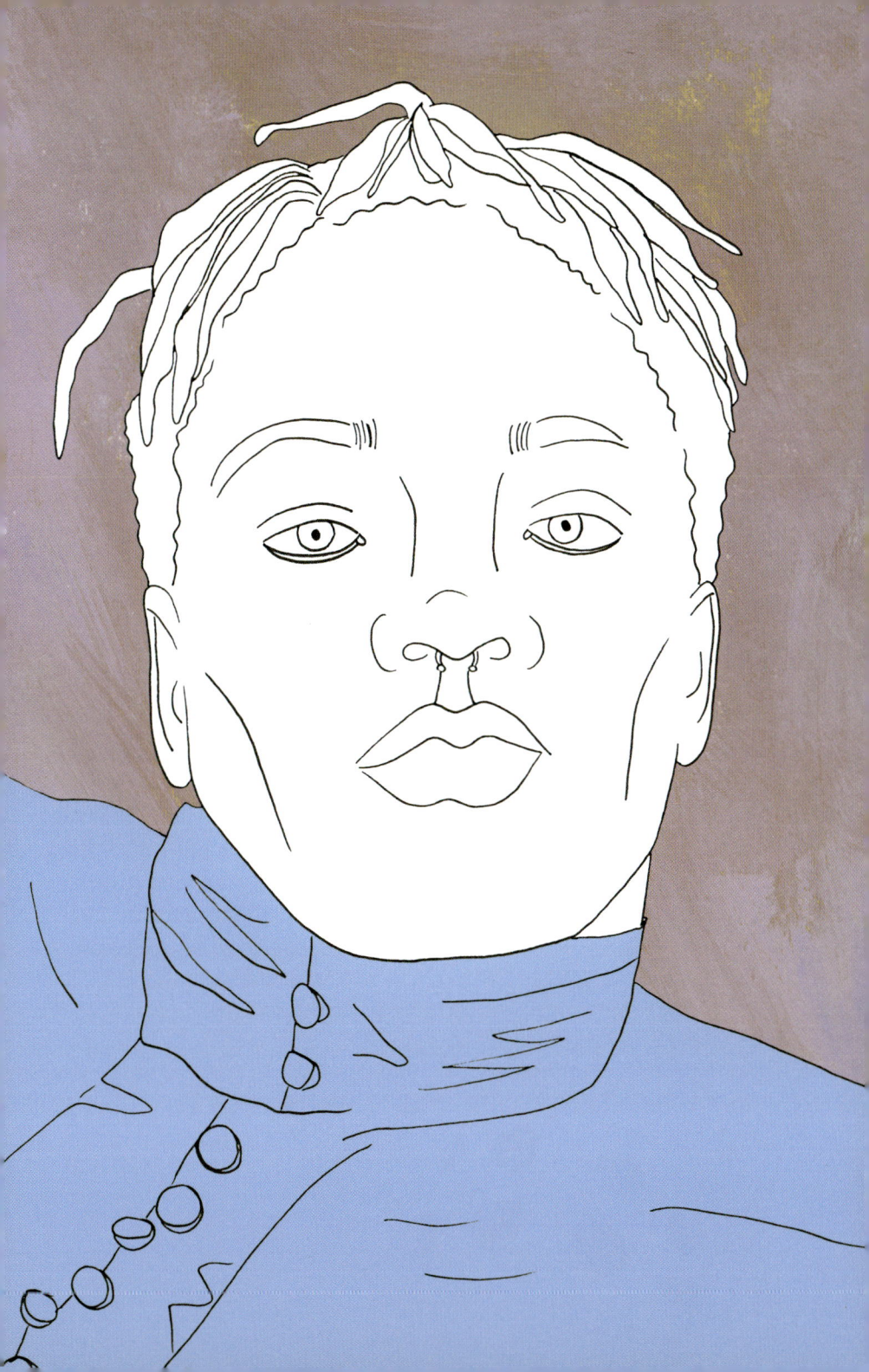

THE FIRST TRANSGENDER, BLACK AND DISABLED WOMAN TO SIGN A CONTRACT WITH A MAJOR MODELLING AGENCY, AARON ROSE PHILIP IS AN ACTIVIST CAMPAIGNING AGAINST ABLEISM, TRANSPHOBIA AND RACISM.

Born in 2001 on the island of Antigua in the Caribbean, she was quickly diagnosed with quadriplegia and could only move around in an electric wheelchair. A few years later, she moved with her family to New York City to access better care. She lived in a homeless shelter for two years, due to financial problems related to the 2007 crisis and high medical expenses, before moving into an apartment in the Bronx. At that time, she told her story on the microblogging site Tumblr and was contacted by its founder David Karp, who was fascinated by her story. At the age of fourteen, she wrote her memoir, *This Kid Can Fly: It's About Ability (NOT Disability)*.

In 2017, she challenged model agencies on Twitter. Her message quickly went viral and attracted the attention of several brands who contacted her and enabled her to start a career as a model without an agency. Aaron Rose Philip became the face of campaigns for H&M and ASOS. In 2018, she signed a contract with Elite Model Management and became a model in one of the largest agencies in the world.

Aaron Rose Philip

"I enter the fashion world with intentions of making the industry more diverse, inclusive, and accessible. I have never seen a physically disabled supermodel or a Black transfeminine model heralded, celebrated, or even working in the way other models are — and I hope to change that," she told *Them* magazine.

Aaron Rose Philip shakes up a fashion industry that is cautious about these subjects but is undeniably powerful. Her courage and determination allow thousands of people to feel represented and finally visible. She campaigns for a better representation of people with disabilities but also Black transgender people and wants to push the boundaries, aware that it will take time.

"PEOPLE THINK BECAUSE I'M PHYSICALLY DISABLED, I'M NOT CAPABLE OF ACHIEVING MOST THINGS... WELL, I'M HERE."

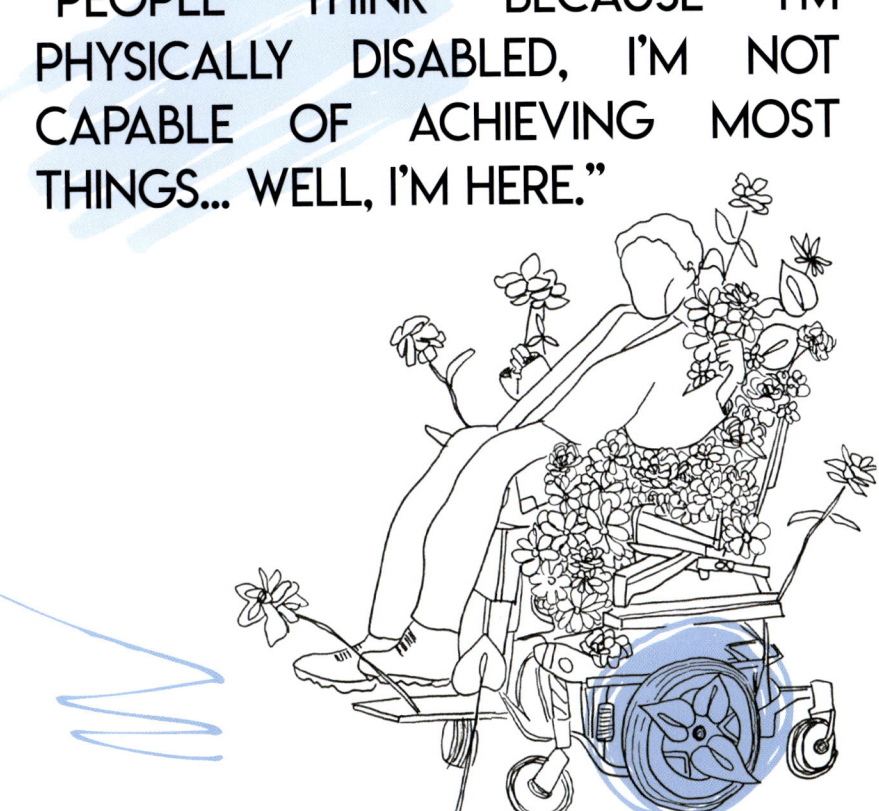

Glossary of terms

Thanks to SOS-homophobie for permission to use these definitions, from or inspired by documents published by the Council of Europe and the European Commission, as well as the Yogyakarta principles.

Bisexuality
Sexual orientation of people who experience emotional, physical and/or sexual attraction to both women and men. Bisexuality can also be defined as encompassing attractions to people regardless of their gender identity and biological sex. This is also called pansexuality.

Biphobia
Attitudes or manifestations of contempt, rejection, or hatred towards bisexual people.

Coming out
Disclosure of their homosexuality or bisexuality by the person concerned. This revelation can be done at different levels: family, professional, social (leisure, neighbours, friends). Also referred to as coming "out of the closet". Coming out can also concern transgender people with regards to revealing one's desire to live in a gender different from that assigned at birth.

Discrimination
Where based on sexual orientation or gender identity, discrimination includes any distinction, exclusion, restriction, or preference based on sexual orientation or gender identity that has the purpose or effect of invalidating or impairing equality before the law, or equal protection before the law or recognition, enjoyment, or exercise, on equal terms, human rights, and fundamental freedoms. Discrimination based on sexual orientation and gender identity can be, and is commonly aggravated, by discrimination based on other grounds such as sex, race, age, religion, disability, health, and place of residence.

Gay
A person who is emotionally, physically and/or sexually attracted to a person of the same gender. For thirty years, the English word gay has been used in the four corners of the world and in all languages to designate homosexual people.

Gayphobia
Attitudes or manifestations of contempt, rejection, or hatred towards gay people.

Gender
Gender is a socio-cultural norm that carries relations of domination between the categories it establishes (especially between the binary categories

Glossary

"woman" and "man"), and within these categories themselves. It is used in the humanities and social sciences to analyse the socio-cultural context, in the same way as other categories such as race, religion, ethnicity, geographical location, socio-professional category or age. Gender provides the framework from which gender identity is built.

Gender Expression
How a person expresses himself through their clothes, makeup, behaviour... Gender expression does not necessarily correlate with a person's gender identity.

Gender identity
This term refers to the intimate and personal experience of one's gender deeply lived by each one, whether or not it corresponds to the sex assigned at birth.

Gender Identity Disorder / Gender Dysphoria
Terms for trans identity in the official literature of psychiatry (DSM, Diagnostic and Statistical Manual of Mental Disorders, and ICD, International Classification of Diseases), and considered stigmatizing by many trans people.

Heteronormativity
Heteronormativity can be defined as the set of norms that make heterosexuality appear coherent, natural, and privileged. It involves the presumption that every person is heterosexual and the consideration that heterosexuality is ideal and superior to any other sexual orientation. Heteronormativity also includes favouring a binary gender expression norm that defines or imposes the conditions required to be accepted or identified as male or female.

Heterosexism
All attitudes, prejudices, and discrimination in favour of heterosexuality, which is then established as the only relational model. Heterosexism claims that it is more normal, moral, or acceptable to be heterosexual than to be gay, lesbian or bisexual.

Heterosexuality
Sexual orientation of people who experience emotional, physical and/or sexual attraction to a person of the opposite sex.

Homophobia
Negative attitudes, feelings of discomfort or aversion to homosexual people or to homosexuality in general. This attitude often results in reactions of rejection, exclusion, and hostility. The victims are homosexuals, but more broadly, people whose appearance or behaviour deviates from traditional representations of femininity and masculinity.

50 LGBTQI+ who changed the world

Homosexuality
Sexual orientation of people who experience emotional, physical and/or sexual attraction to a person of the same sex.

Intersex
(UN definition) Intersex people are born with sexual characteristics (genital, gonadal or chromosomal) that do not correspond to the typical binary definitions of female or male bodies. Because their bodies are considered different, intersex children and adults are often stigmatized and suffer multiple violations of their human rights, such as the right to health, physical integrity, equality and non-discrimination and the right not to be subjected to torture or ill-treatment.

Lesbian
A woman who is emotionally, physically and/or sexually attracted to other women.

Lesbophobia
Attitudes or manifestations of contempt, rejection, or hatred towards lesbians.

LGBT
Acronym meaning Lesbians, Gays, Bi (bisexual) & Trans. Generic term for and speaks of sexual orientations and minority gender identities as a whole. We often talk about LGBTQ+ people. Other initials are now often associated with the acronym LGBTQ+: for example, the Q to designate queer people (LGBTQ) , the I to designate intersex people (LGBTQI) or even the + (LGBT+) to designate queer, intersex, pansexual, two-spirit, asexual and allied people.

Non-binary
People whose gender identity is outside the gender binary.

Outing
The act of disclosing a person's homosexuality or bisexuality without their consent. Outing can also refer to the action of revealing a person's desire to live in a different gender than the one assigned at birth.

PMA
Medically Assisted Procreation, includes all medical methods (IVF, IAD ...).

Queer
A word meaning "strange" and initially used as an insult to LGBTQI+ people. Today, it is claimed by people who do not wish to see themselves defined by the traditional normative categories of gender and sexual orientation. Queer thinking thus profoundly challenges binary social patterns and norms (male/female, homosexual/heterosexual).

Glossary

Sexual orientation
Sexual orientation refers to the ability of each person to feel a deep emotional, physical and/or sexual attraction to individuals of the opposite sex and/or the same sex, and to maintain intimate and sexual relations with these individuals.

Trans identity / Transgender people
Transgender people are people whose gender identity is not in line with the identity assigned at birth on the basis of biological sex. Trans identities thus refer to the fact of living, punctually or durably, according to an appearance and social norms that differ from those assigned at birth. Transgender people can decide whether or not they want to make a transition, i.e. a change in their physical appearance and/or social identity.

Transphobia
All the prejudices and discriminations faced by trans people. These can be manifestations of contempt, rejection, or hatred, at different scales and in different social spheres: rejection by the family, discrimination in housing or hiring, refusal of care, outing, dead-naming...

Transsexualism
A medical term, today rejected and considered stigmatizing by many trans people

Transvestite
Long associated with carnival or disguise practices, cross-dressing is an identity in its own right. A transvestite person uses in part or in whole, on an ad hoc or lasting basis, codes (clothes, attitudes, etc.) that do not correspond to stereotypes of the gender assigned to them at birth. Unlike transgender people, transvestites do not (necessarily) question the gender they were assigned at birth.

Other terms in this book:

Asexuality
The state of a person (asexual) who does not feel sexual attraction to another person. Asexuality is to be distinguished from sexual abstinence and celibacy.

Ball culture / Ballroom
Black and Latino LGBTQI+ movement born in the United States in the 1960s characterized by a competitive grouping around the body as a space of subversion in a performative approach (dance, fashion, music, etc.). Balls are "safe spaces" (places where people who are usually marginalized can feel confident) in which competitions take place. Each person rep-resents a "House" led by a "Mother" and competes for one or more categories.

50 LGBTQI+ who changed the world

Cisgender
Cisgender people are those whose gender identity is consistent with the identity assigned at birth on the basis of biological sex.

Misgendering
Using a pronoun or other term of the wrong kind about a person.

Drag queen / Drag king
A person (regardless of gender) constructing a female (queen), or masculine (king) identity voluntarily based on temporarily exaggerated gender stereotypes.

HIV/AIDS
The human immunodeficiency virus can infect humans and be responsible for acquired immunodeficiency syndrome. AIDS is the most advanced stage of HIV infection. HIV cannot be cured, but due to recent treatments, people are living with the virus and staying healthy.

Voguing
Voguing is an urban dance style born in the 1970s in American ballrooms. Led by the Black and Latino gay and trans community, voguing is characterized by lascivious or acrobatic poses as practiced in *Vogue* magazine or fashion shows.

Photo Credits

Photographs in this book are either in the public domain, or included with permission from the relevant copyright holders below:

Armistead Maupin
San Francisco- pixabay.com/fr/photos/san-francisco-paysage-urbain-3658531/
Armistead Maupin and friend posing at San Jose Pride Celebration in the late 1970s © Ted Sahl photographer

Marsha P. Johnson
Gay rights activists at City Hall rally for gay rights- Sylvia Ray Rivera, Marsha P. Johnson, Barbara Deming, and Kady Vandeurs © Davies, Diana, 1938; Kady Vandeurs and Marsha P. Johnson at gay rights rally at City Hall © Diana Davies

Brenda Howard
Brenda Howard at a meeting © Efrain John Gonzalez- hellfirepress.com; Brenda Howard © Efrain John Gonzalez- hellfirepress.com

Manvendra Singh Gohil
Anjali Gopalan, Gopi Shankar of Srishti Madurai during Asia's first gender queer pride parade in Madurai, 2012; Manvendra Singh Gohgil © Hemant Bhavsar

Useful Websites

aclu.org
amnesty.org
article230.com
asexuality.org
asexuals.net
awesomedude.com
bi.org
biresource.org
blackhistorymonth.org.uk
beaumontsociety.org.uk
britishlgbtawards.com
cairn.info
cestcommeca.net
deportation-homosexuelle.
blogspot.com
draguniverse.com
elop.org
equaldex.com
equalityfederation.org
galop.org.uk
gaycenter.org
gayprideshop.co.uk
gaytimes.co.uk
genderedintelligence.co.uk
glaad.org
gmhc.org
gsanetwork.org
hrc.org
hrw.org
intersexequality.com
jeuneafrique.com
kajalmag.com
ilga.org
isna.org
lambdalegal.org
lesflicks.com

lgbtagingcenter.org
glbtqarchive.com
lgbtqbar.org
lgbtcenters.org
lgbt.foundation
lgbthealth.org.uk
lgbthistorymonth.com
lgbtqnation.com
lgbtqreligiousarchives.org
londonfriend.org.uk
makingqueerhistory.com
matthewshepard.org
mindout.org.uk
mpactglobal.org
nclrights.org
oloc.org
out.com
outandequal.org
PeterTatchellFoundation.org
pflag.org
pride.com
queerarthistory.com
sos-homophobie.org
stonewall.org.uk
stophateuk.org
switchboard.lgbt
thelgbtqshop.com
thepinknews.com
theprideshop.co.uk
theproudtrust.org
thetrevorproject.org
tht.org.uk
transactual.org.uk
transequality.org
transunite.co.uk
ukia.co.uk

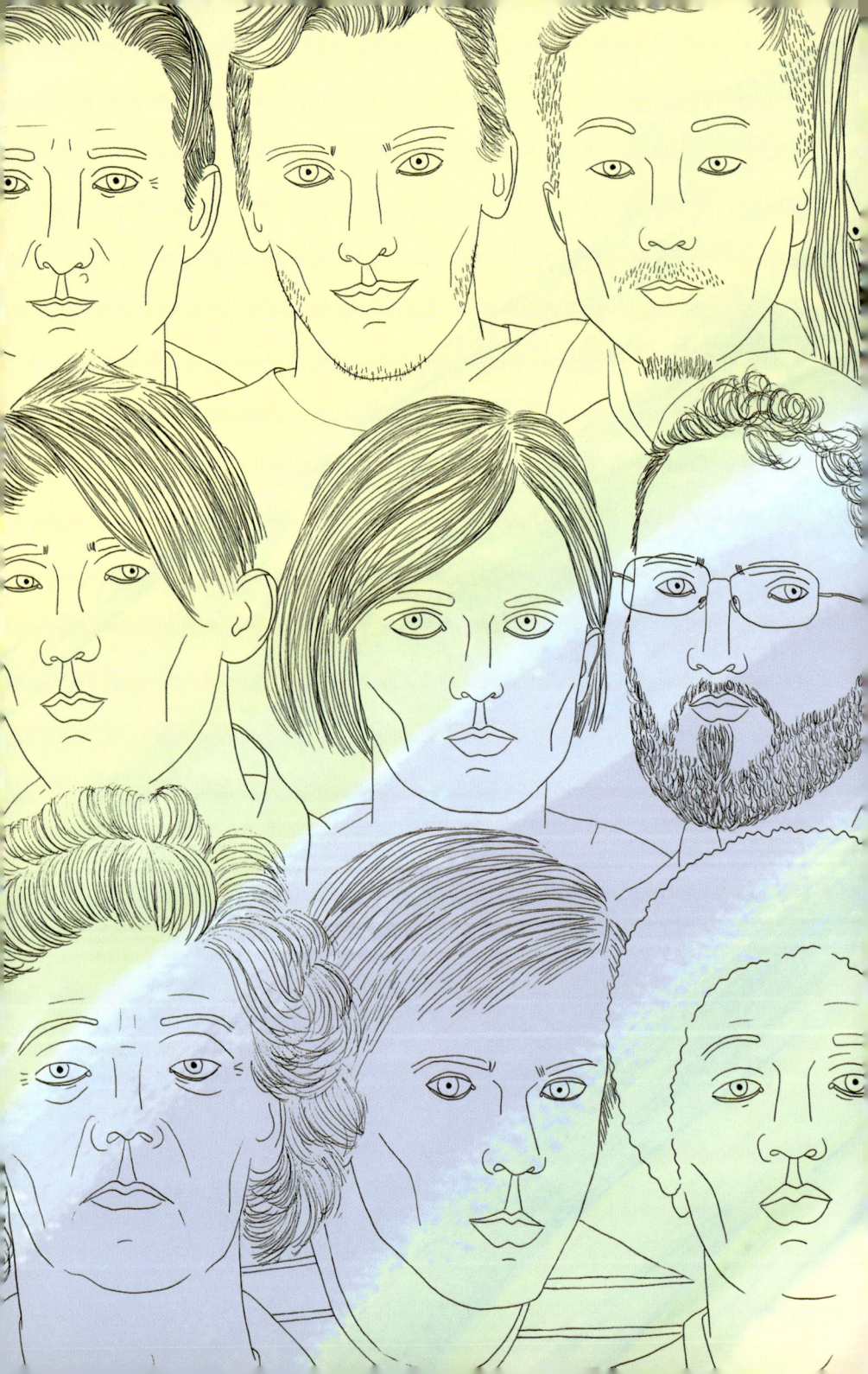

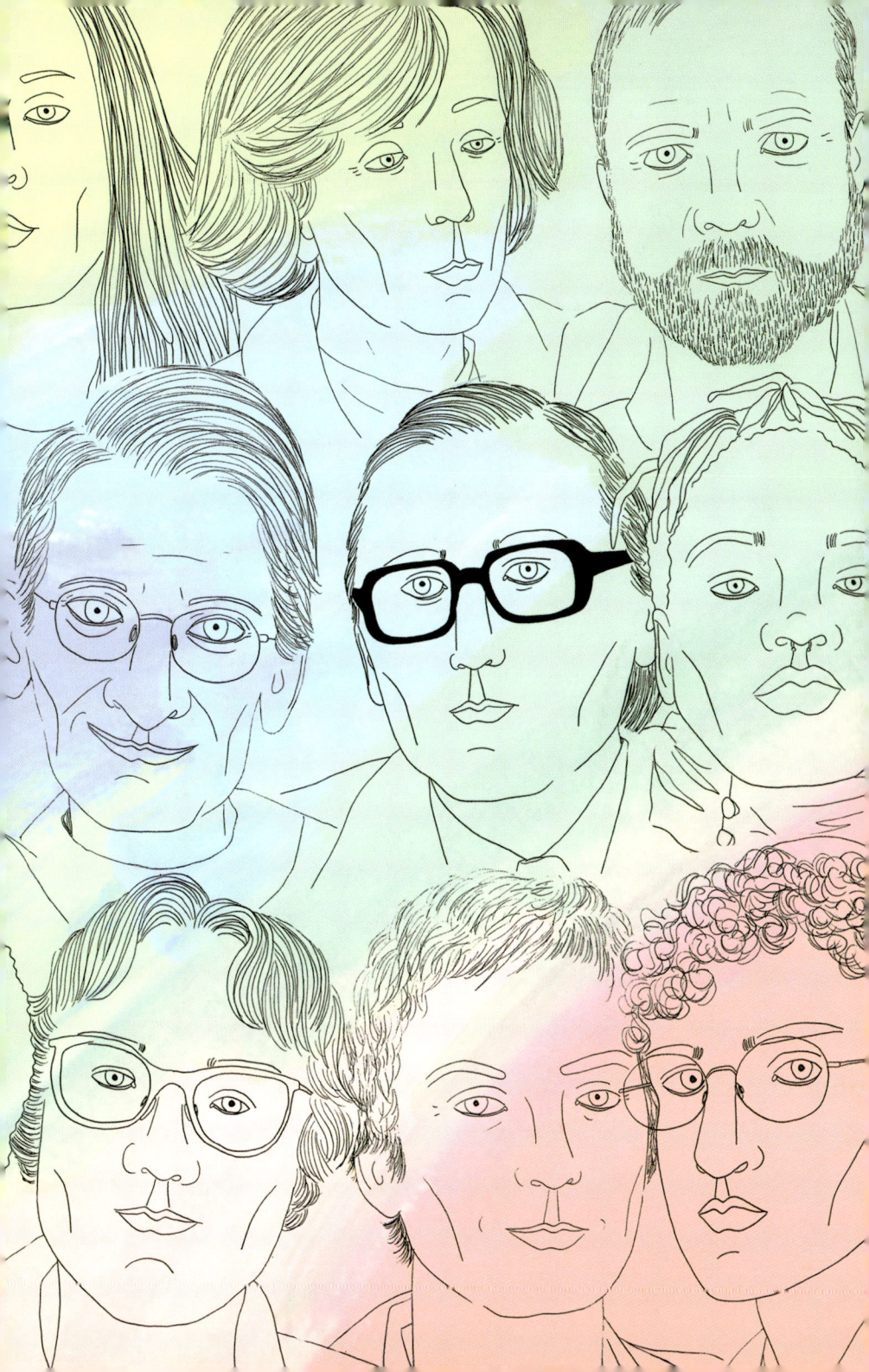

Add your own drawings or information about your favourite LGBTQI+ heroes on these pages

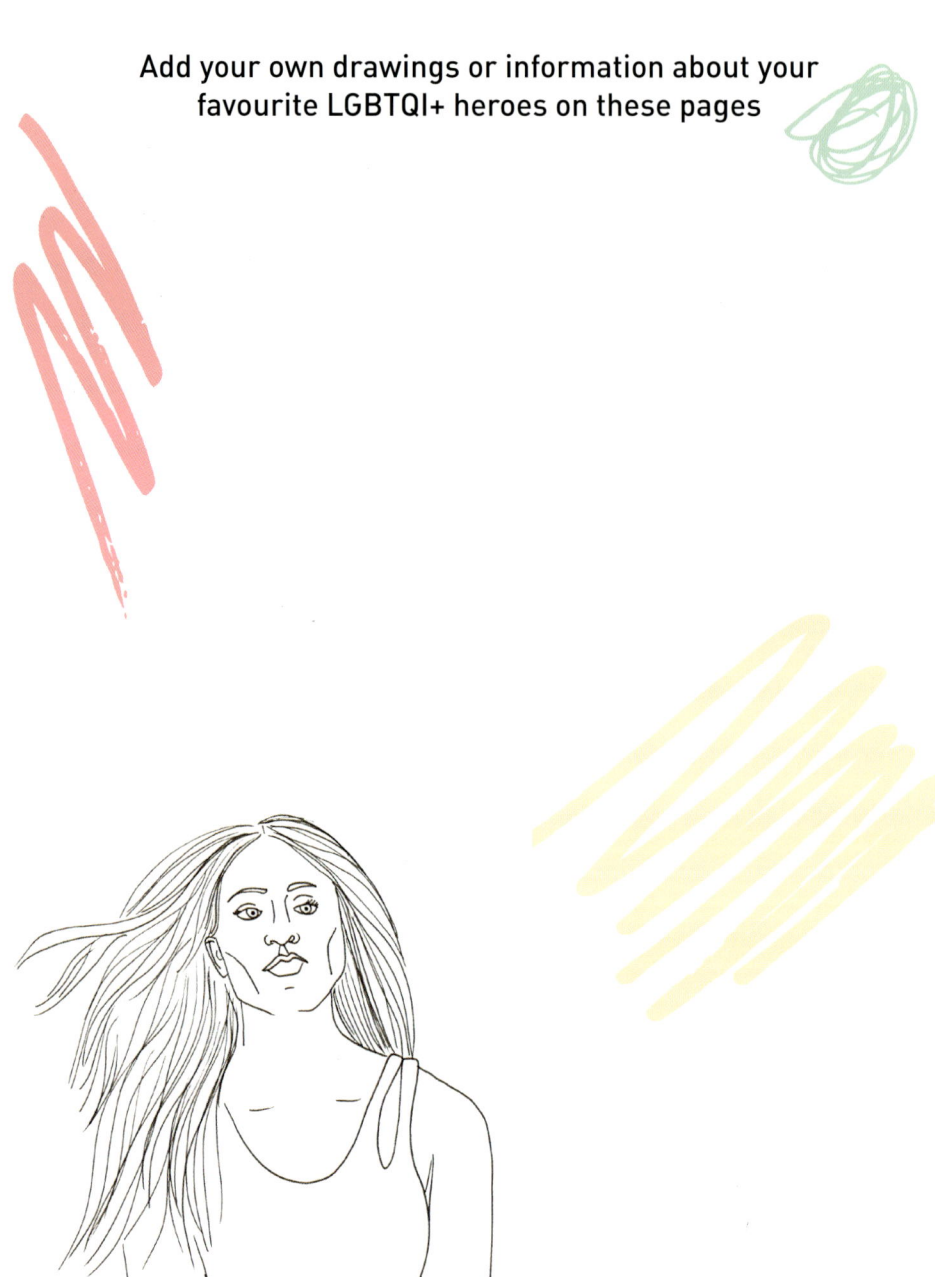

Laverne Cox

Notes and drawings

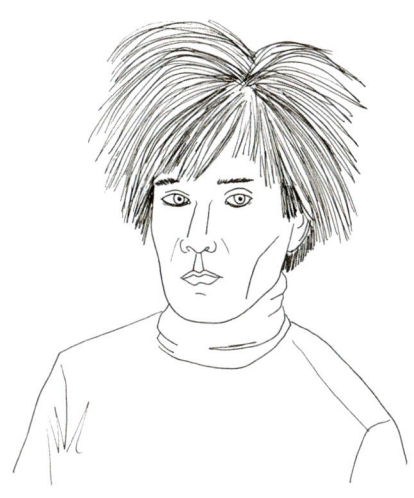

Andy Warhol

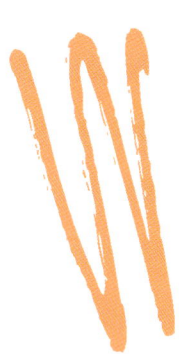
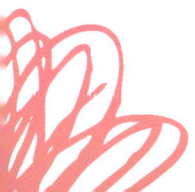

Be creative every day!

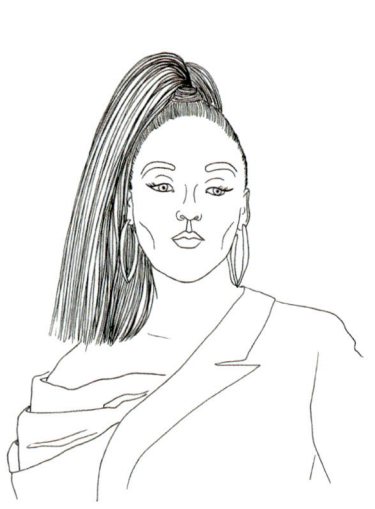

Janelle Monae

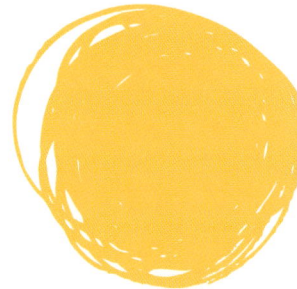

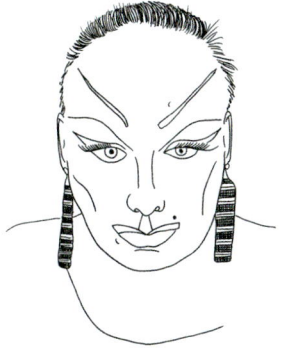

Divine

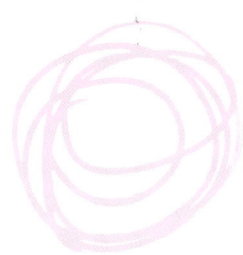

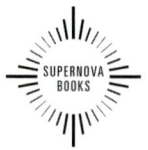

more great books to read

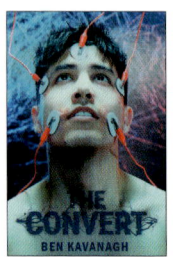

Silent Women; pioneers of cinema
eds M. Bridges & C. Robson
ISBN 978-0-9566329-9-9 | £14.99

Bone Rites
by Natalie Bayley
ISBN 978-1-9124308-7-1 | £9.99

Celluloid Ceiling; women film directors breaking through
eds G. Kelly & C. Robson
ISBN 978-0-9566329-0-6 | £15.99

Next Lesson
by Chris Woodley
ISBN 978-1-912430-19-2 | £9.99

The Convert
by Ben Kavanagh
ISBN 978-1-912430-76-5 | £9.99

Grandmother's Closet
by Luke Hereford
ISBN 978-1-912430-89-5 | £8.99

Unravelling Women's Art
by PL Henderson
ISBN 978-1-913641-15-3 | £19.99

Counterculture UK – a celebration
eds. R. Gillieron & C. Robson
ISBN 978-0-9566329-6-8 | £16.99

Virginia Woolf in Richmond
by Peter Fullagar
ISBN 978-1-912430-80-2 | £12.99

www.supernovabooks.co.uk

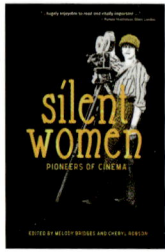
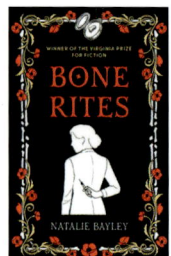
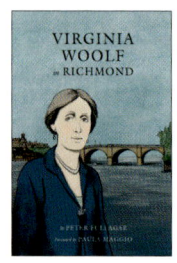
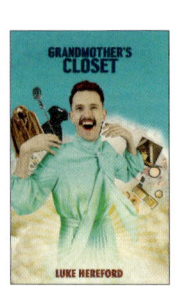
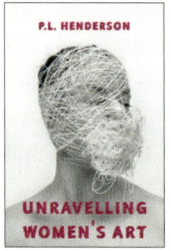
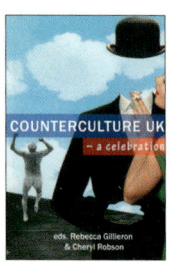
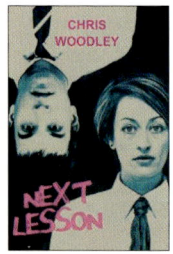